SPOOK

WAR

A MEMOIR FROM THE TRENCHES

WILLIAM NORTHROP

STRATEGIC MEDIA BOOKS

TABLE OF CONTENTS

DEDICATION

This work is dedicated to Lexi, Tali, Rob, Blue and of course, Suzanne. I also want to mention Ari Ben-Menashe whom I have never had the opportunity to thank.

PREAMBLE

THE TRADES

*"How hath the spy dwelt so long amongst us?
What is his utility to the state and the
citizenry? How is he considered - and known -
by the people he serves, often at the risk to his
life? He is at once rogue and useful fellow. We
survive by his information, yet we taunt and
abuse him, and we have scant knowledge of
his theories and his tactics; yea, we do not
even speak his tongue."*

Henry S.A. Becket

History is resplendent with footnotes memorializing good or bad policies by governments influenced by *spooks* … theirs or someone else's intelligence operatives. Sometimes these policies clash with the interests of other nations and often these clashes literally change the world.

This work is a tour of the *Spook War,* a glimpse into the primary and collateral events triggered when the Reagan Administration abruptly shifted three decades of American Foreign Policy to the interests of the Arabs States and to the detriment of our traditional Middle East allies, the Israelis.

It is a dark, unfocused period of American history engined primarily by oil interests, Arab money and

5

America's ongoing, noble if somewhat Quixotic, efforts to bring peace to the most volatile region of the world.

It is a field for careful chroniclers and more akin to walking randomly through a graveyard of events, pausing here and there to examine the inscriptions on selected tombstones.

These are war stories that need to be told – perhaps to draw lessons – but primarily because they happened. It is history lost to denials, cover-ups, secrecy and spins and it is time for its return to the American People, who, we would argue, have a *need to know*.

 C3 80

HUMINT

> *"... it's part of a spy's profession, to prey on the community to which he's attached, to take away information - often in secret - and to translate that into intelligence for his masters..."*

John le Carre

Generally in The Trades, some 60 to 65 percent of all information comes from open sources ... books, newspapers, internet blogs, radio and television ... the media. Probably 25 percent comes from signal sources, satellite, telex, internet, telephone and radio communications. Another 5 or as much as 10 percent comes from liaison sources, friendly intelligence agencies. Only about 3 percent or so comes from human sources ... spies ... and that is the good stuff.

So, the best sources are the spies (agents or cases) run by trained spy handlers (case officers or katzas). This is classified as Human Intelligence (HUMINT) and the key qualification for an agent is access ... access to secrets wanted by his handler or in the case of a "double" agent, access to the enemy's intelligence organization. (Spy vs. Spy)

Keeping it simplistic, avoiding the analytical side and without going too far into the tiresome minutia of categories and tradecraft while wholly ignoring penetrators and provocateurs, suffice to say agents – recruits or walk-ins – live dangerously, completely mortgaged to chance for a quiet, peaceful delivery to their graves. That is a fact.

Making matters worse, beyond their Hollywood entertainment value, the stories of these agents and their exploits are retold in endless shades of gray, mostly unfocused, murky, often misleading, with unconfirmed conjecture presented as fact and in believable yet tantalizing lore comparable to the haunting mystery surrounding the Romanov women.

By far the most interesting of HUMINT agents are the doubles. Double agents – agents or handlers who have come over to you from the other side – are obviously used to ascertain what your enemy knows, his sources and methods and often to confuse him with a little mischief.

One classic example was the Egyptian double, Ashef Marwan (THE IN-LAW), [1] who is to this day publically declared "the perfect spy" by both the Egyptians and the Israelis with each side claiming he worked for them.

On 5 October 1973, the eve of Yom Kippur, Marwan warned the Israelis that the Egyptians and the Syrians would attack simultaneously the following day at 1800 hours. While the Israelis were already strategically surprised ... it took 48 hours to mobilize their reserves ... the actual attack came at 1400 hours, four hours earlier. Because of this, the Israeli Southern Command did not execute their defensive plan – DOVECOATE – on the Suez Canal, which might have stopped or at least heavily hindered the Egyptian assault at the water's edge.

There has been much speculation in *The Trades* as to Marwan's real allegiance and he promised to publish all in a 2007 confessional. Unfortunately, THE IN-LAW was taken suddenly dead in June of that year when he mysteriously fell from the fifth floor balcony of his apartment in London. Not surprisingly, his tell-all manuscript has disappeared.

Hands down, the most flamboyant double was Dusan "Dusko" Popov, known to the British TWENTY COMMITTEE of MI-5 as TRICYCLE and to the German Abwehr as IVAN. A Yugoslav playboy, it is said he made a lot of money from both his sponsors during World War II. He is best known for helping to convince the Germans under Operation BODYGUARD that the 1944 Normandy invasion was only a feint and that the real invasion would come in the Pas de Calais. He also tried to warn the FBI that the Japanese were gathering intelligence on Pearl Harbor for a possible attack. Post-war, TRICYCLE was knighted by Great Britain for his many contributions to the war effort. So lavish was his life-style and so wild were his exploits that the popular British novelist, Ian Fleming, used him as the model for his fictional secret agent, James Bond (007).

The IN-LAW at his wedding to Nasser's daughter and TRICYCLE at play

Finally, we might mention that the CIA was trying to double some of their detainees down at Guantanamo Bay, but their program was terminated in 2006. It is said that likely candidates were moved from their prison cells and comfortably sequestered in what is described as a "bungalow" setting called PENNY LANE in a remote location at Gitmo. The success of this effort is in doubt, especially now that the program has been "outed." Still, it speaks volumes about the utility of doubles.

Overhead: The white bungalows of PENNY LANE at Gitmo

 C3 ℰꙄ

SIGINT

"There will come a time when it isn't 'They're spying on me through my phone' anymore. Eventually, it will be 'My phone is spying on me'."

Philip Kindred Dick

Electronic eavesdropping has always played a critical part in military operations, but it is best known and was particularly valuable during World War II. The

Allied successes in deciphering Axis machine-generated codes – Communication and Signals Intelligence or SIGINT – specifically the German ENIGMA and the Japanese PURPLE codes greatly contributed to our eventual victory. (The work product from these intercepts was known as ULTRA and MAGIC respectively.)

The deciphering of the Japanese diplomatic code known as PURPLE by American Naval Intelligence (OP-20 G) enabled Washington to intercept and read the famous 14-part message warning of war on 7 December 1941.[2] Later, a 20-page report on German military preparedness sent by the Japanese Embassy in Berlin to

German ENIGMA machine and remains of a Japanese PURPLE

Tokyo and encoded utilizing a System 97 – Type B cipher machine (PURPLE)[3] – naturally proved very helpful to the Allies in Europe.

On the tactical level, the American cryptanalysts under Commander Joseph Rochefort, the eccentric genius in charge at STATION HYPO, Pearl Harbor, were able to break the Japanese Navy's operations code known as JN-25.[4] This resulted in the great American victory over the Japanese at the Battle of Midway in 1942. Overcoming bureaucratic resistance from Washington (OP-20 G), Rochefort managed to outwit the

Joe Rochefort

Japanese enabling the US Navy to set their ambush at Midway and defeat the superior naval forces of the emperor.[5]

 C3 80

T & S

*"We have some material on spying by a major
government on the tech industry. Industrial
espionage."*

Julian Assange
WikiLeaks

As technology has become paramount in the military and industrial strength of nations, the second and third world countries often steal information developed by the West. This theft, sometimes called "industrial espionage," is the only way lesser regimes can compete with the wealthy, first world nations. This is especially true in the development of weapons.

Since 1945 when Soviet spies stole the atomic bomb from the American MANHATTAN PROJECT, [6] Intelligence agencies have listed technology and scientific (T&S) collections among their priorities. With the advent of the *computer age,* the illegal transfer of proprietary information and indeed industrial wealth has increased alarmingly.

Among the nations which blatantly "hack" foreign computer systems is China. It is known, for example, that the Chinese have managed to obtain the designs for all of the American nuclear weapons. [7] While this arguably seems to pose no direct threat for a toe-to-toe showdown, China has displayed a penchant for proliferating weapons technology to third-world enemies of the United States.

Chief among the contemporary results is the Lockheed F-35 Joint Strike Fighter on which billions have been spent for development. While still not clear at this writing, the Chinese apparently hacked into the computers of a British sub-contractor to the project, BAE Systems, and have subsequently produced a knock-off version, their J-31, out of the Shenyang Aircraft Corporation.

The Chinese J-31 and the American F-35

This type of industrial espionage, however, is a two-edged sword as was apparently the case in the matter of the Soviet Tupolev TU-144 Supersonic Transport (SST). In the 1960s, a British-French consortium began design work on the Concorde Supersonic Transport at Aerospatiale. In 1965, Aeroflot's representative in Paris, Sergei Pavlov, was arrested in possession of the drawings for the Concorde's braking system, landing gear and airframe. After Pavlov was deported, the KGB sent in another agent, Sergei Fabiew, [8] to continue facilitating their collection requirement. Although alert to the Soviet threat, Fabiew still managed to obtain a complete set of blueprints for the initial Concorde prototype. In fact, the Tupolev TU-144 (the "Koncordski") was a fairly decent copy of the earliest version of the Concorde design, which confirmed the loss of the blueprints.

At that point, British and French Intelligence moved in and at their behest, the Concorde Team produced a complete set of bogus blueprints for the upgraded, production version of the aircraft, inclusive of design flaws. By doubling the Soviet's source at Aerospatiale, they were able to deliver the bogus blueprints to the KGB without suspicion. The apparent result was the spectacular crash of the TU-144 at the

The TU-144 "Koncordski"

Paris Air Show in 1973. The exact cause(s) of the crash remain unknown as the aircraft's "black boxes" mysteriously disappeared. However, in the end, the Concorde enjoyed a career of scheduled passenger service from 1976 until 2003; the TU-144 "Koncordski," did not.

C3 80

Political Policies and Consequences

"The Middle East is obviously an issue that has plagued the region for centuries."

President Barak Obama
Tampa, Florida
28 January 2010

Political policy drives action. In the United States, we have had good policies, bad policies and policies that blew up or simply went quietly sour. The politicians and bureaucrats responsible for our bad policies rarely, if ever, accept that responsibility.

To avoid embarrassment they normally cloak policy failures in "National Security," pretending the truth is too important for *We, the People* or they simply deny it. But, here our old tradition of democracy should hold sway: Our government should not be afraid of the truth. If it is, we can only then conclude that it was doing something wrong.

The CIA told President Jimmy Carter that the Shah of Iran was in no danger of losing the Peacock Throne. Carter then went to the Guadalupe Conference and passed this judgment onto our allies, who all seemed to be aware of the French efforts to unseat the Shah. The direct consequence is the Islamic Republic of Iran, currently the foremost purveyor of terrorism worldwide.

In the matter of Saddam Hussein's Weapons of Mass Destruction (WMD), the CIA informed President George Bush (43) that it was positive about the existence of these weapons, as a matter of fact, they called their analysis a "slam dunk." This led, at least partially, to the Iraq War in 2003 and indirectly to the "goat grope" that has followed.

While it is easy to point out these historical intelligence peccadilloes, most policy issues are not that cut and dried, even in hindsight.

In a time of hard choices, in the midst of the Cold War, the CIA saw an opportunity to attack the "Evil Empire" and took it ... using a surrogate army of primitive Moslem fundamentalists. We armed them, trained them and supplied them and for their part, they went into the Afghan hills and did evil things to the soldiers of the Soviet 40th Shock Army.

Our political leaders admired their perseverance, their nobility and sang their praises as "Freedom Fighters" while the Mujahedin took carnal advantage of the Tennessee mules the CIA provided to carry their supplies.

The Agency "understood" when their officers were not allowed to interrogate the Soviet prisoners, who were sexually assaulted by the Muj before being summarily executed. It was, after all, in their nature and while they never warmed to us infidels or gave us credit for supporting them, we did win that war – a little payback for Vietnam – and that was enough. What we did not realize was in this first Moslem victory over a superpower, the Mujahedin believed they had done it alone, with, of course, Allah's help.

Upon the victory in 1989, we, in typical American fashion, then abandoned Afghanistan, leaving the Mujahedin to its own devices. Soon, a bunch of religious fanatics, the Taliban, a literal creation of Pakistani Intelligence (ISI), took over and established a Moslem state under Sharia, Islamic law. They also gave shelter and assistance to Al Qaeda.

In retrospect, American intervention may have been the right choice at the time, but our abandonment speaks volumes on our long range statecraft and world-view. In the wake of its victory in the Afghan War, Moslem fundamentalism triggered trouble throughout the world. In natural progression, America soon became the target of their fundamentalist rage using the skills we taught them.

Very easily it can be claimed that our near-sighted, foreign policy has burdened us with numerous, unforeseen consequences in our current war against Moslem fundamentalist terrorism. A brief example would be our strategic, Arab ally in the Middle East, Saudi Arabia. For all fundamental intents and purposes, Al Qaeda is Saudi Arabian. Its terrorist leadership was mostly Saudi nationals, its ideology is Wahhabi and its financing comes from Saudi Arabian citizens.

The engine of the any *Spook War* is, of course, that connection between intelligence and political policy. So, throughout this work we are going to be constantly referring to intelligence communities, the sources of information and covert actions on the tactical level that have influenced our political policy in the Middle East. Two in particular, the American and the Israeli intelligence services, were the real players. The British bounced to the aid of one side or the other, as their interests dictated. Naturally the Iraqis were heavily involved, but the rest, while certainly operative in the play, were small participants by comparison.

ଓ ଝ

United Kingdom

"Thank the Queen for me, won't you. But, tell her my brother's a queen, and even he doesn't want me to spy for England."

Robin Williams
Club Paradise

The British are considered the most cultured of practitioners in *The Trades* and are viewed as vastly more experienced in matters of intelligence compared to most. And, they have more friends in far off places as they were, in recent memory, the dominate world power. (*The Empire Strikes Back*).

Their flagship organization is the Secret Intelligence Service ... SIS or MI-6, known colloquially as "The Circus." It is headquartered at Vauxhall Cross, London, and they are rumored to recruit primarily from among the British upper classes.

At their annual Christmas parties during the Cold War, it was said that a Santa Claus, dressed in a traditional red suit, but wearing a Vladimir Ilich Lenin mask, would enter the festivities and lead the assembled host in a rousing rendition of the Soviet National Anthem ... in Russian.

In spite of publicized defections, bizarre stories of scandal and general lore, MI-6 is a very serious player in *The Trades*. When David Barnett (CIA), Edward Howard (CIA), Aldrich Ames (CIA) and Robert Hanssen (FBI) went over to the KGB and burned their entire HUMINT organization[9] within the Soviet sphere, one of the few agents to survive was Oleg Gordievsky (GT/TICKLE), the KGB Rezident[10] in London whom the Brits had initially recruited and run. While MI-6 never exposed him to CIA, Aldrich Ames was detailed to discover his identity by the agency. Initially fingered by a British journalist[11] and having been "confirmed" by Ames on 13 June 1985, he was ordered back to Moscow where he was accused and interrogated, but not arrested. Still free, he alerted his MI-6 handlers, and disappeared from Moscow on 19 July 1986 only to resurface, safe and sound in London.

British Intelligence enjoys a good relationship with the Americans ("the Cousins"), but is often quietly critical, viewing them as "colonials" and generally characterizing their work product as "loose files and

American scramble." The Israelis ("Izzies") are also viewed with caution as former "colonials," but the cooperation is surprisingly close and genuine given successive British Labor Governments' outright, anti-Semitic distain for the Jewish State.[12]

The second organization of British Intelligence is MI-5, often referred to colloquially as "The Nursery" or "Box 500." This group, like the old Second Directorate of the KGB, is responsible for internal security and counter-intelligence within Great Britain. These are the folks who run the doubled agents (The TWENTY COMMITTEE, XX or double X) out of their headquarters in Thames House, London and work closely with Scotland Yard.

The third principle British Intelligence organization is called the Government Communications Headquarters (GCHQ), based in Cheltenham. It is roughly equivalent to the American National Security Agency in that its primary brief is SIGINT. It became famous after World War II for breaking the German ENIGMA codes at Bletchley Park. And, like the NSA, GCHQ has a branch charged with the security of British communications known as The Communications-Electronics Security Group (CESG).

There are other intelligence organizations within the British infrastructure, but they are usually attached to some department such as the Foreign Office and the like. Under law, all of British Intelligence falls under the direction of the government's Joint Intelligence Committee.

CB BO

United States

> *"From the Bay of Pigs to Iran-Contra, (American) covert warriors hatched one   disaster after another. Its analysts misjudged almost every major development in the post-World War II world, including the most spectacular misjudgment of all – the flat-out failure to predict the collapse of the Soviet Union."*
>
> David Wise
> NIGHTMOVER

In the wake of the Second World War, Congress established a central organization, the CIA, into which all intelligence was supposed to flow, be digested and presented to everyone's number one consumer, the President of the United States. A more efficient intelligence flow, it was reasoned, would prevent a second Pearl Harbor. It did not, of course, and a new Intelligence Czar, the National Director of Intelligence (and a new bureaucracy), was appointed in the wake of Nine-Eleven

Over the years, however, the military, terribly unhappy with the CIA's work product, has eroded this initial streamlining with the establishment of the Defense Intelligence Agency (DIA), a sort of mini-CIA that belongs exclusively to the Pentagon. All intelligence from the military branches, Army, Navy, Air Force and

Marines, flows into DIA to be digested and presented to their own number one consumer, the Chairman of the Joint Chiefs of Staff. The DIA, however, is still (allegedly) subject to the authority of the Director of Central Intelligence or now to the National Director of Intelligence.

Within the DIA is a small operational unit called the Intelligence Support Activity. We do not know much about it since "The Activity" was seemingly utilized to avoid congressional oversight. It was, however, a major player in Iraq during the period of the covert American foreign policy known as the "Level Battlefield Doctrine."

By far the largest, most sophisticated and probably least known of the American Intelligence agencies is the National Security Agency. NSA (the spooks call it "No Such Agency") belongs to the Department of Defense and is tasked with signal intelligence (SIGINT). This generally means it listens in on everyone's conversations and it has the capability of penetrating and intercepting any electronic communications in any country. A part of NSA is the Central Security Service, which is tasked with the security of American communications. Worldwide, the NSA is thought to employ some 50,000 people.

Like all of the American intelligence shops, the NSA's mission has been expanded over the years with bigger budgets and has seeped into areas where, some say, it has neither business nor brief. American civil libertarians, for example, hate the idea of the NSA monitoring every overseas phone call going in or out of the United States, not to mention email traffic of individual citizens. And apparently, there is some justification given the Obama Administration's current scandals involving the NSA.

Besides these main agencies, the State Department, Federal Law Enforcement, the Energy Department and most other governmental Departments maintain intelligence organizations. We would not be surprised if the Bureau of Fisheries had a similar unit. In America, the sixteen main organizations are collectively known as the "Intelligence Community" with an annual budget of $75 billion.

Each and every one of these intelligence organizations has a large "operations" section ... clandestine services, black ops, a la James Bond ... and no matter what their brief might be, they are all "shaken not stirred." There is plenty of overlap and duplication of effort but the United States after all, can afford this luxury.

The historical track record of American Intelligence is almost perfect. That is to say 100 percent wrong on its major cases. From the Korean War to the Bay of Pigs to the Vietnam War to Iran-Contra to the collapse of the Soviet Union to Nine-Eleven, American Intelligence has delivered one disaster after another. It never seems to know what is going on in the world and enjoys this reputation among intelligence professionals internationally.

One of the main reasons for this failure is that the American Intelligence Community has a structure that gives it little analytical capability. It is said that roughly the division of resources shakes out at 90 percent for collections, but only 10 percent for analysis ... an exaggeration, no doubt. Still, plenty of information is gathered, but no one knows what it means.

Another aspect of its failure is that no one has ever been held accountable. On the contrary, Congress traditionally rewards the agency. In the wake of failure, the CIA always complains that it did not have the "resources" and with an increased budget, will do better next time. There is, therefore, absolutely no incentive for the agency to become a serious player in *The Trades.*[13]

A final reason is that the CIA has evolved into an instrument of political view,[14] moving away from its primary mission of "preventing a second Pearl Harbor," which it failed to do in any case. It is a matter of dogma over data that finds the CIA telling the government what it wants to hear, rather than what is actually happening or is likely to happen.[15] Among intelligence professionals, this incompetence and politicizing of America's flagship intelligence service has given rise to the "Third Law of Analysis:" *Wherever the CIA is looking, look elsewhere for the answer.*

CR 80

Israel

"The Lord spoke to Moses, saying, 'Send men that they may spy out the land of Canaan, which I give to the children of Israel; of every tribe of their fathers shall you send a man, everyone a prince among them.'"

Numbers 13: 1-2

The Israelis have a similar "Intelligence Community," but their centralized agency belongs to their armed forces. Known by the acronym AMAN, [16] Israeli Military Intelligence is the rough equivalent of the American DIA. AMAN receives the information from the military officers in the field and other agencies, processes it and briefs its number one consumer, the Chief of the General Staff, the Rav Kal.

The commander of AMAN is a Major General and a member of the Israeli General Staff on an equal footing with the commanders of the Army, the Air Force, and the Navy. The Chief of AMAN also reports to the Prime Minister. The reason for this architecture is simple: Israel's primary problem is the physical threat to its existence and surrounded as it is by enemies, only the armed forces (IDF) stand between its population and a Second Holocaust. Israeli Intelligence is literally the first line of defense and consequently rates a slot on the General Staff.

Within AMAN is the signal intelligence (SIGINT) organization, which is called simply "Unit 8200."[17] AMAN also has a small operational unit that works cross-border (Unit 504), which is often confused with the Sayeret Mat'kal (Unit 269) of Entebbe fame … the on-call muscle of the General Staff. AMAN was also formally the home of LAKAM, the T&S unit of the Ministry of Defense and it has also absorbed the sabotage and propaganda unit of the Israeli Foreign Ministry (Unit 131).

The General Security Services (GSS),[18] sometimes called Shin Bet or Shabak, is responsible for internal security, counterintelligence, and is roughly equivalent to the American FBI's Terrorism, Intelligence and Counterintelligence divisions or Britain's MI-5. It works very closely with the Israeli National Police, especially the "Green Berets" of the Border Guard.[19] The Shin Bet is also responsible for the security of Israeli political missions and diplomats abroad and reports to the Prime Minister.

The third major intelligence organization in Israel is, of course, Ha Mossad (The Institute).[20] This small group [21] reports directly to the Prime Minister and operates strictly outside of Israel. Not only does it collect intelligence, but also has a secondary mission of clandestine power projection. This is why the Mossad is much better known to the world than its larger sisters, AMAN and Shin Bet. It also has a third, less publicized mission, which is to keep an eye on Jewish communities world-wide, especially those under threat.

Ha Mossad enjoys a 90 to 95 percent success rate or better and its exploits are legendary. Among their more notable efforts was the stealing a MiG-21 from Iraq, the rescue of 18,000 Falasha Jews from Ethiopia to Israel in a secret airlift and the destruction of the PLO infrastructure responsible for the Munich Massacre.

They have also suffered disasters in their history and have learned bitter lessons about political expediency like relying on the Germans to rescue their hostages at Munich and believing their American counterparts just before Israel suffered the terrible strategic surprise of the Yom Kippur War in October of 1973.

The last Israeli intelligence organization we will mention is LAKAM.[22] This group worked directly for the Ministry of Defense, through AMAN, in a narrow, specialized area, gathering information of a technical and scientific nature. We mention this T&S unit because it figured so prominently, as we shall see, in the American-Israeli Spook War. LAKAM never consisted of more than fifty people, who were tasked, among other things, with chemical and biological warfare (CBW) intelligence. Since there is little rivalry within the Israeli Intelligence Community, LAKAM would often borrow expertise and manpower from the IDF and the Institute for Biological Research, Israel's "Germ Palace," for its collection requirements in the CBW field.

ひ &ひ

Comparisons

"We're both thieves, Harvey Swick. I take time. You take lives. But in the end we're the same:"

Clive Barker
THE THIEF OF ALWAYS

We should make some brief comparisons between the two principle antagonists, because it will give the reader a better feel for the play. Let us take the two "flagship" organization, the US CIA and Israel's Mossad. There are numerous cultural differences  between Mossad Katzas and their CIA Case Officer counterparts.

The CIA notoriously recruits out of colleges and universities and there was a point where no analyst or case officer was without at least a master's degree. The agency is headquartered in Langley, Virginia.

New hires are schooled in a basic training course (CIA 101) at Camp Perry, Virginia, sometimes called "the farm." By all indications, this basic course lasts several weeks, at which point the analyst or case officer goes on to an advanced course in their particular discipline, much like the US Army trains its officers in branches. Some advanced courses for Case Officers are held at Harvey Point near Hertford, North Carolina, incidentally where the Navy constructed a mockup of Bin Laden's home on which SEAL Team Six practiced.

The CIA has its own university and the training of a Case Officer is continual throughout his career, again in the manner of officers in the armed forces.

The CIA is a massive bureaucracy and the number of its employees is a state secret, but thought to be around 25,000. The agency has four major divisions, Intelligence (analysis), Clandestine Services (collections and counterintelligence), Support (logistics, training, etc.) and T&S. Finally there is this: CIA's Counterintelligence currently lists as priority targets China, Russia, Iran, Cuba *and Israel*.[23] Apparently, they are as afraid of the Jews as they are of the Chinese and the Russians.

Compared to the CIA, Israel's Mossad is an entirely different animal, rather miniscule in size and budget. The entire agency consists of approximately 1500 salaried individuals and of that number, only about 35 are Katzas (case officers) who are stationed world-wide.

Mossad officers are recruited from inside Israel after military service and come from 104 different countries, so language training is rarely needed. The selection process is drawn out and rather unusual. It is done through extensive background checks, interviews and psychological testing, because unlike the CIA, they do not recruit for field work based on college transcripts.

The Mossad, like the CIA, has its own university or academy. But, unlike the Americans, "Mossad 101" consists of a three-year course, roughly equivalent to a college degree in the black arts. (Israel Defense Force officers are subject to continuing education like their American counterparts throughout their careers.)

The Katzas are schooled in an isolated "no rules" environment and because of this, they are viewed by the rest of Israeli Intelligence as barely housebroken ... the side of the family one doesn't talk much about.

In Israel, it is understood that the Mossad is not allowed to operate within the borders of the country. There is no written law forbidding it, but everyone understands that this is a chiseled-in-stone rule. Occasionally, Mossad operatives venture out on training exercises or simply go *off the reservation,* breaking this rule. When this happens and if they are caught by the Shin Bet, they are severely beaten for their sins. (It is said that if they are seriously unlucky, they may have an encounter with the Shin Bet's premier water boarder, "Boris the Baptist.")

All of this imparts another advantage over their CIA counterparts ... Mossad officers do not like anybody very much ... certainly not enough to fabricate information or "spin" an analysis for some political agenda.

In all fairness, their missions are not comparable because the United States is a superpower while Israel is a little state the size of New Jersey on the shores of a second-rate sea. Therefore, the CIA has been tasked offensively with bringing down whole governments while the Mossad is usually assigned spoiling or "pay back" missions keyed to national defense.

It should also be mentioned that allies or not, there is no love lost between the American and Israeli intelligence communities. And so, it was with these forces in an Israeli-American *Spook War* that the secret foreign policy agendas of the Reagan Administration were contested.

Cʒ ꙮ

In general terms, the American-Israeli *Spook War* was triggered because Israel took a very dim view of the "Level Battlefield Doctrine." Shortly after discovering the Reagan Administration's secret policy, the Israelis set out to negate it, but did not enter upon their crusade for any noble or even moral cause. They simply viewed the Iraqi military build-up as a *Clear and Present Danger* to their physical survival. From the other side, there is no clear evidence that the Reagan Administration was particularly concerned with Israel's well being or even its continued existence as a nation-state, in spite of all the public pronouncements to the contrary.

The Israelis did not openly confront the Americans. If they had, there might not have been a Gulf War. There was argument among Israel's political leadership, some of whom insisted that going public was interfering with internal American politics. Instead, Israel opted to join the contest in the shadows, where the Americans were implementing their secret military build-up of Iraq. By March 1983, the contest was slowly evolving into a *Spook War*, embroiling the intelligence agencies of both countries.

In this clandestine chess game, the more powerful Americans were very adept at moving the pieces. What they missed for various reasons was that the Israelis simply moved the board. So, let us now lay the foundation, looking briefly at the playing field and the underlying issues.

ରେ ଚ

CHAPTER 1

A BRIEF HISTORY OF
BROWN DISNEYLAND

"If you removed the State of Israel and the crude oil from the Middle East, you might be able to establish a wilderness theme park ... Six Flags over Nothing."

William Northrop
Presentation
ORMA Board of Visitors
2011

The Arabs

"Allah made the desert, Allah made the Arab, Allah made the camel ... and from the camel shit he made the city Arab."

Old Bedouin Saying

There are nine gates into the Old City of Jerusalem and one of them is known as the "Golden Gate," sometimes referred to as the "Eastern Gate," the "Gate of Mercy" or the "Gate of Eternal Life." Located on the city's far eastern wall, it is no longer in use and is therefore not particularly noteworthy unless you are an historian or a religious aficionado.

According to Jewish tradition, the Messiah will enter Jerusalem through the Golden Gate and in fact, it says so in the Hebrew Bible.[24] It was also the Golden Gate through which Jesus of Nazareth entered the city on Palm Sunday.

The Golden Gate

With the spread of Islam and the arrival of Moslem conquerors in Jerusalem, the quote from Ezekiel, Jewish tradition and the Palm Sunday episode triggered their primitive superstitions. It seems that

Islam was not ready for the coming of the Messiah ... first time or second time ... so in 1541 they sealed up the Golden Gate, lest some Hebrew Prince fulfill the prophecy. Not completely comfortable with this solution and believing the anecdote that the Messiah would not walk through a graveyard, the Moslems quickly began to bury their dead just outside the gate.

One can point to the absurdity of all this and label it an indication of the primal mentality of the Arabs. That aside, it seems to have worked ... so far.

ℭ ℬ

There are 22 member states of the Arab League and 57 member states in the Organization of the Islamic Conference. Let us leave aside for the moment the entire Moslem population, currently estimated at 1,476,233,470 souls, and concentrate on the Arabs.

From Morocco to Pakistan, the Arab states cover a land area larger than the United States or all of Europe with a population of some 300 million people and rapidly growing. The Arabs have an extremely high birth rate and over half of their population is under 20 years of age. Disease is rampant, life spans are low and medical care is practically non-existent.

There is not one democracy in the pre-enlightenment, Arab world for there is no middle class and it follows as no surprise that basic human rights are non-existent.

Democracy had a one-night-stand as a result of the so-called "Arab Spring" where the populations rose and overthrew their secular dictators starting in December 2010. In Tunisia, Libya, Yemen and Egypt, the governments were overthrown and Islamists were elected in their place. At this writing, civil war has erupted in Syria, the Egyptian military has overthrown their Islamists leader and Lebanon is controlled by the Shia Islamists (Hizb Allah or Party of God). It had a lot to do with economics and the natural corruption of the ruling Arab governments, not to mention the age-old conflict between Shia and Sunni Moslems. Finally in the mix is Islam, which holds no separation between church and state. *Welcome to the Middle East.*

With all their oil wealth the 22 Arab states have a combined Gross Domestic Product (GDP) less than Holland and Belgium combined. That's about half of the GDP of California. All the media bushwa to the contrary, the Arab states are, in essence, extremely poor.

They are also poor intellectually. Greece alone translates more books into their language than does the entire Arab world. Great Britain annually publishes 2000 books per 1 million citizens while Egypt publishes 20 per 1 million. The 7 million Israelis publish more scientific papers annually than do the 300 million Arabs.

In the entire Moslem world, the literacy rate stands at best around 40 percent whereas at least 15 Western nations have a literacy rate at 100 percent. The Moslem world has around 500 colleges/universities whereas the United States alone has 5,758 and India has almost 8,500.

For all their problems, the Arabs have an answer: It is some one else's fault. It is the Americans, it is the Jews, it is all the "Crusaders" and in a broader sweep, let us not forget the Persians. One is hard pressed however, to find one American or one Jew among the Crusaders of old, much less a Persian, but never mind. It makes absolutely no sense, but it sounds good to the masses.

The entire Arab world is totally dysfunctional, which, we would argue, is the basis for their aggression. It really has little to do with the State of Israel, which is constantly cited as the primary cause. In fact, it is clear that this situation would have been the same had Israel joined the Arab League and an independent Palestinian state existed for the last 100 years.

In our 21st Century world, the Arabs are lost children. Our wealthy, American culture offends their non-tolerant, religious beliefs and in their part of the world, religious beliefs define mind set.

Their religion, Islam, is trapped in antiquity, stuck fast between tradition and modernity, not compatible with other religions and certainly not compatible with democracy. So for starters, the Arabs do not recognize the Western principle of religious toleration or a separation between church and state. Islam is not a religion; it is an emotion, a creed fanatical, a way of life and a convenient fall-back when matters do not work out.

C３ ８０

SPOOK WAR

The Jewish Problem

*"If we do not find the solution to the Jewish Problem,
mankind will never be at peace."*

Julius Streicher
Editor, Der Sturmer
Berlin, 1935

There are certain inane prejudices inherent in all mankind. That the Germans, as a people, have a character flaw is one example that is abundantly supported by history. In the American South, the term "damnyankees" reflects the 150-year-old hostility of Southerners toward Northerners. There are sub-sets … women are not equal to men is supported by religions and blacks are not equal to whites has been supported by governments, but none really compare to the enduring and centuries-old, abject hatred of the Judeans (Jews), the People of the Book.

Throughout history, various cultures have sought a "solution" to what is termed, "the Jewish problem." The European Enlightenment offered up assimilation as the answer, but this was shattered in the 19th Century by the East European pogroms, the Dreyfus Affair in France and in the 20th Century with Germany's Holocaust.

There are only three possible solutions to the "Jewish Question." The first is assimilation, the second is segregation and the third is eradication (genocide).

The Jews themselves came up with a modified segregation solution, which is based on Theodore Herzl's *"Der Judenstaat"* and the political movement known as Zionism. It simply advocates a separate nation-state for the Judean People.

The fact that the world needs a "solution" and it does *need* a solution, is a rather glaring indictment of mankind as a whole for the Jews have evolved into the virtual canaries in the coal mine of civilization. Still, even after this segregation, after the establishment of the Third Jewish State, the hatred still manifests itself even among "enlightened" Western governments.

Take for example, the Yom Kippur War of 1973 when Israel was simultaneously attacked by Egypt and Syria, supported by the rest of the Arab states.[25] In population comparisons at the time, the four main Arab states (Egypt, Iraq, Jordan and Syria) held at 55,177,000 versus 3,180,000 Israelis. The Soviet Union, in supporting their Arab clients, poured in massive amounts of replacement armaments and supplies. Yet when the United States attempted to do the same for Israel, the European NATO nations would not grant the Americans landing rights or over flights, refusing to aid Israel in any manner. (Portugal was the exception.)

Surrounded as they are by implacable enemies bent on their destruction, with Western civilization seemingly tolerant of the blatant Arab hatred, one can understand Jewish paranoia, if for no other reason than it is solidly supported by history. That aside, all is not milk and honey in the Promised Land.

At this writing, the Israelis sit uncomfortably on the horns of their own national dilemma. They want and have proclaimed a democratic, Jewish state. A cruel fate and Arab intransience has given them a non-Jewish minority within Israel. If they accept their Arabs as full-fledge citizens, they threaten the demographics of their Jewish state. If they relegate their Arab minority to the status of second class citizens, they no longer have a democracy.

Could they forcibly expel their Arabs to the surrounding Arab states? They could, but that is not a practical solution. First, the Arab states have made it abundantly clear they will not accept the "Palestinians." Second, it reminds the Jews of the forced exile of the Diaspora and the Holocaust. So thirdly, if it was done, half the Jews in Israel would have to go into therapy for the next twenty years.

Politics in Israel is another factor. Unlike our two-party system, there are numerous political parties in Israel's democracy ... from the militant, religious right to the peace-love-dove, socialist left. Leaving out the parties of their Arab minority, the Israeli political scene amply evokes the old adage: *Two Jews, three opinions.*

Amidst all the political dissention and chaos, the Israeli Jews have one saving grace. Threaten them and they instantly ban together into one of the most formidable forces on earth ... an inherent survival tactic the Arabs have painfully experienced on numerous occasions.

CƷ ՖↃ

The Troubles

"The problem is not that Israel is being provocative, it is Israel's being is provocative."

George Will

There is a beautiful valley in the north of Israel just below the Galilee. It is called the Valley of Yisreel and about half way down on the southern side there is a small mountain. The mountain is man-made and the locals identify it as a "tell." This "tell" covers the ruins of the once-great city of Megiddo. The remains of this city and the valley beneath breathe foreboding mystery, strained juju, bent karma and hard irony. If you are familiar with the biblical significance of this place, it can lay a special darkness on you.

It is an area mentioned in the Bible and was the site of the first great battle humankind ever recorded in any detail. It was here in this beautiful valley on the plains of Esdraelon that the Egyptians under Tuthmosis III defeated the Syrians and laid siege to Megiddo. The narrative celebrating this battle was recorded on the walls of the Temple of Amun-Ra at Karnak, long before Joshua Ben-Nun led the Children of Israel across the Jordan River and back into their Promised Land.

It seems only proper that the "first" battle was fought there in the Middle East, there in the Holy Land, there in the Yisreel Valley, because tradition holds the last battle will be fought there as well. In the Bible, the Yisreel is known by another name. It is called Armageddon.

The Middle East begot the Holy Land; the Holy Land begot the Third Jewish State; the Third Jewish State begot the Arab-Israeli conflict; the Arab-Israeli conflict begot the *Spook War.*

To understand these "begots," it is incumbent upon us to briefly comment on the Arab-Israeli hostility. It is a common misconception that it is a "centuries old" conflict, unless you count the Crusades. Those "holy wars" actually pitted the Christians against the Arabs and the Jews, although nowadays, the Jews are conveniently lumped in with the other "infidels." The troubles between the Arabs and the Jews actually began in the late 1920s and have not abated.

The religious component is now paramount in the conflict as it always has been, if even sub-rosa. It is, after all, the home of the three great desert religions, which is why this small slice of burnt desert on the shores of a second-rate ocean is called the "Holy Land."

Simplistically, Judaism is the father, Christianity is an ever-evolving modification of Judaism and Islam is the "super religion" that incorporates elements of both predecessors. All three are monotheistic and believe in the same God. The Moslems and the Christians believe they have the "true religion" and adopt a missionary approach to convert "non-believers," often by force. In the process they have made war "holy." The Jews have a more introverted, tribal view of their religion and do not, as a rule, solicit converts.

The territorial component of the Arab-Israeli conflict also has a religious flavor. The Jews believe that the God of Abraham promised them a small slice of land (now) between the Mediterranean and the Jordan River. (We currently use the Jordan as the eastern boundary, but originally the land included the area from the Jordan River eastward to the Iraqi border and also portions of what is now southern Lebanon.) In any case, this "Promised Land" was to be theirs for eternity.

In this aspect of the argument, the late Yitzhak Walker[26] would say, "First, you have to believe that God promised this land to the Jews. After that, everything falls into place." John Anthony Claro, an Oklahoma City trial lawyer and Middle East scholar, calls this notion "the concept of the divine warranty deed."

That being said, the Jews have continually inhabited their "Promised Land" throughout history, occasionally ejecting competing tribes by force of arms and just as often being subjugated by outside invaders. Thus they have the distinction of being the only people indigenous to the Land of Israel who have ever ruled as a sovereign nation.

The Palestinian Arabs make the claim that they have continually inhabited the land and thereby claim ownership. There is a modicum of truth to the fact that non-Jews have lived in the Land of Israel since the 8th Century AD as non-sovereign inhabitants. The vast majority of present-day Palestinians, however, can only trace their arrival back to the 1920s when their Egyptian forefathers arrived looking for work in the fields and farms then being developed by the Zionist Jews.[27]

The Holy Land was occupied by the Ottoman Turks in the late 19th Century when a new Jewish, political movement - Zionism - rose among the young Jews of Europe.[28] Based on the writings of Theodor Herzl, Zionism was promoted as the only solution to the "Jewish question." The Enlightenment dream of total assimilation had died and Zionism's stated goal was the re-establishment of a Jewish State in the ancient Land of Israel, which was by then called by its' old Roman name, "Palestine" – land of the Philistines.

By ones, twos, and in small groups, the Jews of Europe began returning to their ancient homeland, joining with the resident Jews who had never left. They began buying land and expanding the existing Jewish community in order to establish a third Jewish nation-state in the land of their forefathers.

These industrious European Jews attracted Arab workers from nearby countries and as both populations grew in numbers, the friction began. Before that happened, however, war broke out in Europe. As a result, possession of the Holy Land passed from the hands of the Moslem Turks into the hands of the Christian British.

Prior to the First World War, there were no Arab states. On the religious level radical Moslems viewed the post-war results as simply the 20th Century extension of The Crusades; the Moslems were back out, the Christians were back in. A vast majority of Moslems and Jews in the Middle East, however, viewed *The Great War* as political and not religious in nature, which in retrospect is hard to imagine.

The great tribes of Arabia are Bedouin and during the war they sided with the British, helping to defeat the occupying Ottoman Turks.[29] Their promised reward for this cooperation was to be an independent Arab State. The Jews, who also sided with the British, were promised an independent state as well. In 1917, Lord Alfred Balfour, the British Foreign Minister, codified this promise to the Jewish people in his famous "Balfour Declaration"

The Arabs got a reduced, independent Arabia almost immediately, but because of Arab pressure on the British, the Jews had to wait. Palestine then encompassed all of the area from the Mediterranean eastward to the border of Iraq, but in 1922, the British chopped off that portion east of the Jordan River and established the Emirate of Transjordan for the Hashemite tribe. That was the first partition of Palestine.

During the Second World War, the Palestinian Jews sided with the British,[30] while the Palestinian Arabs sided with the Germans. The Grand Mufti of Jerusalem, the leader of the Arabs in Palestine, spent the war in

The Grand Mufti of Jerusalem and his wartime friend

Berlin as the guest of Adolph Hitler and raised two Moslem SS divisions in Yugoslavia [31] for the armies of the Third Reich.

The destruction of the European Jews in the Holocaust of the Second World War imparted the moral high ground to the Zionist cause and helped implement its' aspirations for a Jewish State in Palestine. After the war, the British, bled white and broke, tired of their mandate over Palestine and the United Nations voted to further divide the land into a Jewish segment and an Arab segment. It was understood that the Jews would declare an independent state in their portion while the Egyptians and the Jordanians would divide up the areas apportioned to the Arabs. (There were no "Palestinians" in those days.)

This second partition of Palestine was a watershed event and led directly to the establishment of the State of Israel. The idea of a Jewish State in their midst did not sit well with the Arabs and it was soon clear that there would be war over the issue. [32]

As the battle lines were drawn, the Arab world enjoyed a superiority of numbers and wealth, but they lacked leadership and national structure. The Arab states were and are now, feudal monarchies, dictatorships and religious oligarchies, which are further divided by the Sunni – Shia disputation.

On the other hand, the Jews structured their future state based on First World, Western concepts. They infused Democratic Socialism, European economic efficiency and a love of education and technology into the backwater of Palestine.

The Jews also enjoyed superiority in leadership. Among the Zionist immigrants were the men and women who would lead their people to independence and establish the Third Jewish State dreamed of by Theodor Herzl. One, David Green, a young Russian immigrant to Palestine, was destined to become Israel's "Prophet of Fire," David Ben-Gurion. Another, Goldie Myerson, a schoolteacher from Milwaukee, Wisconsin would become Israel's first woman Prime Minister, Golda Meir.

Ben Gurion   *Golda Meier*

The Palestinian Arabs had no visionary leaders. The man who might have curtailed the growing animosity between the Arabs and the Jews was the Hashemite King, Abdullah of Transjordan. Unfortunately, he was undermined and later assassinated on the orders of the spiritual leader of the Palestinian Moslems, Mohammed Said Haj Amin el Husseini, the aforementioned Grand Mufti of Jerusalem. Without King Abdullah, war between the Jews and the Arabs was inevitable.

In May 1948, the British withdrew from Palestine, the Jews declared the State of Israel, and the surrounding Arab nations attacked the fledgling state with five armies. Instead of dividing up the allotted Arab portion of Palestine, the Arabs made war on the Jews and lost. Ironically, an Arab state in what is now Israel is currently being negotiated, some sixty-five (65) years later.

As matters turned out, the real losers in what is now called Israel's War of Independence were the Arabs living in Palestine. Convinced to leave their homes to make way for the invading Arab Armies or in some cases frightened out by the Israelis, approximately 650,000 Palestinians found themselves on the losing side and could not return afterward. They ended up in refugee camps scattered throughout the Middle East, because the Arab states would not take them in. Those who remained in their homes in the Jewish area - approximately 32 percent of the pre-war Arab population - became Israeli citizens in the new Jewish State.

Often overlooked in the wake of the Israel's War of Independence are some 850,000 Jews who were consequently expelled from the Arab countries. Their property, which was confiscated by Arab governments, has been estimated at $2 billion. These Jewish refugees were absorbed by the new Jewish State.

As noted, the Palestinians were not allowed the opportunity of settling in any Arab State, which while cruel, was a brilliant strategic move by the Arabs. Their status as "stateless persons" gave the world its "Palestinian Problem," which at this writing, has not been solved. It also gave rise to the virtual if celebrated "injustice" now embraced by many, as if losing a war, which they started in the first place, was some how grossly unfair to the poor Arabs. (One must also keep in mind that at the end of the Second World War there were an estimated 20 million displaced persons – refugees – in Europe and ten years later there were none. So, the Palestinian refugee "problem" is clearly for propaganda value only.)

Israel was born in war and has been continually plagued by it. In the mid-1950s, President Gamal Abdel Nasser of Egypt turned to the Soviet Union for arms and dragged the two superpowers into the Arab-Israeli conflict. It then evolved that a majority of the Arab states became Soviet clients while Israel enjoyed the general (and selective) support of the Western democracies.

During the Cold War, the Soviets supplied their Arab clients with the latest weapons based on the concept that military parity between the warring parties would lead to peace. Mutually Assured Destruction (MAD) worked between the Soviets and the Americans during the Cold War, but it never worked in the Middle East where the mentality is radically different.

Each and every time the Arab states felt they were militarily equal to the Israelis, they attacked. And in each instance, they lost. This blind aggression, this passionate hatred of the Jews is beyond all Western reasoning and conception but, is the basis for the Arab-Israeli conflict. Israeli Prime Minister Golda Meir once commented that peace between the Arabs and the Jews would only come when "they learn to love their children more than they hate us." In the light of ongoing Palestinian terrorism, her point is abundantly clear.

Since their displacement in 1948 and throughout the continuing conflict, the future of the stateless Palestinian Arabs settled at the perceived heart of the matter. Confined to UN-supported refugee camps throughout the Middle East, they festered with frustration over the Arab states' inability to destroy the State of Israel. So in the 1960s a new Palestinian political movement took root. A terrorist group, the Palestine Liberation Organization (PLO), was formed with the specific goals of the destruction of the Jewish State and the establishment of a Palestinian Arab State in its place. While the Palestinians were not at all successful on the battlefield, they soon became the wealthiest transnational terrorist group in history.

Interestingly, the PLO became more dangerous to the feudal governments of the Arab states than they ever were to the Israelis. One of the most grievous examples was the war in Jordan in September of 1970 ("Black September") where the Israelis were forced to mobilize their army in order to save King Hussein and his kingdom. Yet another example is the destruction of Lebanon and the attempt by the Palestinians to take over that nation, which will be covered in some detail later. Responsibility in both of these cases has to be laid directly on the doorstep of the PLO, now known as the "Palestinian Authority." Terrorism, many argue, is in the nature of the Palestinians.

Militarily, the strategic view holds a fine military balance between the Arabs and the Israelis. (Hence the efforts by Iraq, Syria and currently Iran to obtain nuclear weapons.) This balance ensures the existence of the Jewish State, but also curtails any expansionist ideas that might arise in Israel. It is understood by both parties that the destruction of Israel is a national priority of the Arab states and indeed the entire Moslem world. Thus, when the Arabs feel militarily superior to the Jews, war breaks out. This, in essence, feeds the continual cycle of war in the Middle East.

CB EO

Peace Would Be Nice

"In order to be sheltered against every act of hostility, it is not sufficient that none is committed; one neighbor must guarantee to another his personal security."

Immanuel Kant
PERPETUAL PEACE

If one defines nationalism as the belief that there are peoples with a clear cultural indemnity and these people should be independent, it gives us some perimeters to view the Arab-Israeli conflict.

There are prancers and dancers in the West who believe peace is the only answer to the Arab-Israeli conflict and that without it, the Jewish State cannot survive. These folks also harbor the false concept that Arab Terrorism cannot be dealt with by force and often conclude that Nine-Eleven was America's fault.

For their part, the Israelis will listen to anyone who cares enough to put forth their (often annoying) ideas and indeed there are "peaceniks," compromisers and appeasers among the Jews themselves. (They are known in Hebrew slang as "beautiful souls.") But, as a general rule, their physical security is non-negotiable and they cannot depend on anyone else to provide it. Once again, it is important to note that this Jewish paranoia is fully supported by history.

On the Arab side of the argument, their position is also clear. The destruction of the Jewish State is now and has forever been the ultimate goal. Since they cannot accomplish this militarily, they have become dependent on Western democracies to do their bidding and force the issue. In the United States, Arab political cajolery based on the oil threat, oil money and the subsequent rise of the American political left has imprinted the "Two State Solution" paradigm on all matters Middle Eastern.

The concept that the State of Israel cannot survive without peace indicates an acceptance that sooner or later the Jews must reach for their suitcases. At this writing, the Jewish State is 66-years-old and in that time, they have built a viable democracy, the only one in the Middle East. Internally, Israel has moved politically from a social democracy to more of a free enterprise nation state, which has resulted in an annual economic growth rate of around 5 percent.

Israel has become the technological power house with all the major computer and software manufacturers having established their R&D facilities there. The cell phone was invented at Motorola Israel. The computer operating systems Windows NT and XP were written at Microsoft Israel. The Pentium MMX chip along with the Pentium-4 and Centrino microprocessors were invented and are produced at Intel Israel. Voice Mail, the iPhone, Play Station and AOL Instant Messenger were invented in Israel. In fact, Israelis file more patents per capita than anybody in the world.

They also publish more peer-reviewed scientific research papers than any other nation ... 109 per 10,000 people. They utilize more scientists in the work place ...

145 per 10,000 workers. In context: The US has 85 per 10,000 workers, Japan 70 and Germany is at 60. Israelis hold more college degrees per capita than any nation and the World Health Organization rates Israel's medical care as 2nd or 3rd in the world. (The US is rated 57th ... right above Slovenia.) They have also recently discovered massive natural gas fields off their coast. They are the smallest among a mere handful of nations that have put satellites into space. I will not bore you with the military technology understandably developed in Israel, the point is this: In its 66 years of existence, Israel has never had peace.

Still, there are many tea leaf gurus, palm readers, rocket scientists, academics and other mental leprechauns who believe there must be peace. It would, of course, be wonderful and Israel would thrive, but in the reality of the Arab states bent on Israel's destruction, it would seem an unreachable goal.

෦෫ ෭෮

Pax Americana

> "...the ironclad (American) belief that our secular tradition of toleration, moderation and compromise can transcend the religions and animosities of older societies has led us to see others as we would want them to see themselves."

Reuel Marc Gerecht
The Price of America's Naiveté
The New York Times
14 October 2000

America's entry into the quagmire of the Middle East in general and the Arab-Israeli conflict in particular is based on two common myths. The first is there must be Peace … that there is no alternative to peace, one must take chances for peace, people on both sides want peace, a Palestinian state next to Israel is the only chance for peace and terrorism cannot be defeated by force. All this diplomatic stagecraft would be grand if it was not completely devoid of reality.

Pax Americana holds that the Israelis and the Arabs, two peoples who have entirely different cultures, who speak different languages, who have different religions, and who maintain an historical blood feud, can somehow live together in peace on the same small piece of real estate although they have never been able to do so in the past.

This American naiveté has played an important role in the constant turmoil of the Middle East, especially in recent years. Hard to define in understandable terms, we like the lines from the 1970s movie, *The Best Little Whorehouse in Texas.* In the film, the press questions the Governor of Texas about his weekly prayer breakfast. He replies that he "prayed for the Jews and the A-rabs to settle their differences in a Christian manner." And, that about says it all.

C3 80

Ms. Condoleezza Rice was a professor of political science at Stanford University in California before answering her political calling and eventually becoming our 66th Secretary of State. The Department of State is now and always has been notoriously pro-Arab in the contest of interests in the Middle East and the fact that the Israelis are not willing to be voluntarily driven into the Mediterranean goes a long way toward explaining why there has been no peace settlement up to now.

The Bush (43) Administration, like all before it, nobly sought a peaceful solution to the Arab-Israeli conflict with Professor Rice on point. She advanced a new theory, which she believed would deliver the goods. (We say "new theory," but in truth all solutions involve heavy doses of Israeli concessions since the Palestinian Arabs, in essence, have nothing they can bring to the party.)

Rice called it "Transformational Diplomacy" and while no formal definition has been forth coming, it appeared to mean the Israelis would make concessions and the Palestinians would agree, bringing peace between the parties. It was a pragmatic approach, because the Arabs are intransigent and the Jews will at least talk to the US State Department.

In truth, "Transformational Diplomacy," like its predecessors, "Land for Peace" (aka "Territorial Compromise") and the "Road Map" had all the appearances of another underachiever. By 2005, the Israelis had decided to buckle under to American pressure and trade "Land for Peace." For this, according to the American formula, they would get peace in return and could rely on Arab rationality and assurances. There were, of course, Western guarantees that the new Arab entity would be terrorist-free, so to speak. So, the Israelis completely abandoned the Gaza Strip in August of 2005, which they had taken from Egypt in the Six Day War some 38 years before. (One should note that it was never "Palestinian" land, but actually belonged to Egypt.)

"Not to worry," Ms. Rice intoned, "we shall have peace when the Palestinians in Gaza go to the polls in their first free election." *Arab Democracy will triumph.* So, the Gazans went to the polls in January 2006 and 83 percent [33] of them voted to oust the (somewhat) moderate Sunni Palestinian Authority (read: the PLO) and bring to power the Shiite HAMAS (Harakat al-Muqawamah al-Islamiyya or Islamic Resistance Movement). HAMAS is of course, the Shia terrorist organization backed by Iran and best known for its suicide bombers and rocket attacks on Israel. It is even listed by the State Department as a terrorist organization.

In June 2007, HAMAS attacked the remnants of the Palestinian Authority (PLO) in a bloody putsch that completely consolidated their democratically-procured hold on the Gaza Strip. They decided against moderation in favor of a proper, Shia-Islamic entity.

So, matters did not quite hold to plan and the Israelis got in exchange a continuous barrage of rockets from the Gaza Strip. (Not surprisingly those Western guarantees were never implemented.)

Thus having to abandon "Land for Peace" and "Arab Democracy," Secretary Rice apparently fell back on "Transformational Diplomacy." In 2008, she asked the Israelis for more concessions to the Palestinians, including providing the Sunni-Moslem, Palestinian Authority with arms and armored vehicles to off-set the rise of the Shia-Moslem HAMAS in Gaza. In the end, "Transformational Diplomacy" has delivered up another typical "goat grope. "

While your humble servant earnestly believes that there is a village in the Silicon Valley being deprived of its idiot, Secretary Rice is in good company. Hilary Rodham Clinton, who superseded Rice as Secretary of State has subsequently attempted an Arab-Israeli fix with the same results. At this writing, her successor, John Kerry, has leaped into the breach and played the only card available to him … forcing Israel makes massive concessions to the Palestinian Authority and sweetening the PLO with massive American financial aid.

There have been numerous attempts in the past to bring about that ever-elusive "Peace in the Middle East" and all have only one similarity … they all ended in failure.

CB BO

The Super Powers

"Peace is that brief glorious moment in history when everybody stands around reloading."

Thomas Jefferson
(Questionably attributed)

In the midst of the Cold War, the two superpowers took sides in the Arab-Israeli conflict, wading into this quagmire with both feet. Their respective superpower sponsor armed each side and thus the Cold War was superimposed on the tumultuous, seething cauldron of the Middle East.

As a practical matter of survivability, the Israelis have always been disdainful of outsiders arming the Arabs, because it invariably leads to war. It always has and it always will. The late Yitzhak Walker once summed up the Israeli view when he caustically noted, "You don't give real guns to children." The modern history of the Middle East supports his view. The primary objective of the Arab States remains the destruction of the Jewish State. This has not changed nor will it in spite of the best intentions of outsiders. Arming the Arabs only brings on war ... if not with the Israelis, then with each other. This, it can be argued, is the way of the pre-Enlightenment Arabs.

The fall of the Soviet Empire gave rise to the Islamic Wars of Insurgency, which are seemingly aimed at establishing the mythical Islamic Caliphate. At the turn of the millennium, every trouble spot in the world ... Somalia, Sudan, Chechnya, the Philippines, Sri Lanka, Bosnia ... were holy wars being perpetrated by Moslem insurgents. Many in Russian Intelligence believe that there is a central funding source for these "wars of liberation" and are looking hard at Wahhabi-Sunni, Saudi Arabia. American Intelligence officials agree, but it was not "politically correct" to openly express this view until "Nine-Eleven" and then never publically and only with caution.

NATO's intervention into a Moslem War of Insurgency in Bosnia set a bad precedent for the Middle East. While CNN and the rest of the western media downplayed the Moslem insurgency (the Moslems, those same folks who provided Adolph Hitler with two SS Division, were magically transformed into "Ethnic Albanians"), they overplayed government atrocities until NATO, led by the United States, intervened militarily. It was not the first time the media brought political pressure on the United States to intervene in a foreign dispute or leave one. The American intervention in Somalia ... as in "Blackhawk Down" ... comes immediately to mind. But, NATO's intervention into a European civil war on the side of Moslem insurgents had a special significance for the Palestinians. Especially since then, they have been seeking intervention by outside forces in their war on the Israelis.[34]

Unlike the Reagan Administration, which sided with the Arabs, the United States under Bill Clinton made efforts to be fair to both the Jews and the Arabs in the Middle East. Of course, that did not work either. And, Barak Obama ... forget about it.

Additionally, the American Government's view of the Middle East has normally reflected the political party in power. Very generally speaking, the Democrats have favored the Israelis while the Republicans have favored the Arabs up until 1973. This is not however, a hard and fast rule in changing times and media perceptions. Jimmy Carter was actually very pro-Arab and has grown more so with age[35] while Republican Richard Nixon was always pro-Israeli. The bias was shifting again to pro-

Arab under George Bush (43) ... right up to Nine-Eleven when everyone woke up and discovered the Arabs hated us. Barak Obama is definitely a pro-Arab appeaser, while the challenging Republicans have swung strongly to the pro-Israeli side. *One needs a scorecard to keep matters straight.*

Interestingly, the secular American Jews support the Democrats no matter their stance on Israel, while the American Orthodox Jewish community supports the Republicans. *Go figure.*

The Israelis understood that the Reagan Administration, top-heavy as it was with appointees from the petroleum industry, was going to shift American political support to the Arabs. As we shall see, when the Reaganites began to secretly arm Iraq in an updated version of the old Mutually Assured Destruction scenario, a dynamic was set in motion that eventually triggered the First Gulf War.

For all its efforts, for all its agendas, for all the exalted promises of a "fairness doctrine," successive American policies have changed nothing. Depressingly, the strife will continue until the issue is decided militarily. The conflict also spread globally and it was not until Nine-Eleven that our American naïveté was dealt a serious dose of reality, which sadly did not last long.

So in spite of various administrations leaning toward one side or the other, in spite of lofty, noble pronouncements out of Washington, nothing much is going to change in the Middle East until the people who live there decide it will, most probably by war.

CHAPTER 2

TILTING THE MILITARY BALANCE

"I will execute judgment upon him with plague and bloodshed; I will pour down torrents of rain, hailstones and burning sulfur on him and on his troops and on the many nations with him."

Ezekiel 38:22

The Arabs and the Jews, both fractious peoples, have a common ancestry in the founding patriarch of the Hebrew tribe, the *First Hebrew* if you will, a man called Abraham. He was a revolutionary of sorts, because in defiance of tradition, he had only one god to whom he answered. The "God of Abraham" became the One God of the Hebrews and Judaism became the first monotheistic religion. The other two great desert religions are also monotheistic and trace their lineage back to Judaism and the One "God of Abraham."

Abraham sired two sons from two women. His first son, Ishmael, was the off spring of Hagar, an Egyptian servant. His second son, Isaac, was the off spring of his wife, Sarah. Tradition casts Ishmael as the "father" of the Arabs, while Isaac is the "father" of the Hebrews. Both tribes view Abraham as their patriarch and refer to each other as "cousins." Thus, the troubles between these two tribes could and should, be viewed as a "family affair."

Both tribes have a tendency to spawn prophets and holy men whose main calling seems to be telling the people how to live, most especially in the eyes of their One God. In retrospect, one might proffer that this could be the baseline cause of all hostility. And, while Arab aggression in the last century causes the world to view them as whining troublemakers, one must remember that the One God of the Hebrews took to calling them "Israel," which loosely translates, "He who struggles with God."

Thus, war has become the common state of the Middle East; peace is simply an interlude. It is the military balance, therefore, between the two tribes that brings and perpetuates those peaceful interludes. What upset this balance are the Arab oil revenues, Soviet and Russian foreign policy that has generously supplied military hardware and mischief, and a wildly-fluctuating American foreign policy.

A working definition of this "military balance" would have the State of Israel in a military posture capable of defeating the combined forces of the Arab states. It must be this calculation since a military defeat would end the existence of the Jewish State. On the other hand, Israel's military objectives have never been the annihilation of the Arab People or even the annexation of their land. Thus, the Arab states can and have suffered devastating military defeats and lived to fight another day.

When that delicate balance tilts in favor of the Arabs, they attack Israel. It has always been that way and will be so until day and night come to an end. Occasionally, the Israelis will preemptively attack a threatening Arab project as they did the nuclear facilities of Iraq in 1981 and Syria in 2008. Mostly, however, the Jews are content to be left alone.

The Arabs, on the other hand, are constantly jonesing to tilt the military balance, in spite of the fact that they have lost every time they have gone to war. We suppose it is probably a matter of principle and machismo. And, the Arab states, most of which cannot properly feed their populations, still manage to afford new military purchases from a plethora of outside sellers … all with a handful of "gimme" and a mouthful of "much obliged."

Byzantine conspiracies, plots and schemes have always been woven into the fabric of the Middle East in general and the Arab-Israeli conflict in particular. The East, an early Greek philosopher once noted "has a way of swallowing men and their dreams."

CB EO

Säenger's Choirboys

"The Lord hath mingled a perverse spirit in the midst of it; and they have caused Egypt to err in every work of it..."

Isaiah: 19

Historically, the Arabs' primary objective has remained constant. You can dress it up by calling it the "Level Battlefield Doctrine" and you could make it look nice by promoting it as the "New Saudi Peace Plan" or the "Road Map" or "Transformational Diplomacy" but, in the end, it is the same old agenda, warts and all. The Arab effort in the 1980s sucked in additional outside players - the Americans - but the Germans and the Arabs have continually conspired in their genocidal wet dream, which remains at the core of matters. *(As the Germans are wont to say, "The Arabs have our oil; the Jews only have our guilt.")*

The Israelis, looking at the 1980s experienced a serious dose of déjà vu. It harkened back to 1956 when Israeli Intelligence was focused on Gamal Abd el Nasser's Egypt into which Soviet-supplied weapons were then pouring in unbelievable numbers in order to ostensibly "level the battlefield." The Middle East military balance was tilting toward the Arabs every day as Soviet tanks, aircraft, artillery and munitions arrived. [36] The Israelis knew the moment Egypt felt sufficiently strong, there would be war ... such is the tried and true way of these matters.

When the Egyptians felt the military balance had tilted enough in their favor, they nationalized the Suez Canal. But, they miscalculated the European reaction and the French and British in particular were not amused. Soon tensions were peaking and trouble was in the wind.

Then, as sometimes happens when one focuses intelligence assets too hard in a single place, on a single threat, the Israelis misread a seemingly unrelated scrap of information.

Earlier that year, an Egyptian businessman named Hassan Said Kamil had stumbled across a Mossad tripwire in Switzerland. From first indications, Kamil was apparently recruiting former Nazi rocket scientists for an Egyptian Government project in the sleepy Cairo suburb of Helwan. The Israelis quickly determined that the industrial center for this project was coded BASE 333, a rather ominous indicator. Beyond that, nothing definitive washed up, so they back-burnered it.

While initially, the Israelis read no immediate threat into it, soon a young Mossad agent[37] in Cairo began peppering Tel Aviv with radio traffic warning that the Egyptians were employing a large number of German scientists and engineers who had formerly worked in the Nazi regime. At the time, Mossad was actively tracking fugitive Nazi war criminals, many of whom had sought and had been given refuge in Egypt where their "Jewish experience" was in demand. There may have been some initial confusion that lumped the scientists in with the common criminals, but in any case, Tel Aviv Center had bigger fish to fry at that moment in the spool-up for the Sinai Campaign of 1956.

During this second Arab-Israeli War, the French and the British attacked Cairo and took the Suez Canal. The Israelis struck into Sinai and destroyed the massive Egyptian Army concentrated there. It was a quick and complete victory, but the Republican administration of President Dwight Eisenhower reacted badly.

The Americans forced the French, the British and the Israelis to withdraw and Egyptian sovereignty was re-established over the Suez Canal and the Sinai Peninsula in the name of anti-colonialism. There were, of course, promises and guarantees given to the victors to help induce their withdrawal. Among these were the right of free passage through the Suez Canal for all ships, the Sinai was demilitarized and the deployment of a 3,400-man UN peacekeeping force on the border between Egypt and Israel. The United States signed on as a guarantor to this agreement.

As the Israelis pulled out of Sinai, they shipped back to Israel or destroyed in place, the bulk of the Egyptian Army's Soviet-supplied equipment. It would be eleven years before the Arabs would again feel militarily strong enough to make war on the Jews.[38]

It took a while, but when the dust finally settled in the wake of the 1956 War, Mossad decided that the Helwan situation begged a closer look. What they found terrified them. The German scientists in Egypt were specialized in the fields of aviation and rocketry and all of them seemed to be part of a newly-revamped, Egyptian military build-up.

And, the Germans were not your garden-variety players, but rather the creme de la creme from the former Nazi military-industrial complex. They were men like Willi Messerschmitt, the pre-eminent aircraft designer, and former SS Standartenfuhrer Ferdinand Brandner of Junkers, who had recently designed the NK-12 power plant for the Soviet Tupolev-95 "Bear" bomber.[39]

In 1960 the Israelis found rocketeers such as Eugen Säenger[40] who had run Nazi Germany's original rocket research unit at Luneberg Heath. Paul-Jens Goerke and Wolfgang Pilz, who worked with Säenger at Peenemunde during the war, were also employed at Helwan.[41] All worked under the direction of Dr. Wilheim Voss, one of the deans of German rocketry.

As the Israeli intelligence collection emphasis shifted from the war criminals to the scientists, additional reports began to flood in from Europe. Nasser had sent his agents to purchase machinery, technology and materials for his new projects from the Europeans, exactly like Saddam Hussein would do some 30 years later. Companies like MECO and MTP of Zurich, Switzerland, and INTRA of Stuttgart, West Germany, were identified as major suppliers.

Initially, the Israelis attempted to stop this growing threat through diplomatic means, but serious talks with the West German Government about its nationals building ballistic missiles in Egypt produced little reactions and no solutions.

Shortly after these diplomatic talks began, many more wanted war criminals washed up in Egypt in addition to the Peenemunde retreads. These were real Jew-haters with blood on their hands. Among them was former SS Standartenfuhrer Leopold Gleim, aka Ali al Nahar, wanted in Poland for Crimes against Humanity, but now in Cairo working for Egyptian State Security in charge of political prisoners. SS General Oscar Dirlewanger, the former commander of the 36th Waffen SS division and a former Nazi bureaucrat, Willi Brenner,

71

who had organized the Mauthausen death camp, where thousands of Jews, political prisoners and Allied POWs perished were also identified as gainfully employed by the Egyptians. And while these ex-pat Germans were distracting, the real threat was centered in the rocket scientists and engineers.

The Helwan industrial complex had been overlooked during the Sinai Campaign, but in its aftermath, the language du jour was once again German at BASE 333 (later rebuilt as the Sakr Factory for Developed Industries) [42] and the secret Egyptian weapons projects were soon back up and running.

Israeli Intelligence began calling the Germans "Säenger's Choirboys" and on 22 July 1962, the fruits of their labors splashed into the international headlines when Nasser unveiled his three new ballistic missiles[43] in a military parade through Cairo. As frenzied crowds screamed for Jewish blood, Nasser told them that his missiles were capable of hitting any targets "south of Beirut." The crowds and the Israelis believed him.

In September 1962, apparently on the direct orders of Prime Minister David Ben-Gurion, [44] Israeli Intelligence implemented their own "Final Solution" to their German problem under the codename DAMOCLES. It was decided to terminate the Germans' employment in Helwan; to terminate it with *extreme prejudice.* All over Europe and even within Egypt, Israeli agents began hunting down "Säenger's Choirboys" and killing them.

Dr. Heinz Krug, chief of Antra, the Munich front company supplying critical components to the Egyptians, disappeared in September 1962 while on home leave from Egypt. His body was never found.

On 27 November 1962, a letter arrived at the office of Wolfgang Pilz in Egypt and when his German secretary opened it, it exploded, blinding her. Only two days later, a package arrived in the office of the project's Egyptian administrator in Heliopolis, General Kamal Azzaz. When it went off, five Egyptian engineers were blown to pieces ... make that little pieces.

Dr. Hans Kleinwachter, another Peenemunde alum who headed the development of the missile guidance systems at Helwan, went back to Germany for a visit in February 1963. Driving along the back roads in the small town of Lorrach, Kleinwachter was forced off the road by another car. An Israeli agent jumped out and shot Dr. Kleinwachter full of holes. The German miraculously survived, but he got the message. Hans Kleinwachter never returned to Egypt.

In the beginning of the "hunting season," some of the German scientists could not fathom why heartless, determined men were murdering them. Most rationalized that they were "only doing their jobs," that it was "science" and therefore endowed with a purity that somehow exempted them from the normal restrictions civilized society places on most endeavors. Many never made the connection between the mentality of the gangster state that spawned them and the relentless anger driving the Jews. It was the same astonishing mindset that surfaced some 30 years later.

In the spring of 1963, Swiss authorities arrested an Austrian physicist named Dr. Otto Joklik and a shadowy Israeli, Joseph Ben-Gal. Both men were charged with attempting to intimidate Dr. Paul-Jens Goerke, an Austrian-born Peenemunde veteran then working for the Egyptians in Helwan.

At first pleased with the arrests, the West German Government soon changed its mind when Joklick and Ben-Gal demanded a public trial. Dr. Joklick had been previously recruited to work in Egypt, but when the overall plan was explained to him, his personal revulsion forced him to quit and return to Europe. Joklick, it seemed, could not justify the Egyptian Government efforts as "science."

From the witness stand in a Swiss courtroom, the world learned first hand about the projects then under way at BASE 333 in Helwan, Egypt. Joklick outlined the development of aircraft and missiles that would carry chemical, biological and eventually nuclear warheads to Israel. He detailed how Wolfgang Pilz had sent agents to North America to purchase Cobalt 60 and other radioactive materials for use in the missile warheads.[45] Dr. Joklik went on to tell of Egyptian experiments with deadly pathogens and nerve gases on live animals. These revelations along with the mix of the former Nazis, stunned and outraged the world. After all, millions of people had died during the Second World War to stop this exact thing.

Both Joklik and Ben-Gal were found guilty and sentenced to 60 days ... time served ... and served with an expulsion order.[46] In reaction to the public disclosures out of Switzerland, the West German Government quickly passed legislation forbidding its nationals from working in Nasser's armament industries. Shortly thereafter, the German scientists left Egypt and returned home. The Egyptian projects at BASE 333 ground to a halt. Four years later, during the Six-Day War, the Helwan industrial complex was completely destroyed by Israeli air strikes.[47]

While its objective was reached, Israel did not come through the Helwan Affair unscathed. When the DAMOCLES operation went "loud" in that Basle courtroom, the director of Ha Mossad, Isser Harel, was forced to resign by Prime Minister David Ben-Gurion. This precipitated the additional resignation of the officer-in-charge of the operation (and later Prime Minister), Yitzhak Shamir. Three months later, Ben-Gurion resigned as Prime Minister.

ଔ ଓ

The APD Blueprint

> *"With the basest of companions, I the streets of Babylon."*

Augustine
Confessions, II, 3

By the mid-1970s, prior to the Iran-Iraq War, Saddam Hussein was attempting to construct manufacturing facilities to produce "aslihatul dammar ashammel," Arabic for weapons of mass destruction. It was all about regional dominance among the Middle Eastern states and also part of the old Arab game of gaining enough military strength to destroy the Jewish State.

The manufacture of nuclear, chemical, and biological weapons, and the military vectors to deliver them had been recommended in a study done by a Beirut-based, Palestinian consulting firm, Arab Projects and Developments (APD). The APD study, which was circulated to several Arab States, concluded that this was the only way the Arabs could reach military superiority over Israel and ultimately destroy the Jews.

APD was organized as a non-profit organization to promote economic, social, and cultural progress in the Arab countries. It was run by two Palestinian businessmen, the late Kamal Abdel Rahman and Hassib Sabbagh[48], both close to Yasser Arafat.[49]

The now-famous APD study was a strategic blueprint for an Arab state to reach military superiority over their Zionist enemy. It proposed that a state should not become dependent on one source of weapons making it vulnerable to embargoes or political whims. It suggested a diversity of sources, making suppliers compete for the business. It took the question of armaments one step further and proposed that the state become independent of those sources by insisting on purchasing manufacturing facilities from those same weapons suppliers. This, ironically, was patterned on the Israeli model.

As to weapons of mass destruction (WMD), it suggested that the acquisition of chemical and biological weapons should be undertaken initially because it was far simpler than the homegrown development of nuclear weapons. Nuclear weapons should be developed in parallel, but would take longer. Finally, the report recommended that delivery vector (ballistic missile) development should also proceed in parallel.

Iraq was the first Arab country to put money into implementing the recommendations in the study. APD personnel working for the Iraqis contacted the Pfaulder Corporation of Rochester, New York, which they retained to design Iraq's first chemical weapons plant. The site chosen for the facility was at Samara, 115 miles north of Baghdad.

It was a nice piece of business for Pfaulder, but in 1978, when they attempted to export the plans, machinery and materials necessary for the construction of the Iraqi "pesticide" plant at Samara, the Carter State Department said "No way."

APD [50] was able, however, to smuggle the Pfaulder drawings and technical specifications out of the United States and turn them over to the Iraqis. Several months later, the Iraqis contracted with Karl Kolb GmbH of Drieich, West Germany to build the Pfaulder-designed, "pesticide" plant at Samara. [51]

In a parallel effort, the West German firm of Thyssen AG began planning the construction of a biological weapons research and development facility at Salman Pak, south of Baghdad.

The success of the Salman Pak facility was off-set by a debacle when two other ADP alumni, a Palestinian named Merwan and his brother, pulled together the Al-Hazen Ibn Al Haitham Institute. Given millions of dollars by Saddam Hussein to acquire foreign military technology, the brothers attracted foreign scientist to Al-Hazen and even forged a partnership with the Optics Science Center of the University of Arizona in Tucson. In the end, however, it turned out to be a gigantic scam, which landed Merwan in the Abu Ghraib Hilton, but who was saved temporarily from execution by the personal intervention of Yasser Arafat. But, when Arafat betrayed Saddam by siding with Iran, the star-crossed Merwan was cut up in pieces, boxed up and returned to his mentor.[52]

Thus, the Iraqis began developing non-nuclear weapons of mass destruction. Their nuclear weapons efforts are better known.

 C8 80

SPHINX

*"He had to fiddle around with the atom, when cancer
was still uncured, and hunger, hate and avarice still
strode the earth untouched, unharmed and nearly
unnoticed by this ignoble animal, man. And now he
has the atom just where it wants him. He can
compress, into six square inches, enough hate and
malignity to kill half a million people, blot out the sun,
uproot fertile fields and steal the smell of preach
blooms from the air."*

Robert Ruark
I DIDN'T KNOW IT WAS LOADED

The story of Saddam Hussein's efforts to produce
a nuclear "Islamic Bomb" involves a Byzantine maze of
plots and counter-plots. It is standard fare for the Middle
East and like all Arab military build-ups, it inevitably
ended in a shooting war.

It was the Soviet Union that provided Iraq's first
nuclear reactor in 1963. In a five-year project, a
complex of nuclear facilities and laboratories was
constructed at Al Tuwaitha, some 16 miles south of
Baghdad, which was later coded TAMUZ 17. [53] The
Soviet-supplied research reactor was an IRT2000-type
with a 2 megawatt (thermal) capacity and it went on line
in July 1968. It was reportedly upgraded some years
later to 5 megawatts (thermal) by increasing its fuel
enrichment. [54]

One must classify the Iraqi experience with
Soviet nuclear technology and equipment as a defining
underachievement. First, even upgraded to 5

megawatts, the Soviet reactor was too small to produce fissile material for a bomb. Second, the Soviets piled on long-outdated equipment and worthless service-contract technicians and sold the package to the Iraqis by weight. Finally, when the reactor needed cleaning, the Soviet technicians shied away, leaving it to the Iraqis, who promptly screwed up the process, causing dangerous radioactive leakage.[55] All-in-all, it was not a shining example of Soviet technology.

By late 1971, the Soviet flim-flam was discovered and by early 1972, Saddam Hussein ordered the Russians out. He then refused to pay his obligations under the contracts and when he did give them a pittance, it was in Russian Rubles, not hard currency.

Flush with new-found oil money as a result of the Arab boycott in the wake of the 1973 Yom Kippur War, Iraq continued looking for a supplier of nuclear technology and equipment and by late 1975, they had connected up with the international, nuclear equivalent of the friendly, neighborhood drug dealer: France.

France agreed to provide Iraq with two additional nuclear reactors. The first, a small Isis-type teaching reactor and a second, a dual-purpose, gas-graphite reactor of the Osiris class.[56] The second, an advanced reactor called "Osirak" (the acronym for Osiris-Iraq), had a capacity of 500 megawatts (electrical) and 1,500 megawatts (thermal). The reactor, which would be built at the French manufacturing facility in Sarcelles, north of Paris, was touted as a "research" reactor, but it was designed to produce both electricity and plutonium.

The French Prime Minister, Jacques Chirac, justified the sale because of renewed interest in alternative sources of power in the wake of the oil crisis created by the OPEC countries. A reasonable person might only conclude that the Iraqis, who were sitting on top of the second largest proven oil reserves, were not especially interested in "alternative sources of power."

In return, the French got a contract to purchase 70 million barrels of Iraqi crude per year for ten years at current market prices. Iraq would also make massive purchases of French military equipment … helicopters, tanks, missiles, radars and 100 Mirage F-1 fighter aircraft, along with the attendant service and training contracts and spare parts. Saddam Hussein also agreed to purchase 100,000 Peugeot and Renault automobiles … 50,000 each … and to give the French a contract to develop a billion-dollar lake resort near Habbaniyah, west of Baghdad. On the face of it, it was a "strike-up-the-band" deal, unless, of course, you consider the potential, minor consequences of giving a tin-pot, blood-thirsty, Arab dictator a nuclear bomb.

A sidebar comment is now indicated: The French as well as the myriad sub-contactors were not idiots and knew full well that there were humorless people out there who would take a dim view of their efforts to provide Saddam Hussein with his nuclear wet dream. Those particular folks were of the Jewish persuasion and had the maddening habit of holding individuals personally responsible for what they considered irresponsible behavior. This was most especially true if that irresponsible behavior had the potential to threaten the physical existence of the Jewish State.

The French made a reasonably successful effort to assuage the concerns of the Israelis, up to a point. The contract dictated that all the necessary equipment was to be manufactured in Sarcelles, shipped to Iraq and assembled in the TAMUZ 17 complex. The French would also supply two nuclear cores and it was these nuclear cores that became a critical sticking point for the Israelis.

Under the terms of the agreement, the French were to supply 72 kilograms of weapons-grade, enriched uranium (U^{235}) in two cores fabricated from 93 percent Uranium Oxide ore, also known as "Yellow Cake." The Israelis pointed out to the French (and anyone else who would listen) that if the reactor was going to be used for the production of power as advertised, a core of non-weapons-grade "Caramel" would do nicely.[57]

When the French, like little gentlemen, broached the idea with the Iraqis, they were turned down flat and even threatened. Not wanting to lose the massive revenues, the French pushed ahead with the project, knowing full well that the Iraqis intended to use their new reactor's by-product, plutonium,[58] to build nuclear weapons. In fact, it was calculated under a "worst case" scenario that the reactor could produce enough plutonium for one nuclear bomb annually. Still, the French insisted on their tired, old prognosis of Iraq's renewed interest in alternative sources of power.

This talking point held right up until Israeli Intelligence discovered a contract the Italian firm, SNIA, had received from Iraq to construct a facility to extract plutonium from the spent fuel rods at TAMUZ 17. While the French denied knowledge, the battle lines were thus drawn.

CB BO

Israeli diplomatic efforts had begun under Prime Minister Yitzhak Rabin back in 1974 when Ha Mossad first informed the Government of Israel about the French deal. Shimon Peres, then-Foreign Minister, contacted his old friend, Jacques Chirac, who vaguely promised to see "what could be done after the (French) elections." Based on this, Rabin decided to wait and see.

In 1975, the influential French investigative reporter, Jean-Pierre Van Geirt of *Paris Match,* broke the story of the French-Iraq nuclear deal with all its sordid details. Who his sources were is unimportant, but it did have the effect of pressuring the French government, alas to no avail.

In May 1977, the newly-elected Prime Minister of Israel, Menachem Begin, convened a secret meeting of what has been called his "shadow security committee" on the Iraqi nuclear question. Among others in attendance, was General David Ivry, Chief of the Israeli Air Force, and his superior, General Raphael "Raful" Eitan, the IDF Chief of Staff. Also attending were Yitzhak Hofi, Chief of Ha Mossad and General Yehoshua Saguy, head of AMAN, Israeli Military Intelligence.

It was clear from the photographs presented that unexpected and alarmingly, rapid progress was being made by the Iraqis at their TAMUZ 17 facility and quite obviously Israeli diplomatic efforts had failed. Further,

Israeli scientists upped the estimate of the Iraqi capability to "2 to 3 bombs annually."

No consensus on a plan of action was reached, but it was clear that military planners had to begin work on an operational option. Formally, a State of War still existed between Israel and Iraq and being ignored by "friendly" allies, the Israelis decided to quietly intervene to "slow things down." They initiated their clandestine operations under the code name SPHINX.[59]

※ ※

With the completion of the preparations at the TAMUZ 17 facility at Al Tuwaitha in 1979, it remained only to ship the reactor's nuclear core to Iraq and install it. The French stored the first two reactor cores at a guarded, high-security warehouse[60] in the Riviera town of La Seyne-sur-Mer near Toulon and scheduled their shipment for 6 April 1979.

Sometime during the night of 5 April 1979, seven Israeli operatives penetrated the secure storage area and blew up the nuclear cores. It was a letter-perfect covert operation, causing $23 million in damages, which was calculated to set back the French-Iraqi timetable by more than two years.

While Paris screamed that the sabotage was an "act of war," the Israelis smugly denied any connection and called the French accusations "anti-Semitism." It was clear to all, however, that the Israelis meant business.

There was, however, a problem. The La Seyne-sur-Mer operation completely destroyed one of the reactor cores, but left the other only heavily damaged. Iraq decided to accept the damaged core with the intention to salvage and repair it. Thus, the setback was not as lengthy as Israel desired.

A little more than a year later, yet another act in SPHINX played out. On 13 June 1980, one of the key Arab scientist working on Iraq's "Islamic Bomb" project at TAMUZ 17, Dr. Yahia El Meshad, was beaten and stabbed to death in room 9041 of the Meridian Hotel in Paris.[61]

Born in Egypt, Meshad was a noted physics professor and nuclear engineer at the University of Alexandria. After his death, Zamuba Meshad, his widow, stated, "He used to tell me he would continue the

Dr. Yahia El Meshad

assignment of creating the bomb even if he had to pay for it with his life." Obviously, someone took him at his word.

In spite of the public pronouncements of Madam Meshad, the French were still determined to see the project completed, although it was crystal clear by then that the Iraqis had no interest in "alternative power sources." Explaining this indifference years later, Dr. Khidir Hamza, the Iraqi scientist in charge of the TAMUZ 17 project, stated simply, "no one cared."[62]

In the late summer of 1980, business executives of Iraq's three key suppliers in France and Italy - SNIA-Techint, Ansaldo Mercanico Nucleare and Techniatome - began receiving threatening letters. On 2 August 1980, a bomb exploded on the front porch of the home of the Chairman of SNIA in Rome. Soon other bombs followed at private homes and offices throughout Italy.

The toll on the Iraqi nuclear scientists was far greater. Of the 20 principal scientists involved, 17 were threatened outright. Two of them were killed by poison … one while attending an official state dinner in Paris. An additional three or four died in "accidents." Understandably, morale plunged, but the Iraqi Government shored up their flagging scientific cadre with cash bonuses and new Mercedes automobiles.

In the meanwhile, the French labored to replace the reactor cores destroyed by the Israelis in 1979. They completed repairs to the damaged core of Yellow Cake and secretly delivered it to the Al Tuwaitha facility in 1981. The Osirak reactor (coded TAMUZ 1) was scheduled to go "hot" between the second week in June and 1 July 1981.

C8 80

OPERA

"Before your eyes I will repay Babylon and all who live in Babylonia for all the wrong they have done in Zion, declares the Lord."

Jeremiah 25:12

In September of 1980, Saddam Hussein attacked Iran, initiating the 8-year Iran-Iraq War. Cross-border firefights built into a full-scale invasion when Iraqi forces crossed over on 22 September. Six days later, General Yehoshua Saguy, chief of Israeli Military Intelligence (AMAN) told journalists that he was surprised the Iranians had not destroyed the Al Tuwaitha nuclear complex during the first week of the war.[63]

On 30 September 1980 and again on 1 October, Iranian Air Force F-4 Phantoms attacked the Iraqi nuclear complex at Al Tuwaitha. The raids were poorly executed and missed the reactor building entirely. It did, however, blow out the water cooling system and plumbing in addition to damaging some outer labs. In reaction, the Iraqis surrounded the complex with a high, earthen, blast wall and fortified it with dedicated radar-controlled, anti-aircraft artillery and SAM-6 missile batteries. Seven months later, there being no further Iranian raids on the complex, the construction work was continued.[64]

On Sunday, 7 June 1981, Israeli Air Force units attacked and destroyed the reactor only days before it was to go on line.[65] There are several excellent accounts of this raid, which was coded OPERA, and it is not our intention to recount the details here. There are, however, certain aspects of the operation having to do with the intelligence and planning that beg our attention in the context of this work.

It was a 1200-mile mission Israeli planners had to cope with that had to be completed without refueling. Luckily, the Israelis had the right aircraft, the American-made F-16A, to do the job. Those F-16s had come to Israel by way of a political upheaval ... the overthrow of the Shah of Iran in 1979. The Shah had ordered 160 of the fighters, but after the fall of the Peacock Throne, the United States refused to ship them to the new Islamic Republic of Iran. The manufacturer, General Dynamics of San Diego was stuck with 76 aircraft in various stages of production. The Americans offered those 76 to Israel.

Israeli Military Intelligence, AMAN, had prepared the battlespace and had the target "lined and defined." It knew that the Iraqi defenses around Al Tuwaitha faced east, toward Iran. It knew that the security shifts changed at 6:00 PM in the evening when the personnel went to supper and the defensive radars were turned off. It knew that the French technicians did not work on Sunday. These and other tidbits were vectored into the operational attack plan.

It was 90 minutes to the target, two minutes time-over-target and 90 minutes back home ... 182 long minutes, half the time flying nape-of-the-earth to avoid radar at "econo-cruise" power to conserve fuel. The Air Force planers decided to strike late on a Sunday afternoon to take advantage of the known routines and with the quick arrival of night, making it less risky for Israeli Search and Rescue should any pilots be downed.

Fuel was a major consideration. Normally, the F-16s carried enough fuel for the flight to the target and a return trip as far as Jordan. (Israel's conformal fuel tanks for the F-16 had yet to be developed.) Defensive systems were pulled from the F-16s to save weight and extra fuel was added. New centerline fuel tanks arrived from the United States and "hot topping" was utilized to add fuel while the bombers awaited their turn for departure. The F-16s took off from Etzion Air Force Base (now Taba International) at twice their operational weight.

Other than the two Mk 84 free fall, non-guided, general purpose, 2000 pound bombs each aircraft carried, the F-16s flew unarmed. A flight of eight F-15s accompanied the bombers flying low cover, but hung back out of Iraqi airspace ready to intervene should Saudi Arabia or Jordan decide to intercept. Two F-15Bs flew high over the Saudi desert acting as communication relays and an additional six F-15s flew top cover and radar suppression to the target. The last element was composed of CH-53 helicopters loitering at Israel's eastern border ready to rush in and snatch any downed pilot. Altogether, some 50 aircraft were involved. Additionally, elements of a paratroop brigade stood by ready to be inserted should a knock-down-drag-out develop around the rescue of a downed pilot.

Before launch, there was one humorous incident that begs mention. A Mossad officer arrived with a large black briefcase. As he wandered onto the tarmac, the latch of his briefcase snapped and thousands of dollars worth of Iraqi dinars spilled out. It was, of course, bribe money for the pilots, but the incident destroyed any operational security as to the target.

The reactor was destroyed and all aircraft returned safely to base. It would take the United States ten years to appreciate the attack.

The OPERA bomber pilots

CR &O

Ironically, Kuwait led the condemnation of Israel for this attack. The Reagan Administration, led by Vice-President George Bush, quickly joined the fray in a show of solidarity with its Arab friends.

In a meeting of the Senate Intelligence Committee, Bobby Ray Inman, the Deputy Director of the CIA, noted his outrage at the Israelis. In justification he stated:

"The US is engaged in a sophisticated and very successful effort to turn Saddam Hussein into a pillar of American foreign policy in the Middle East."[66]

The French swore to rebuild the reactor, but this time with the secret agreement of Israel, they supplied the Iraqis with "Caramel" nuclear cores. Thus, the Iraqis were forced to seek weapons-grade "Yellow Cake" nuclear fuel for their reactor elsewhere and eventually sourced it from Brazil.

When the Israelis destroyed the building housing the nuclear reactor in TAMUZ 17, the Reagan Administration was only six months old. The American reaction spoke volumes about the new political attitudes toward the Middle East in Washington. One might have hoped for at least a smooth bit of duplicity, but the reality was simply angry, utter confusion.

The administration's condemnation of Israel and a subsequent "embargo" on the delivery of the American-made F-16 fighter-bombers was orchestrated by the Vice President and Secretary of Defense, Caspar Weinberger. It was done without the knowledge of Secretary of State Alexander Haig, who only learned about it from the media and quickly reversed the "embargo." There was obviously a case of *"Who's On First"* in Washington, which added more confusion to a confused Middle East policy.

Cʒ ᘒ

CHAPTER 3

COMES THE GIPPER

"Men in authority will always think that criticism of their policies is dangerous. They will always equate their policies with patriotism, and find criticism subversive."

Henry Steele Commager

The Boys in the Oil Business

"We have always played down the American oil interests, and it would certainly not be popular if the impression should be given that we were risking military action to protect investments of American oil companies."

John Foster Dulles
Secretary of State
30 January 1956

President Jimmy Carter introduced his national energy program in April of 1977,[67] which challenged the supposition that "demand for energy grows more or less automatically." The basic tenet of his program was his belief that the United States could cut back its dependence on Middle East oil through conservation measures and the development of new energy sources.

This, he felt, would be economically beneficial to the nation as a whole.

Carter also "deeply resented that the greatest nation on earth was being jerked around by a few desert states," read: the Arabs. He was bound and determined to reduce the country's need for imported, Middle Eastern oil and he called his program the "moral equivalent of war." The Republican oilmen, who were financially threatened by the Carter energy initiative, derisively referred to his program by its acronym, MEOW.[68]

Oil money, the energy crisis and the tedious Iran hostage situation defeated Jimmy Carter in the election of 1980. His one-term presidency had not been long enough to kill off the old Nixon-Watergate crowd within the Republican Party and when Ronald Reagan went to Washington in 1981, the old Watergaters and the oilmen went with him. It did not bother them being "jerked around by a few desert states" as long as the oil and their profits flowed.

The "suits" came to Washington with no experience in foreign policy, no experience in economics and little sense of history. Their new economic vision, soon dubbed "Reaganomics," ended in a disastrous depression by the end of their first year in office.

Shifting gears, they began an unprecedented military buildup that spent $34 million an hour during both Reagan administrations. The reasoning held that whopping tax cuts plus unprecedented spending on the military would magically balance the federal budget by

1984. The American economy bumped along unsteadily with unemployment hovering at 7 percent until the stock market crashed in October 1987, leaving in its wake the largest government deficit in American history up to that time. While shocking at the time, it was nothing compared to our current deficit.

They did, however, outspend the Soviet Union, precipitating its economic collapse in 1989 and ending the Cold War. Nothing else the Reagan Administration did can take away that magnificent accomplishment.

Critics are quick to point out that during the two Reagan Administrations, the homeless population in America grew to the size of the city of Atlanta and AIDS became a pandemic, which in the end, would take more human lives than the Black Death in Fourteenth-Century Europe. The focus of our inquiries, however, is the Republican Administrations' view toward and relations with the Middle East. It was obviously influenced in no small measure by the presence of numerous oilmen in the Reagan Administration.

For instance, George Bush, the Vice President, was the former president of Zapata Off-Shore, while George Shultz, the Secretary of State, and Caspar Weinberger, the Secretary of Defense, were from Bechtel. All three men had served in the Nixon Administration.

If the oilmen dominated the Reagan Administrations, they *really* dominated its' successor, Bush Administration. On the eve of the Gulf War, President Bush had to grant a conflict-of-interest waiver for ten of his top administration officials, so they could *legally* prosecute the war against Iraq.[69]

Most political historians agree that during the

George Bush, George Shultz, Caspar Weinberger

first Reagan Administration, the day-to-day running of the country was left in the hands of three, non-elected officials. The first was James Baker III, a Bush minion and Texas oilman who was the White House Chief of Staff. Michael Deaver, a close friend of Nancy Reagan and the "King of Spin" was the Deputy Chief of Staff. The third member of this troika was Edwin Meese III, an old Reagan loyalist from California who was the Counselor to the President.

It was a government by troika, not by Cabinet, or as Alexander Haig observed, "government by staff."[70] Everyone agrees that these three men were not far-sighted statesmen. Their sights were set on the public image of Ronald Reagan and their ears were attuned to the daily popularity polls. They were also heavily influenced by their proximity to the petroleum industry and their foreign policy, such as it was, reflected it.

The Troika: Baker, Meese and Deaver

The impact on America's attitude toward Israel was immediately apparent. Why was that so important? Most will argue that Israel is the only democracy in the Middle East and our only tried and true ally in the region. The shift in American "friendliness" toward the totalitarian Arab regimes was a direct result of the presence of Reagan's oilmen. Right or wrong, good or bad, this was the long-term, underlying cause of the 1991 Gulf War.

The writing was on the wall early. In late 1981, Israel sent Dr. Moshe Arens to Washington as its new ambassador to the United States. While Arens enjoyed good relations with the Secretary of State, Alexander Haig, and with the President (Reagan liked everybody), he was never able to meet with members of the troika despite his best efforts.[71]

The White House told the Israelis that it was improper for any of the troika members to meet with foreign ambassadors. All three White House staffers, however, met regularly with Prince Bandar, the Saudi Arabian Ambassador to the United States.[72] In later years, Arens would treat this small point with political correctness, but in hindsight, it is always sad when a bad omen is misread.

Bandar   Arens

American foreign policy in the Middle East was marked by utter chaos beginning with the first Reagan Administration and continuing on through that of George Bush (41). Alexander Haig was Ronald Reagan's first Secretary of State, but there were numerous other "Secretaries of State" on the White House staff and in the Cabinet. There was no "unity of one voice" in matters of foreign policy and foreign states having to deal with this situation were dumbfounded and rarely able to adjust.

The Israelis were able to cope because of their long experience with the diplomatic maneuvers of the Arab States and with the duplicitous interference in the Middle East by foreign governments. They also enjoyed the support of the Democrats, who were then the majority in Congress. The Saudis were able to work through it because they were, in essence, inside advisors on the Reagan Administration's Middle East policies. On reflection, this goes a long way toward explaining why Reagan's policies were in such chaos.

Cʒ ʒO

The Level Battlefield Doctrine

"Yet in the early months of Reagan's Presidency, the assumption that the United States would always unreservedly support Israel in a contest of interest with its Arab neighbors ceased to apply...the atmosphere of American-Israel relations underwent a change...the energy crisis had developed and the United States had become steadily more interested in improving its relations with the Arab countries.... To a considerable degree, this establishment of stronger ties to Arab states depended on the sale of sophisticated arms."

Alexander M. Haig, Jr.
CAVEAT

While it can be said the liberal Carter Administration was quietly sympathetic toward Palestinian aspirations in the Middle East, they never allowed American participation in the sale of sophisticated arms to the Arab states. The British were less inhibited especially after Iraq invaded Iran in 1980.

In January 1981, the British Cabinet's Overseas and Defense Committee met to discuss the "commercial possibilities" inherent in the Iran-Iraq War that began the previous September. The British were keen to "exploit Iraq's potential as a promising market for the sale of defense equipment" and in the spirit of capitalism, caution was thrown to the wind.[73] There was a singular lack of thought given to what the military balance might look like in the post-war Middle East.

Ronald Reagan had just taken office and his oilmen were scheming to get into the play. Opportunity, they exclaimed, was presenting itself. If exploited properly, Iraq presented a fertile market for American goods, but could also become the strategic American base in the Persian Gulf, replacing Iran in the global scheme of things. This became chiseled-in-stone Republican Party doctrine and helps explain the American invasion of Iraq in 2003.

It was not until 1982, however, when Alexander Haig resigned his post as Secretary of State, that this secret policy was enabled resulting in a whole series of controversial misadventures like "Iraqgate."

George Shultz was the president of California's Bechtel Group when he was tapped as Al Haig's replacement at State. Bechtel's major customer was the Kingdom of Saudi Arabia, and when Shultz took over the helm at Foggy Bottom, he brought with him a pro-Arab political attitude that dovetailed with that of Reagan's

White House troika, not to mention the entrenched view of the State Department bureaucrats.

Caspar Weinberger, the former vice president, director and legal counsel of the Bechtel Group, was already the Secretary of Defense by the time George Shultz arrived to take up his duties in Washington. The United States Justice Department had previously brought a lawsuit against Bechtel for complying with the Arab boycott of Israel in violation of U.S. law. This was during the tenures of Shultz and Weinberger at Bechtel.

In 1982, the Kingdom of Saudi Arabia was a feudal Arab monarchy whose main concerns were the Iran-Iraq War and that old Arab bugaboo, Israel. With *their men* from the petroleum industry now in the key positions of authority in Washington, it was time for the Saudis to exercise a little political leverage.

There were two main political agendas for the Saudis to push forward in Washington. The first was to shore up the flagging fortunes of Saddam Hussein, who in September 1980 had invaded Iran hoping to take advantage of the internal turmoil generated by the previous year's fall of the Peacock Throne. Unexpectedly, the Iranians had rallied against their hated Arab enemy and had delivered Hussein some crippling, military setbacks. By 1982, the invading Iraqi Army had been driven completely out of Iranian territory.

The Saudis believed the United States could help swing the military situation in favor of Iraq. They reasoned that Iran was not only the enemy of Iraq, but also the enemy of the Arab people as a whole, at least the Sunni majority. It did not have to be pointed out that it was the Iranians who had humiliated the Americans with the embassy hostages, who were released only in 1981 after more than a year in captivity.

There was, however, a problem in Washington. The Reagan Administration had taken the public, election-campaign stance that there were two great evils in the world: the Soviet Empire and International Terrorism. The Administration planned to economically strangle the Soviets while to combat Terrorism, it attempted to isolate those Moslem nations supporting it. In the latter case, there were four states on the State Department's list of terrorist sponsors. Known as the *"Sleaze Bucket Four,"* those states were Libya, Iran, Syria and Iraq.

There was no way to publicly aid Iraq in its war against Iran as the Saudis wanted, without first removing them from the State Department's terrorist list, and then to re-establish diplomatic relations. While these two steps were quietly undertaken by the administration, aiding the Iraqis with a military build-up, which required congressional approval, was quite another matter.

The Saudis were pushing hard for American military support of Iraq, but the Reagan Administration was forced to maneuver behind the scenes in Washington, all the while blaming their "inability to make foreign policy" on the "Jewish lobby." Never mind that Congress was then solidly controlled by the

Democrats, who had quite a different view of Saddam Hussein.

In its political maneuvers, the administration employed a vehicle, which it touted as a new *Peace Plan for the Middle East.* The premise for this new (Saudi) Peace Plan was based on the supposition that Israel, not the Arab States, was the real aggressor in the Middle East. The Israeli invasion of Lebanon in June 1982 came just in time to bolster this position if the proper "spin" was applied.

Israel, the Saudis held, was the real cause of Middle Eastern unrest and there was only one solution: The United States had to bring the Arabs up to military parity with the Jews. Once this was done, peace would surely follow. This tired old concept was the same idea that had been attempted numerous times by the Soviet Union. Without exception, every time it has been tried, it ended in a shooting war. Shultz, Weinberger and the White House troika, who were never accused of being direct descendants of the Enlightenment, liked the concept and made it their own.

Supporting the Reagan Administration's tilt toward the Arabs was another factor. The personal animosity Caspar Weinberger felt toward Israel most certainly advanced the Saudi agenda. Even lower-level players like Oliver North at the National Security Council, felt it and later wrote:

"Weinberger seemed to go out of his way to oppose Israel on any issue and to blame the Israelis for every problem in the Middle East. In our planning for counter-terrorist operations, he apparently feared that if we went after the Palestinian terrorists, we would offend and alienate Arab governments - particularly if we acted in cooperation with the Israelis. Weinberger's anti-Israel tilt was an underlying current in almost every Middle East issue." [74]

Once the Reagan Administration accepted the Saudi Arabian premise, the military build-up began. In fact, it was memorialized in June 1982 in a National Security Decision Directive (NSDD). The old idea of military parity was given a new American name, "The Level Battlefield Doctrine," and a spate of new military sales (FMS)[75] began filling Arab arsenals, which in turn, filled Iraqi arsenals.

When the administration decided to sell the Saudi Arabians five E-3 Sentry AWACS[76] aircraft, 17 KC-135 refueling tankers and upgraded F-15 fighter aircraft, the American-Israel Political Action Committee (AIPAC) - the so-called "Jewish Lobby" - waded into the fight.

The Administration's effort to push through this massive sale was led by James Baker at the White House. [77] Interestingly, two military men, Air Force General Richard Secord and National Security Council staffer, Marine Lieutenant Colonel Oliver North, both later of Iran-Contra fame, were assigned to help the White House effort in Congress.

In the end, the administration managed to squeak the massive sale by (54 to 48), obtaining congressional approval with certain caveats, which were promptly ignored by the Saudis.[78]

On congressional insistence, the Israelis were thrown a small bone meant to offset the new military disadvantage the American sale placed on them. This was an official agreement to share intelligence between the US and Israeli Intelligence communities and was meant to avoid a repeat of the strategic surprise Israel suffered in the Yom Kippur War of 1973. It was formally known as the US-Israel Bilateral Intelligence Sharing Agreement and will be discussed in some detail later.

Behind the scenes, outside of congressional oversight, the Reagan Administration began to seriously undertake the clandestine, military build-up of Iraq. This effort was run by Weinberger out of the Department of Defense, with the strict oversight of Vice President George Bush. Acting on a Presidential Finding, a National Security Directive,[79] military advisors from a secret unit of the Defense Intelligence Agency, the Intelligence Support Activity, began to put backbone into the Iraqi Army in the field.

There was yet another downside to the "Level Battlefield Doctrine," that was unanticipated by all parties. The Israel Defense Forces (IDF) is deeply dependent on their qualitative edge in weapons to defeat their Arab foes in a shooting war. Since the French weapons embargo in the wake of the 1967 Six-Day War, Israel purchased the majority of their weapons systems from the United States. The Israelis' advantage in weapons was thus negated by the sale of those same weapons to the Arabs. The Israelis were then forced to fall back on their own ingenuity, closing their doors, to a certain extent, to American arms manufacturers. This resulted in the Merkava (Chariot) main battle tank (in lieu of the M-1 Abrams), the Lavi (Lion Cub) fighter aircraft, the Ofek (Horizon) satellite and the Hetz (Arrow) ballistic missile interceptor among other new weapons systems. [80] Upgrades to existing American weapons were also developed such as the conformal fuel tanks for the General Dynamics F-16 fighter-bomber.

In total, it represented a marketing loss for American weapons manufacturers. Markets previously open to American tank manufacturers now faced competition from the Israeli Merkava tank. Not only did they have new competitors, but when ordering new weapons, Israel always specified their own upgrades. Thus, in 2006 when Israel purchased new F-16s, it specified they include their own conformal fuel tanks. This new variant is classified the F-16I and even Saudi Arabia demanded it for their aircraft purchases, which required the US to purchase the fuel tanks from the Israeli manufacturer.

ɔʒ ଞ

Since Iraq was not financially viable, *moderate* Arab States often transferred arms and equipment to the Iraqis in violation of American Third Party Transfer policies, after having purchased the material for their own defense needs.

American equipment taken from Iraqi armed forces

Later, a funding scheme was established by the Secretary of State, George Shultz, using the Commodity Credit Corporation of the U.S. Department of Agriculture to guarantee Iraqi loans from American banks. The Banco Nazionale del Lavoro (BNL), the largest Italian State bank, soon jumped onboard the Iraqi loan program. BNL had branches in New York, Chicago, Los Angeles, Miami and Atlanta, qualifying as an "American" bank for the loan guarantees.[81]

While all this was en train, there was still one matter that perplexed American policymakers. It is understood that Israel possesses nuclear weapons. How then could they bring the Arab States into military parity *without* passing out atomic bombs? The answer was simple: chemical and biological weapons ... *aslihatul dammar ashammel* in Arabic ... weapons of mass destruction, sometimes called the "Poor Man's Atomic Bombs" by the press.

Of course the Arabs did not consider themselves "poor men" and preferred the "Rich Man's Atomic Bomb." But in keeping with the strategies outlined in the study done by Arab Projects Development (ADP), which was previously discussed, and not wanting to upset their American benefactors, they contented themselves with a parallel development program to produce nuclear weapons.

The new relationship between the Americans and the Iraqis had some practical benefits for both parties. Everybody's military likes to test new weapons in someone else's war. That's a given. The Defense Department's reasoning was straightforward in the case of Iraq. The United States had the technology in chemical and biological weapons, Iraq had the delivery vectors, and the Iranians had the target army to provide the developmental testing. The Cold War justification for this insanity went: *We would rather have these weapons in the American arsenal than in the Soviet.* Never mind that Iraq was the key Soviet client in the Middle East, a supporter of international terrorism, and the United States was forbidden to do this as a signatory to an international treaty.

The wild card in this new Middle East equation was, of course, Israel. Even a blind man could see the threat implications to the Jewish State by the introduction of chemical and biological weapons into a renegade nation like Iraq. It really did not matter how the Reagan Administration *hoped* it could influence Saddam Hussein; at the end of the day, Iraq would still be Iraq and *hope* is not a *plan*.

Unfortunately, Israel would become completely unpredictable when threatened and was more likely to attack the Iraqis - as it did in June of 1981 - than be intimidated. This issue worried the Reagan Administration, but any immediate concern about an Israeli reaction was mitigated by the administration's efforts to keep the whole agenda "dark" and deniable.

Like the British, the American policy makers missed the point that the military build-up of Iraq presented a future threat to Kuwait and Saudi Arabia. But, the Reagan Administration was focused on the Iran-Iraq War and Lebanon in 1982, with little thought given to what Iraq might do after its war with the Persians was concluded.

The Iraqis have never shed their bellicose machismo or their penchant for braggadocio. In late 1982, Israeli signal intelligence (Unit 8200)[82] recorded a radio broadcast from Iraq's *Voice of the Masses* station in Baghdad. In this broadcast, an Iraqi military officer claimed that the Army had prepared "a certain insecticide for every kind of insect."

Knowing that Iraqi officers normally referred to Iranian troops as "insects," and that the broadcasts were meant to inspire the Iraqis in their war against Iran, the recording was sent to the AMAN analysis group for further study. With hindsight, the message seems crystal clear, but at the time the Israelis attached no particular significance to it, because, most certainly, their intelligence assets were concentrated on the PLO terrorists in Lebanon. It was an early and lucky break for the Reagan Administration's "Level Battlefield Doctrine."

The Iraqi military build-up continued and growing in momentum became too widespread by late 1983 and early 1984 to stay out of intelligence reports.[83] American Intelligence elements, which were not involved with the "Iraqi account," had begun picking up the first indicators in 1983, and by 1984, had begun to issue "alert memos" to the rest of the government. The Reagan Administration's covert approval, however, forestalled any law enforcement action being taken against the American suppliers when they washed up.

Everything seemed to be running smoothly for the Reagan Administration, but then the Israelis became more concerned with the reckless, free wheeling build-up of Saddam Hussein's Army far beyond normal support for its continuing conflict with Iran. When Israeli Intelligence operatives began probing the build-up, they discovered the Iraqi supply infrastructure and ran head-on into American "spooks."

During that same time frame, American Intelligence suffered a series of disasters from which they have barely recovered some 30 years later. The year 1985 has forever been dubbed the "Year of the Spy."

CB BO

Reds

"We have suffered very serious losses ... In fact I am not aware of any Soviet case (agent) we have left that is producing anything worthwhile."

Paul Redmond
Chief of Counter Intelligence
Soviet Division
CIA

All intelligence communities suffer disasters, ranging from an irritating speed-bump with the loss of an agent or code to a mega-devastation event like the loss of an entire in-country network or basic sources and methods.

In 1985, the intelligence community of the United States suffered a mega-disaster from which it arguably never fully recovered. And, while these stories have been covered by many experts, we feel it is important to briefly note some of the damages to the United States, briefly viewing what a determined *spook* can inflict.

The nightmare began to unravel in 1985 with the KGB's "discovery" of two American "moles" working inside their embassy in Washington. The first was Major Sergei Morotin, a KGB Line PR (counterintelligence) officer, who had been recruited under an FBI program coded COURTSHIP. Morotin was known to the CIA as GT/GAUZE and to the FBI as MEGAS and was apparently the agent who fingered a CIA officer, who had ironically fingered him to the KGB. Morotin was ordered back to Moscow, arrested on his arrival and tortured to death all within a month or so of being exposed by the Soviet moles within American Intelligence.

The second case was that of Major Valeri Martynov, a KGB Line X (T&S) officer, who had likewise been recruited under the COURTSHIP program and was known to the CIA as GT/GENTILE and to the FBI as PIMENTO. Martynov was ordered home and arrested in November 1985, but unlike Morotin, he was initially "turned," which delayed his execution until May of 1987.

Morotin and Martynov

Nothing was known at the time other than these two assets "went dark" ... disappeared ... within four months of each other. And, since the exposure of agents is very rarely, if ever, the work of counterintelligence, it is always meet and right to suspect a "mole." So, by early 1986, American Intelligence knew it had been penetrated. It was the extent to which that was the shocker, not only to the Americans, but to their friends as well.

CB ⊗O

John Anthony Walker (coded WINDFLYER by the FBI) was an American sailor and Soviet agent whose career spanned some 18 years. Starting in December 1967 as the Vietnam War raged, Walker provided radio cipher cards for US fleet communications, which afforded half the ability to read those communications. The Soviets then needed the cipher machines themselves, specifically the KL-7 ADONIS and the KW-37 JASON systems, which Walker could not provide.[84] A collection priority was issued for the acquisition of these machines and apparently triggered the seizure of the *USS Pueblo* by the North Koreans a month later during which the cipher machines were taken. As a result, the Soviets knew exactly where all American submarines, both boomers and attack boats, were located at all times. The boomers comprised fully one third of America's nuclear deterrent.

Reports on weapons ... strengths, weaknesses, problems ... also passed through the Naval communications system to the Soviets. Additionally, Walker explained the US SOSUS submarine acoustic tracking system to the Soviets. This triggered a new Russian submarine project coded SHCHUKA – B (Project 941) that produced the new *Typhoon* class boomer, called the *Akula* by the Soviets. In 1983, the Soviets purchased the Norwegian Kongsberg technology from the Japanese Toshiba company, which enabled them to produce submarine propellers that completely reduced the tell-tale cavitation. Thus in 1986, the massive, new *Typhoon* class ballistic missile submarine that was undetectable by the US SOSUS system, joined the

Soviet fleet. Old spooks call this boomer the "Walker class."[85]

When he was arrested in 1985, the FBI floated a story that he was snitched off by his ex-wife, but that appears to be a repositioning of history. While the estranged Ms. Walker obviously assisted *after* the arrests, in truth, he was fingered by the double, coded PIMENTO by the FBI and GT/GENTILE by the CIA. [86] There is also evidence that the bizarre case of Vitaly Yurchenko, a defector-redefector from the KGB, confirmed.

Aldrich Hazen Ames (coded NIGHTMOVER by the FBI) was an American career intelligence officer with the CIA who served the Soviets for 9 years. Working in Counterintelligence in the Soviet and Eastern Bloc Division, he was privy to all of the American assets and compromised the second largest number of agents. Starting in April of 1985, Ames exposed 25 American agents to the Soviets/Russians and of those 11 died as a result and only 1 escaped. The others received long prison sentences.

During his career as a "mole" within CIA, Ames compromised over 100 clandestine operations in addition to the exposure of the agents in the so-called "Nasty Circle," meaning he exposed them before they could expose him.

Ames was assigned to the Counter-Intelligence Center and thus had access to all of the CIA and FBI assets plus at least some of those run by US allies like MI-6 and Mossad.

Because Ames and Hanssen (of whom more shortly) were working simultaneously, the CIA was initially confused when whole networks were rolled up by the Soviets. Originally, the CIA believed their cases were compromised by a previous defector, Edward Lee Howard (coded ROBERT by the KGB). He was cleared at some point because he did not know three of the American agents who disappeared.

Practically everyone in *The Trades* knew there was a Russian mole working within CIA and the agency's ability to recruit cases quickly dried up. In one bizarre incident, not totally uncommon in *The Trades*, Ames was tasked to debrief Vitaly Yurchenko, a KGB defector who shortly re-defected back to the Reds, but not before he fingered John Walker. He did not, however, give up Ames, although Yurchenko clearly knew he was a Soviet agent.

To find their mole, the Agency established a task force, coded SKYLIGHT. Meanwhile, the FBI had lost two of its agents and formed a similar task force of their own, PLAYACTOR. Later in 1991, the task forces were combined and their investigation took four years before Ames was identified and arrested. The CIA's handling of the Ames case caused the Director, James Woolsey to resign in 1995, a year after the arrest. Still, the FBI was not satisfied, believing they still had a mole in the Bureau, because some of the compromised agents had not been shared with the CIA and they were right.

Robert Philip Hanssen (coded GRAYSUIT by the FBI) was a career FBI counterintelligence agent who served the Soviets/Russians off and on for 22 years, first for the GRU and later for the KGB. He was bright and had excellent tradecraft, in fact, not only did the FBI not know who he was, neither did the Soviets. There was Aldrich Ames in the analytical mix and other problems inherent with opening a new investigation, so the FBI decided on what might be described as a typically American solution. They would simply buy the Soviet's file on RAMON (GRAYSUIT).

Their interlocutor was a Soviet business man and former KGB officer. The price was $7 million and relocation for the seller and his entire family to the United States. The price was paid and the file was delivered.

The problem was that Hanssen was very careful and as the file revealed, he only slipped up twice. There was a tape recording of a phone call, in which the investigators recognized Hanssen's voice and there were two fingerprints left inadvertently on a plastic garbage bag he had used to deliver treasure.

Having identified their mole, the Bureau employed a ruse that put a young FBI agent next to Hanssen, who was able to purloin personal files that gave the US Attorney enough for an indictment.

Hanssen knew the game and bargained his damage assessment for life over death. He also secured his government pension and a non-prosecution agreement for his wife.

Not only had he given the KGB the American agents-in-place, he had turned over lists of Russians the FBI and CIA were setting up to recruit. He delivered the super-secret Continuation of Government plan that would have been used in the event of war and the methodology the FBI used in tracking Russian "legals" within America. Hanssen warned the Russians that the FBI was closing in on a Soviet agent in the US State Department, Felix Bloch, which compromised the investigation. He also disclosed that the FBI had dug a secret tunnel under the Soviet Embassy in Washington for the specific purpose of bugging communications.

That a lot of folks consider his greatest sin was initially reveled in his debriefing. Being a computer expert, Hanssen had downloaded the entire program the FBI used to track terrorists and threats against the United States. The Soviets sold this program to Osama bin Laden who used it to plan Nine-Eleven and other attacks. This was confirmed by material taken from bin Laden's Abbottabad residence in 2011.

Walker, Ames and Hanssen

CG 80

The three spies discussed above were all "walk-ins," having not been recruited by Soviet Intelligence. And, there was of course, massive collateral damage to the intelligence services of America's friendly allies. First, it paralyzed ongoing operations since no one could determine what or who had been compromised and secondly, it called into question the validity of information received from American Intelligence, not to mention the exposure of assets. For the British it was especially hurtful as the previously mentioned case of Oleg Gordievsky illustrates.

There were other Soviet spies within the American Intelligence community during this time frame, which left their intelligence efforts in shambles. A short list would include:

- Edward Lee Howard   CIA
- David Henry Barnett   CIA
- James Hall II   Army Intelligence
- Earl Edwin Pitts   FBI
- Harold James Nicholson   CIA
- George Trofimoff   Army
- William Kampiles   CIA
- Ronald Pelton   NSA

Israeli Intelligence was well aware that the Americans had been penetrated and tried to assess the damage they suffered as a result. It was the time frame of the US-Israel Intelligence Sharing Agreement of 1983 and what treasure given to the Americans filtered through and out to the Soviets was difficult to ascertain. Still, the Israelis had a bigger problem. One of the spies caught during 1985 was the Israeli agent, Jonathan Jay Pollard of US Naval Intelligence.

CB EO

CHAPTER 4

THE LEVANT

"Confusing the words wish, faith and pray with each other usually just results in a minor grammatical faux pas, but when any of these words, especially hope, is confused with action, the results are much more devastating."

Bo Bennett

SNOWBALL

FRONT
"Siege of Beirut
Summer 1982"

BACK
"Visit Israel
Before Israel Visits You"

Tee Shirt Art
Worn by Israeli Soldiers
Beirut, Lebanon
August 1982

The first real crisis faced by the Reagan Administration in the Middle East was in Lebanon. In general terms, the American People instinctively supported the Israelis while the entrenched bureaucrats of the State Department and the political appointees within the Reagan Administration supported the Arabs.

What happened between 1982 and 1984 clearly illustrates the disasters the Reagan Administration's befuddled Middle East policies produced. This recounting is informative because it was the same confused policies, of the some of the same policymakers, in the same region that led to the 1991Gulf War and the 2003 Iraq War.

When the Palestinians were driven out of Jordan in "Black September" of 1970, their arrival in Lebanon completely upset the country's delicate Christian-Moslem balance. Sectarian civil war broke out in April 1975 between the Christians and the Moslems. The Government of Lebanon, such as it was, requested the intervention of the Syrian Army to stop the fighting and restore some semblance of order. The Arab League then mandated Syria's action in June 1976, giving it legitimacy among the Arab States.

By November, the Syrian Army had suffocated the fighting north of the Litani River and Lebanon settled into a fragile existence where two foreign, armed forces, the Syrian Army and the PLO, ruled the Lebanese.

In this new quasi-peaceful climate, southern Lebanon remained in a state of anarchy as the Moslem PLO and the Christian Phalange happily continued killing each other. When the Syrians decided to intervene, the Israelis began growling and not wanting to tangle with its archenemy, the Syrian Army remained out of southern Lebanon. Syria opted instead to enter the fight against the Christians and the Israelis by using the PLO as its proxy.

Along the Israeli-Lebanese border, the PLO deployed their Soviet-made, long-range artillery, which was supplied by the Syrians. And when they were not pounding the Christians, the guerrillas indulged in a little cross-border bombardment of Israel's northern towns and villages. By February 1977, it was clear why the Israelis wanted to keep the Syrian Army out of southern Lebanon: The Jews did not want the Syrians in the area should they choose to react biblically to the PLO's cross-border attacks.

For over a year there were Israeli retaliatory raids and air strikes every time its northern villages and towns were shelled. The Christian militia in southern Lebanon, which was allied with the Israelis, attempted to curb or even preempt the PLO attacks, but were badly outnumbered and outgunned by the Moslem terrorists.

Then in March 1978, nine PLO terrorists came ashore in northern Israel, killed several innocent civilians and hijacked a bus full of passengers. They then drove the bus down the Haifa Road toward Tel Aviv, shooting up every automobile they encountered on the highway. They were finally stopped north of Tel Aviv and shot it out with the Israeli Ya'amam. When the smoke cleared, 37 Israelis were dead along with the nine Palestinian terrorists.[87]

Israeli bus from Coastal Road Massacre in 1978

There is an old Middle East saw that holds, "Trouble rides a fast horse." When the news of the terrorist attack in Israel reached southern Lebanon, the civilian population and most of the PLO gunmen suddenly remembered they had pressing, personal business in the north. They were only hours ahead of the first Israeli Army units.

Long in the planning, the Israeli Army's Operation LITANI had the simple objective of driving the PLO and other hostile elements north of the Litani River, beyond the range from which their artillery and Katyusha rockets could bombard Israel. Thus displaced, the guerillas simply re-established their position north of the river and began bombarding southern Lebanon. In Israeli eyes, this was preferable to them bombarding the Galilee.

After six days of operations, the Israelis ceased their advance, began withdrawing back across their border and turning over the area to their Christian allies and the new United Nations Interim Force in Lebanon (UNIFIL). Operation LITANI was all over in a month and as all Israeli units withdrew, the PLO gunmen began filtering back into southern Lebanon. UNIFIL as "peace keepers" was ineffective. Thus by the end of 1978, there were four dominate armed forces ruling the Lebanese ... the PLO, the Syrians, the Christians (backed by the Israelis) and the UN, plus the various Moslem militias.

It should also be noted that the introduction of UN peacekeepers to separate warring factions in the Middle East is and always has been an exercise in futility.[88]

At the time the Reagan Administration took the reins of power in January 1981, the situation in southern Lebanon was more or less back to where it had been prior to the Israeli invasion (Operation LITANI) in 1978. The Syrians had supplied the PLO with Soviet-made artillery and the Palestinians were shelling Israel's northern towns and villages once again. These attacks were provoking the Israelis to strike back militarily. Israel's Christian allies were also attacking the PLO units at every opportunity.

Finally in July 1981, Philip Habib, the American Special Envoy to Lebanon, worked out a cease-fire. This cease-fire held, but during the first six months, from July 1981 through January 1982, the PLO violated the truce on at least ten occasions. Those violations resulted in Israeli losses of 17 killed and 288 wounded.

Additionally, the PLO took advantage of the cease-fire to deploy more artillery in southern Lebanon.

By February 1982 matters had come to a head. The Israelis informed the Americans that they intended to invade, push up to Beirut and drive out the PLO out of Lebanon. The Reagan Administration advised against it and counseled patience. For the following three months, the Israelis followed the advice of the administration in Washington, but by late May and early June of 1982 there had been no cessation or progress on the Lebanese problem.

Although then-Secretary of State, Al Haig, was later accused of "green lighting" Israel's invasion, that was not the case. Haig pressed the Israelis not to "overreact," but Begin had had enough. At the eleventh hour, there was a last exchange of letters between the American Secretary of State and the Israeli Prime Minister. Begin's final reply was:

"You advise us to exercise complete restraint and refrain from any action ... Mr. Secretary, my dear friend, the man has not been born who will ever obtain from me consent to let Jews be killed by a bloodthirsty enemy and allow those who are responsible for the shedding of this blood to enjoy immunity."[89]

During Thursday evening, 3 June 1982, a Palestinian gunman shot down Israel's ambassador to Great Britain, Shlomo Argov, in front of the Dorchester hotel in London.[90] On 4 June, Israeli Air Force units struck PLO targets in Lebanon, including the Beirut Sports Stadium where tons of ammunition had been stored. When the PLO began shelling Israeli towns the following morning, Lebanese civilians and Palestinians alike took to the roads in southern Lebanon heading north. As expected, in the early hours of 6 June 1982, the Israeli Army executed Operation SNOWBALL[91] and poured into Lebanon on a 35-mile wide front.

(Left to Right)
Shlomo Argov, Philip Habib, Menachem Begin, Al Haig

As the Israeli units drove northward, they clashed with the Syrian Army in the Bekaa Valley. In the political context of the Cold War, the threat of a potential confrontation looked like this: A Treaty of Friendship existed between Syria and the Soviet Union and any threat against Damascus would involve Moscow. If Moscow chose to intervene against Israel, Washington would become involved. Admittedly it was thin, but it was possible that Israel's invasion of Lebanon might trigger World War III.

Much to the world's surprise, SNOWBALL was not a reenactment of Israel's LITANI operation of 1978. No one anticipated the size, the sheer ferocity or the speed of the Israeli attack and by the evening of 8 June 1982 IDF forward units were just south of the Beirut International airport. By 13 June, Israeli forces had cut the Damascus - Beirut Highway north of the Lebanese capital, effectively trapping an estimated 15,000 PLO gunmen and a large Syrian Army contingent in Beirut.

While most would agree in retrospect that it was in American interests to bring about an immediate cease-fire, the Reagan Administration was not sure if it presented an opportunity or a massive threat to world peace. Philip Habib, Reagan's special envoy to the Middle East was dispatched back to the Lebanese capital. Acting under the orders of Al Haig, Habib then hurriedly shuttled back and forth discussing and receiving commitments from various Arab States, the PLO and the Israelis in an all-out effort to stop the shooting.

In Washington, Haig approached the crisis pragmatically, while the non-policy of the Reagan Administration and its "government-by-staff" began creating a wondrous spectacle of confusion.

First, the Defense Secretary, Caspar Weinberger, held a news conference and "explained" the American position. At the United Nations in New York, the American Ambassador, Jeane Kirkpatrick, then "explained" a different American position. From the White House, James Baker then leaked his "explanation" of yet another American position to his favorite journalist, Tom Friedman of *The New York Times*. All this "whip-sawing" made Washington appear to be running more than usually amok.

In the shadow of this Tower of Babel epic, the actual American policy was in serious question. Michael Deaver, one of the White House "troika," later observed:

"Of course, this strategy risked a Mideast nightmare that might have ignited the Third World War. Could we really afford to take that chance? And, I wondered, could we continue to stand by, publicly denounce the Israeli incursion, and privately encourage them, even as the civilian casualties mounted?" [92]

Meanwhile Alexander Haig, the man actually in charge of the American position, did not "explain" anything, because he believed that crisis diplomacy should be conducted quietly out of the glare of publicity. Besides, the United States was reaping a number of indirect benefits from the Israeli invasion.

In its drive up the Bekaa Valley, the Israelis had indeed tangled with the Syrians. In a series of spectacular air clashes, Israeli pilots flying American-made fighter aircraft destroyed almost 90 Syrian MiGs without sustaining a single loss. Additionally, the Israelis destroyed all of the Syrians' SAM-6 missile batteries deployed in the Bekaa Valley. In the context of the Cold War, this piece of Israeli one-upmanship certainly illuminated the superiority of American hardware.

Everyone in Washington saw the crisis as a superpower confrontation. The Soviet Union through its surrogates, Syria and the PLO, was clashing with the United States through its surrogate, Israel. Al Haig's approach to the solution was to back Israel and use the invasion to get both the PLO and the Syrian Army out of

Lebanon. The oilmen in the White House saw quite a different solution.

Reagan's government-by-staff imagined an opportunity to wean the Arab world away from the Soviets and then use Arab influence and persuasion to get the Syrians out of Lebanon. This would offend no Arab sensitivities. They would get the PLO out of Lebanon by the establishment of a Palestinian State in the Israeli-occupied West Bank, which they believed would satisfy the Arabs. They gave little thought to the Israeli reaction. *("The Jews always vote for the democrats anyway," James Baker was wont to say.)*

While the White House was trying to formulate its solution, the Israeli Army entered Christian East Beirut. Trapped in West Beirut, the PLO gunmen deployed their heavy weapons in and beside civilian structures. The Moslem population of West Beirut was the PLO's only real shield against the Israeli forces. Some observers - Westerners mostly - opined that the Palestinians believed the Israelis would not fire on them for fear of killing Lebanese non-combatants. This naive view was for Western consumption only for the old Middle East hands knew it was a media ploy set to embarrass the Israelis who would take out the terrorists anywhere they found them.

In one instance near Sidon, the Palestinians placed a ZSU-23-4 anti-aircraft gun system on top of a hospital. This Soviet-made system consists of four 23mm automatic cannon guided by radar, which can deliver literally a solid wall of shot at an attacking aircraft. Militarily ignorant, Western journalists covering the fighting called this weapon "ancient" as though it belonged in a museum and was incapable of making a long division problem out of any plane in its general vicinity.

The inevitable happened. Israeli jets flying over the hospital in Sidon were fired on and, of course, the Israelis fired back. Some 90 Lebanese civilians died along with the PLO gun crew. Western journalists were outraged, calling the attack "disproportionate" as if a scorecard really mattered and there was a difference between a dead Palestinian child and a dead Israeli child. Like Vietnam, this was a war for public opinion and the media emerged as a primary weapon.

Alone in the Reagan Administration, Alexander Haig knew the difference. He was not interested in the media images. He saw an opportunity to defeat Syria and the PLO, the two destabilizing forces in Lebanon. If played right, the Israeli invasion could be used to restore the legitimate Lebanese government by removing all foreign forces from the country. And in truth, he was not the only cabinet member who saw it that way. Still, there were those who were only interested in media images not lasting results, so Haig was fighting an uphill battle.

Even Haig's own foreign policy bureaucracy at the State Department was an obstacle, being as Haig described it "overwhelmingly Arabist in its approach to the Middle East and in its sympathies." These bureaucrats saw the Lebanese crisis as "an opportunity to open direct negotiations between the United States and the PLO"[93] and little more.

131

Haig soldiered on alone, subjected to continual sniping by the White House "troika" and various cabinet members under pressure from their Arab friends. The Arab States' diplomatic position was "get the Israelis unconditionally out of Lebanon" as a precondition to any peace talks. (In keeping with the ways of Middle East diplomacy, the Arabs are very good with "preconditions," while an Arab "commitment" is the epitome of the diplomatic oxymoron.)

To compound Haig's problems even further, the Reagan Administration with its pro-Arab posture had precious little political coinage with the Likud government in Jerusalem. In spite of Haig's best efforts, including threats and cajolery, the Israelis were determined to do some bad things to some bad people, and generally ignored the State Department's overtures when it did not suit them.

On the ground, the Israelis had laid siege to West Beirut, trapping approximately 15,000 Palestinian terrorists and several battalions of Syrian soldiers among the 500,000 Moslem civilians. Outside the Lebanese capital, Pax Judica reigned. Knowing the Israelis would brook no nonsense, the sectarian militias put away their guns and became civilians again. Soon, the shops were open, business was brisk and rebuilding had begun.

As Haig and Habib worked for a solution, the Israelis notched up the pressure on the PLO trapped in West Beirut. It was clear that Israel wanted the PLO out of Lebanon completely and most Lebanese wanted the same thing.

On 30 June 1982, the Israelis cut the water and electricity into West Beirut and finally on 2 July, Yasser Arafat cried "uncle." Haig and Habib then hammered out the agreement between the parties.

According to the terms of the agreement the PLO would begin departing for Syria on Friday 9 July 1982. The trapped Syrian battalions would leave with the PLO. The Israelis would not hinder the evacuation. After the departure, the Israelis would pull back and allow an international peacekeeping force, including an American contingent, into Beirut to enforce the peace between the sectarian factions. This agreement was kept quiet by Haig, although naturally the White House knew the details.

There was only one problem: the oilmen in the Reagan Administration were not happy campers. Haig wanted to keep the agreement quiet, but Washington wanted "photo opportunities" and press releases. Public image and oil were their main considerations, so they prevailed upon President Reagan and on 5 July 1982, only four days before the PLO was to depart Lebanon, Alexander Haig resigned.[94]

The following day, 6 July 1982, Haig's hard-won agreement lost momentum and fell apart because the White House wanted to take advantage of the opportunity to shine in the media. The Reagan Administration's black adventure in Lebanon was about to begin with the announcement that American troops would be deployed to Beirut. The announcement was made without considering the Soviets or the public reaction in the Arab street.

The Soviet Union immediately protested the deployment of US forces into Lebanon and its ally, Syria, decided it could not take in the PLO. Haig was livid.

On 13 July 1982 during his Senate confirmation hearings, Reagan's new Secretary of State designate, George Shultz, stated that American foreign policy in the Middle East would emphasize the "legitimate needs and problems of the Palestinian people." It was a meaningful public shift away from Israel to a more pro-Arab stance in the Middle East. With this, the PLO renounced their agreement to quit Lebanon and the Israelis countered with an announcement of a logistical build-up in order to "winter in Beirut."

Leaping into the vacuum, George Shultz announced his support for the administration's plan for peace in Lebanon. The details, worked out in conjunction with the Saudis and touted as the re-establishment of the sovereignty of the Lebanese people over their own country, was to be in three phases:

Phase 1   The removal of the PLO from Lebanon.

Phase 2   The removal of all foreign forces from Lebanon.

Phase 3   The solution to the Palestinian problem.

As part of Phase 1, American, French and Italian troops would be deployed into Beirut in order to "protect" the evacuation of the PLO. Everyone was in agreement until astonishingly, not one Arab State would agree to take in the departing terrorists ... at least not all together. Talk of Arab brotherhood, a Pan-Arab Middle East, mutual hatred of the Jews and the solidarity of the Islamic people, suddenly *went south*. As long as the PLO was killing Jews, the Arab States would fight to the last drop of Palestinian blood. Giving those "heroic martyrs for Islam" a home was an entirely different matter, however. *Welcome to the Middle East.*

This turn of events might have been viewed in the West as bizarre, but one can certainly understand the Arabs' position as a practical matter. Everywhere the Palestinians find a home they cause trouble for their hosts, usually attempting to overthrow the existing government as they did in Jordan, Lebanon and subsequently in Kuwait. Additionally, they were always stirring up trouble with the Israelis, which is never a good idea when one lives within tactical flying distance of the Jewish State.

To the eternal consternation of the Reagan Administration, they could muster no influence with their Arab friends and were reduced to "tin cupping" among the Islamic nations for a PLO home.

Finally, the Tunisians stepped up like little gentlemen and agreed to take in a majority of the PLO gunmen. Syria, Sudan, Iraq and South Yemen agreed to take in small numbers. So, on 21 August 1982, 12 years of the "Palestinian state-within-a-state" came to an end in Lebanon. Their departure from Beirut also ended Israel's 10-week siege of the Arab capital.

As the first deportees - some 400 gunmen - moved down to the port for embarkation, they fired their rifles, anti-tank rockets and mortars into the air in celebration. This "celebration" killed more Lebanese civilians.[95]

On 25 August 1982, American Marines landed in Beirut for the first time in almost 25 years. Along with the French and the Italians, the 800 American Marines constituted the "disengagement force" between the PLO and the Israelis.

Then on 30 August 1982, Yasser Arafat declared a "victory" and personally protected by the US Navy's SEAL Team Six, departed for Tunisia. The last PLO gunmen left West Beirut on 1 September 1982, prompting a "photo opportunity" for the American Secretary of Defense, Caspar Weinberger. In a press conference at the Beirut harbor, Weinberger stood among the American Marines and declared a "victory."

It was good media, which was what the Reagan Administration was all about, but it was long on form and short on reality. As Weinberger claimed the completion of "Phase One" of the new American solution on the Beirut quayside, both Menachem Begin of Israel and Hafez Al-Assad of Syria had already rejected the remaining phases of the plan. And that was the best of it.

While almost 13,000 PLO terrorists had been evacuated from Beirut, at least 10,000 additional Palestinian gunmen remained in eastern and northern Lebanon, where the Syrian Army remained in control.

The irony of Weinberger's "photo opportunity" was not lost on the old Middle East hands present. Some 40 rag-tag soldiers of the Lebanese government's Christian "army" stood around re-establishing Lebanese sovereignty over the city. While only 400 yards away from the press conference, four Israeli armored vehicles sat menacingly as their crews watched the macabre circus through binoculars.

President Reagan also sent a message to the Marine contingent to mark the occasion.

"We are now on the eve of achieving what we set forth to accomplish: an end to the bloodshed in Beirut and the re-establishment of Lebanese government sovereignty over their capital."

The PLO had departed from West Beirut after declaring a victory. The Weinberger press conference had also ended in a "victory." Everybody had a "victory" and it was actually quiet for the next few days in the Lebanese capital. Then, the first of the Multi-National Force soldiers - a French paratroop officer - was shot in the chest and killed. At that point, the "disengagement force" decided to cut short their 30-day commitment and departed after only 17 days in *The Root*.[96] Reality was setting in a little too soon.

Only a few days after the departure of the MNF, the Israelis and the Syrians were back at it in the Bekaa valley. On 14 September 1982, the Syrian Mukhabarat (Intelligence) managed to kill the newly elected Christian President of Lebanon, Bashir Gemayel. In West Beirut, Christian and Moslem militias were at each other once again and the Israelis were moving in to restore some sort of order. In the process, the Israelis not only drew Moslem militia fire, but also drew the ire of their Christian allies, who were bent on some "pay back" for the death of their beloved leader, Bashir Gemayel.

As Israeli forces moved into Moslem West Beirut, their Christian allies followed. What happened then between 16 and 18 September 1982 defies description and years later screams at us from the darkest part of memory. The word atrocity, which was a commonplace description of events in the nightmare that was Lebanon, did not begin to cover it. The enduring description is "War Crime" and it stains the honor of the Jewish State to this day.

ଓ ଛ

North of the Beirut airport there were two Palestinian refugee camps, Sabra and Shatila. Two Lebanese militia units allied with the Israelis, followed the IDF infantry into the area. There is no doubt that as the Israelis surrounded the camps they did draw some small arms fire, but by and large, the inhabitants of the camps - women, children and old men - were unarmed and unprotected since the evacuation of their men from Beirut.

Under the Reagan Administration's "Phase I" solution, the American government guaranteed the safety of the PLO families left behind in Lebanon, but like most American guarantees, it was only talk. [97] Generally speaking, no one in the Middle East believes in American guarantees, they go along because of the funding that inevitably sweetens the deal. And, this is the historical problem in negotiations for a comprehensive Middle East settlement.

On 16 September 1982, Christian Phalange militia units under the command of Major Elie Hobeika[98] entered the Sabra camp to dispose of the remaining Palestinian "terrorists." Apparently, the Christian Arabs loosely defined exactly who the "terrorists" were for they killed everyone - men, women and children - they could find and the massacre continued for two days.

In the Shatila camp, just south of Sabra, units of Major Saad Haddad's South Lebanese Army went about rooting out the (alleged) remaining PLO terrorists in the

Bashir Gemayel

Saad Hadad

Elie Hobeika

same manner. Interestingly, a majority of Haddad's SLA gunmen were Shiite Moslems, not Christians. They too massacred everyone in the camp.

Some of the dead from the Sabra Camp

During the morning of 18 September, Beirut-based international journalists began sneaking into the Shatila camp to check out rumors of a "slaughter." Soon word flashed out to the world ... *tape at ten.*

Of course, the world was stunned and outraged. A gloom descended over the Israeli Army and morale plummeted. After all, they controlled the area and were, in the end, responsible notwithstanding the protestations and excuses of their leaders. That same weekend, President Reagan and Secretary of State George Shultz decided to re-deploy the Multi-National Force (MNF) back into Beirut less than two weeks after its departure.

As of 19 September 1982, when the 3,800 MNF troops went back into Beirut, Phase 1 had been accomplished, at least in Beirut, with disastrous results. Phase 2 was a non-starter because the Syrians were not going to leave Lebanon and the Israelis, like the Syrians, had already rejected Phase 3. *Pax Americana* in Lebanon was stillborn.

The Reagan Administration called the Lebanese situation "complex" in the fall of 1982. That was more than understatement; it was insanity. There were at that point in time 33 different armed forces deployed in Lebanon. There were the Israelis, the Syrians, and the Iranian Revolutionary Guard. The Americans, the French and the Italians constituted the MNF. There were the UN contingents in Southern Lebanon. And there were the militias ... the Christian/Shia SLA, the Christian Phalange, the Sunni Moslems, the Shia Moslems, the Druze, the PLO and the outlaws.

A reasonable person might conclude that Lebanon was like a forest fire in a high wind. The only way to bring it under control was to step back and let it burn itself out. Further dabbling by the amateurs of the Reagan Administration only set the scene for further catastrophe.

A day or so after the re-deployment of the MNF, the Shia Moslems in West Beirut began a guerilla war against the Israeli troops and soon sniper attacks and ambushes rose to the level of at least one every five hours. The streets of West Beirut became a virtual shooting gallery.

In the early morning hours of 26 September 1982, the Israeli units in West Beirut unexpectedly and without fanfare pulled out. Their "peace keeping" between the warring Arab factions had become too costly. Their withdrawal left the Multi-National Force and its Christian Phalangist allies of the "legitimate Lebanese authorities" with the job of policing Moslem West Beirut. Small wonder the Moslems took exception.

The first US Marine was killed on 30 September 1982. Eleven days later, another Marine was wounded in a car bomb explosion. It was the same day a Shiite Moslem drove an explosive laden car into the Israeli military headquarters in Tyre. The explosion brought down the eight-story building, killing 75 Israelis and 15 Palestinians. This first suicide bombing marked the first appearance of the Shia Moslem terrorist group, Hizb Allah (Party of God) and was a portent of things to come.

Over the winter of 1982 – 1983, matters seethed as sides consolidated with the arrival of a new player in town: the Iranians. Israeli Intelligence tried to warn the Americans of the Iranian involvement, but to no avail. Then on 16 March 1983, there were three attacks on the Multi-National Forces in Beirut. Ten Americans and five Italians were wounded, but there were no French casualties. The significance of these attacks was that it marked the emergence of another Iranian-backed, Shiite Moslem group known as Islamic Jihad. It also put the MNF on notice that it had become a target.

Meanwhile, fighting had broken out between the Christians and the Druze Moslems in the Shouf Mountains, just east of and overlooking Beirut. At first, the Israelis were able to control most of the outbursts, but the intensity of the fighting grew steadily.

The Reagan Peace Plan took another crippling hit on 10 April 1983 when King Hussein of Jordan terminated his involvement in Phase 3, the solution of the Palestinian problem. Under the American plan, the Jordanians were to have negotiated with the Israelis on behalf of the Palestinians, but Yasser Arafat decided to change his agreement with King Hussein. For once the Israelis and the Palestinians were in agreement ... there would be no negotiations, even by proxy. So much for Phase 3 of the Shultz plan.

If all this was not enough, the Reagan Administration's honeymoon in Lebanon brutally ended on the morning of 18 April 1983. A Shia Moslem from the Hizb Allah (Hezbollah) drove an explosive laden truck into the forecourt of the American Embassy and detonated it. The main embassy building was destroyed and 63 people were killed, 17 of them Americans. Many of the dead Americans were CIA operatives.

George Shultz apparently saw this attack as nothing more than a speed bump and pushed ahead with Phase 2 of the administration's plan. Under Phase 2, all foreign armies - read: the Israelis and the Syrians - were to withdraw from Lebanon.

On 17 May 1983, an agreement was signed between the Israelis and the Lebanese. The US State Department brokered the agreement, which called for the withdrawal of Israeli forces. Philip Habib, President Reagan's special envoy, guaranteed the Israelis that

Syrian forces would follow suit and depart Lebanon in short order. (It was yet another American guarantee.)

Specific terms of the 17 May Agreement called for the absorption of Major Saad Haddad's South Lebanese Army (SLA) into the Regular Lebanese Army and the stationing of Israeli observers in Southern Lebanon. Further, the state of war that had existed between Israel and Lebanon since 1948 ended.

While the Reagan Administration was applauding itself for the 17 May Agreement, there was a small difficulty. The Syrians refused to withdraw their forces from Lebanon and the Americans knew this before the Israelis agreed to withdraw. Furthermore, Hafez Al-Assad had made it clear to George Shultz on 8 May 1983 that Syria did not recognize the Christian Phalange Government of Amin Gemayel as "legitimate." This did not deter George Shultz from assuring the Israelis of a Syrian withdrawal.

The facts on the ground negated the Shultz promise. In Lebanon's Bekaa Valley, the Syrian Army was digging in, bringing up heavy weapons and anti-aircraft missile batteries.[99]

Meanwhile, hundreds of PLO guerrillas, who had been evacuated from Beirut the previous fall, were returning to Lebanon down the Beirut-Damascus highway from the Syrian capital. When Israeli Intelligence informed the Americans, it was treated as an embarrassment best ignored.

On 15 June 1983, the Lebanese Parliament formally ratified the 17 May Agreement with Israel. Calling the ratification a "sell out," Syrian radio urged the Druze and Shia militias to turn their guns on the Lebanese government forces as well as the Israelis. That same day, Yasser Arafat returned to Lebanon to take over command of the PLO units in the Bekaa Valley and northern Lebanon. To emphasize its truculence, the Syrian Government informed the Americans that the presidential envoy, Philip Habib, was persona non grata in Syria.

For all intents and purposes, the Lebanese Civil War between the Christians and the Moslems had been re-ignited in the Shouf Mountains east of Beirut and would soon spread. With their ticket to withdraw in hand, the Israelis had grown tired of separating the warring Arab militias in the Shouf.

On 20 July 1983, the Israelis announced that they would soon withdraw to positions south of the Awali River and leave the Shouf to its intractable anarchy. At that point, everyone who blamed the Lebanese catastrophe on the Israelis and had been screaming for their withdrawal suddenly went into cardiac arrest. [100] The Israelis were the only stabilizing forces in the Shouf, so they were prevailed upon to remain. Still, the Jews felt that it was not worth one Israeli life in the effort to separate the warring sectarian militias.

On 22 July 1983, the Druze Moslems in the Shouf loosed a barrage of 122mm Katyusha rockets on the Beirut International Airport. The American Marines who controlled the airport were powerless to keep it open and all flights were immediately suspended.

The Druze continued to randomly shell the airport and the Christians in East Beirut. On 10 August 1983, the Government of Lebanon ordered its army to respond. Thus the "legitimate Lebanese authorities" entered the civil war on the side of the Christians. Lebanese artillery units based around the airport opened fire and the Druze replied with more Katyusha rockets. Ironically, Robert McFarlane, Phillip Habib's replacement, arrived at the airport during the artillery duel to consult with the American Marine commander. For McFarlane, later of Iran-Contra fame, it was an exciting welcome to *Brown Disneyland.*

During the summer of 1983, the Kahan Commission, which had been established in Israel to investigate the Sabra and Shatila massacres, issued its final report. The charge of negligence fell squarely on the shoulders of the Israeli Defense Minister, Ariel Sharon. [101] Moshe Arens, the Israeli Ambassador to Washington, was recalled and replaced Sharon in the Defense Ministry.

The first matter on Moshe Arens' agenda was Lebanon. On 16 August 1983, Arens arrived in Beirut for consultations with the "legitimate Lebanese authorities," Amin Gemayel. The Israeli position was simple: Israel was not going spend lives disarming the warring Christians and Druze militias in the Shouf. The Lebanese Government would have to open negotiations between the two factions because the Israeli forces were going to withdraw down to the Awali River. The Israeli withdrawal was set and would happen even if the sectarian fighting continued.

Over the months since the second deployment of the Multi-National Force, the Lebanese Government, dominated by the Christian Phalangists, had grown continuously stronger, thanks to American training and equipment. Still, it hesitated. In late August, the issue was decided when the Moslem militias emerged in West Beirut and began attacking the government forces. It was a sustained effort and while the fighting continued in West Beirut, Syrian artillery in the Metn hills, north of the Shouf, began shelling Christian East Beirut.

Soon the Lebanese Government forces were fully engaged in Moslem West Beirut. Bringing to bear their superior firepower, the Lebanese forces slowly drove the Moslem gunmen back into the southern section of West Beirut.

In retaliation, Druze militiamen in the Shouf massacred 24 Christians - mostly women and children. Large units of the Druze militias then emerged in the Shouf and began systemically attacking the Christian villages. It was at that point, the Israelis notified the Lebanese Government that they intended to withdraw from the Shouf within 24 hours.

During the night of 3 September 1983, the Israeli units in the Shouf Mountains began to convoy up and move south. They had driven the PLO out of Beirut, rescued the beleaguered Lebanese Christians, but had failed to secure the peace in the quagmire that was Lebanon. By dawn the following morning, the Israelis had completely evacuated the city and Beirut was left to the Multi-National Forces and the warring militias. With the Israeli withdrawal, *The Root* sank back into the boiling cauldron of intense sectarian war.

 G8 8O

The Root

> *"They now ring the bells, but they will soon wring their hands."*

Sir Robert Walpole

It was the irresistible nature of the Middle East along with the Reagan Administration's confused, pro-Arab policies that sucked the United States into the quagmire. In and around Beirut, the Moslems were on the offensive. They were taking Christian villages in the Shouf, massacring the inhabitants, and moving on at an alarming rate.

On 6 September 1983, the Multi-National Force, now bolstered by a company of the Queen's Dragoon Guards of the British Army, came under deliberate artillery attack. Two Marines and a French paratrooper were killed. Under orders, the MNF units did not return fire.

On 8 September 1983, a Druze artillery battery shelling the Marines was spotted and the American frigate *USS Bowen* glided effortlessly up to the shoreline and took it under fire. A Moslem mortar team attempted to fire in return, but its one round struck the Mediterranean over a mile away from the frigate. It was the first exchange of fire, however insignificant, between the Americans and the Moslems.

During the night of 18 September 1983, a year after the Sabra and Shatila massacres, the Moslems had

practically driven the Lebanese Government forces out of the Shouf and were threatening Christian East Beirut. President Reagan's envoy, Robert McFarlane, made a momentous decision that brought the United States into the Lebanese Civil War on the side of the Lebanese Christians. McFarlane, a former Marine officer himself, decided that the US Sixth Fleet

Robert "Bud" McFarlane

should lend gunfire support to the Lebanese Government Army. Washington approved.

The following morning, 19 September 1983, the American destroyer, *USS John Rogers,* sailed up close to the shoreline and opened fire on Moslem artillery batteries in the Shouf Mountains. In short order, the guided missile cruiser, *USS Virginia*, joined the *Rogers*. Two French warships and the American amphibious assault ship, *USS Tarawa,* joined them. By the end of the day, the forests in the Shouf had been set ablaze and a massive smoke canopy hung over the city of Beirut.

The naval shelling settled into a routine. American, French and British warplanes also buzzed the city at low level. And when the Moslem gun batteries in the Metn hills opened up on the French MNF headquarters, French fighter-bombers attacked the positions and destroyed the guns.

In the waters off Beirut, there were almost 30 NATO warships and one bright morning, an ominous speck appeared on the horizon. On shore, the American Marines watched the dark object grow as it sailed steadily toward the Lebanese coast. She was the massive 45,000-ton battleship *USS New Jersey* and her 16-inch guns were capable of throwing a one-ton shell some 25 miles into Lebanon. The Marines now had their "big iron" and there was definitely going to be a gunfight.

Back in Washington, the White House apparently did not see the parallels between the tar-baby of Lebanon and Vietnam. The Lebanese Christian forces were crumbling and the United States had come to their aid, just as the Syrians and the Israelis had done previously. The Reagan Administration's Arab friends were of no help and in fact, were starting to view the Americans as aggressors against the Moslems fighting to rid their country of foreign invaders... "Crusaders." The ugly specter of *Jihad* (Holy War) was starting to rear its head, while the White House seemed enamored with heroic images from the "big screen." Both the Arabs and the Israelis tried to caution the Reagan Administration, but their pleas fell on deft ears.

On 22 October 1983, the Syrian Government warned the Americans that they were prepared to use missiles against the Sixth Fleet if President Reagan attempted to "terrorize" Syria. It was an ominous warning, but something was lost in the translation.

More Marines landed to reinforce those already entrenched in *The Root.* The Marine Battalion Landing Team or BLT was headquartered in a large four-story building located at the northern end of the Beirut International Airport, between the two main runways. Beneath the BLT as the structure was called was a small underground parking garage with a ramp leading up to the large exterior parking lot.

The French headquarters of the 1st Chasseurs Parachutists Regiment (Foreign Legion) was located northeast of the airport in a nine-story building called the "Drakkar."

Around 6:15 AM on Sunday 23 October 1983, a Mercedes truck turned left off the airport road and drove into the parking lot outside the BLT. The driver circled the parking lot twice, apparently coordinating the timing, then gunned his engine and smashed through the front gate of the Marine compound where the guards had not been issued ammunition. At 6:20 AM, 4000 pounds of explosives carried in the truck detonated just inside the underground garage. The entire BLT collapsed in fire, smoke and dust.

Twenty seconds later, a second truck sped toward the Drakkar, but the Foreign Legionnaires immediately took it under fire and stopped it about 75 yards from the building. Still, it was close enough and when it exploded it moved the entire 9-story building twenty feet away and collapsed it into a pile of rubble. Only a burning crater 20 feet deep and 40 feet wide remained to mark the former location of the structure.

When the smoke cleared 241 Americans and 58 Frenchmen of the MNF were dead. It was the worst casualties the United States had suffered since the Vietnam War and few in Washington could understand how the Reagan Administration's pro-Arab Middle East policy had gone so terribly awry.

The Marines had returned to Beirut to protect the Moslems against the Christian, but when the Israelis pulled out, the United States had supported the Christian "legitimate Lebanese authorities" against the Moslems in the reignited civil war. The view from Washington was confused, after all the Marines were supposed to be peacekeepers.

Slowly it occurred to the Reagan Administration that Syria - without the Israelis to hold her in check - was the dominate force in Lebanon, but by then, it was too late. And Syria was a surrogate of the "Evil Empire" and Shiite Iran. Not surprisingly, the administration's perceived influence with the Arab States proved as worthless as any American guarantees in controlling the Syrians.

In the wake of truck-bomb attacks on the American Embassy, the BLT and the Drakkar, American Intelligence thrashed around before concluding that Shiite Iran was behind them. No culprits were readily identified, but the general consensus held that it was the Hezbollah with the help of the Syrian Mukhabarat, backed by Iran that planned and engineered the attacks. The suicide bombers were Lebanese Shiite Moslems and shortly after the bombing, a group calling itself the "Islamic Jihad" claimed responsibility. Still, everyone on the ground in Lebanon knew it was the Hezbollah with Iranian backing.

Caspar Weinberger, still trying to cozy up to the Arabs, blamed the Israelis. A story circulated that Israeli Intelligence had known about the planned attacks, but had not warned the Americans or the French. It was nonsense, of course, and just another attempt by members of the Reagan Administration to discredit Israel in the media. In fact on 4 November 1983, only days after the destruction of the American and French military headquarters in Beirut, a suicide bomber blew up the Israelis' new military headquarters in Tyre. Sixty Israelis were killed in that attack.

There is another footnote to the attack on the Marines that deserves mention because it illustrates Weinberger's misguided agenda and continuing anti-Israel posture.

Minutes after the truck bomb exploded in the BLT, the Israelis alerted Rambam Hospital in Haifa to expect a "mass casualty." Rambam was only 15 minutes away from the scene by helicopter, well within the "golden hour" trauma specialists so dearly love. Caspar Weinberger, however, would have no part of Israel's offer to help with the American casualties. Instead, he ordered the wounded Marines flown to the American

Army hospital in Germany, some seven-air hours from Beirut. Several more Marines, who might have been saved, died en route.

The French, however, had no qualms about Arab sensitivities and immediately attacked Syrian Army positions in and around Beirut. In a like gesture, a full-blown Alpha Strike was launched from the American carrier, *USS Eisenhower.* Ostensibly, the strike was headed toward Syrian forces in the Bekaa Valley, but in reality, the aircraft dropped their bombs into the sea so as not to impugn Arab sensibilities.

ᘓ ᘔ

Almost immediately, Hizb Allah (Hezbollah) began kidnapping American citizens in Lebanon ... mostly ex-pats ... as an insurance policy against American retaliation for the BLT attack. This ran on for the next decade and as time progressed, the Iranians saw an opportunity to squeeze political, military and financial concessions out of the Reagan Administration and they were right.

The long and tedious hostage crisis in Lebanon found the Reagan Administration out of air speed and ideas. In the end, 7 of the hostages lived through their long ordeal to be ransomed, 9 were killed by their captors and 11 escaped or were rescued. It was a successful tactic that forced the Americans, the French and even the Israelis to trade for theirs or someone else's nationals. The exception was the Soviets.

Emboldened, by 1985 as the Reagan Administration began trading arms for American hostages in Lebanon, Hezbollah decided to test the waters with the Soviets. The motive was said to be the fighting in Tripoli by and between the Communists and Fundamentalist Moslems. *(Yes, one needs a scorecard.)*

On 30 September 1985, Hezbollah gunmen stopped a car with Soviet diplomatic plates in Moslem West Beirut. They forced the four Russian diplomats into another vehicle and drove off. Taken were Valery Mirkov, Oleg Spirin, Nikolai Virsky and Arkady Katakov ... all Soviet diplomats attached to the Soviet Embassy in West Beirut. (Two were thought to be KGB officers.)

Demands were soon made public by a group (heretofore unknown) calling itself "the Islamic Liberation Organization" offering the release of the Soviet diplomats if the Russians called off the Communist Moslem forces in Tripoli, otherwise the hostages would be murdered. To add emphasis, the kidnappers executed Arkady Katakov and dumped his body in West Beirut on 2 October 1985.

Immediately upon learning of the kidnappings, KGB officers in Beirut contacted Israeli Intelligence. *Saving innocent lives takes priority over politics.* Mossad officers checked their traps and soon informed the Soviets that the Islamic Liberation Organization was just a front for the Shiite Hezbollah. By then the body of Katakov had been recovered, so the gloves came off.

While KGB officers began back-grounding the Hezbollah leadership, a team from their Spetsnaz Alpha

Group was dispatched to Beirut. A close relative of Hezbollah spiritual leader and founder, Mohammad Hussein Fadlallah, was identified and kidnapped. His "manhood" was removed and sent to Sheik Fadlallah along with a list of names of additional close relatives. The kidnapped relative was then executed and his body dumped in the spot where Katakov was found.

The three surviving Russian diplomats were set free within walking distance of their embassy in West Beirut. There was some announcement in Damascus that the release of the Soviet diplomats was the work of Ghazi Kanaan, Chief of Syrian Intelligence in Lebanon, but everyone in *The Trades* knew that was smoke. The whole affair lasted a little less than a month and no other Soviet citizens were kidnapped in Beirut.

All told, some seven Lebanese groups were involved in kidnapping foreigners in Lebanon. Of these, most were interested in the Arab penchant for ransom, not politics. This proved beneficial to the Israelis, who lost only one hostage, if temporarily, to kidnappers.

Moslems kidnapped what was later described as a "driver" for Israeli diplomats in Beirut, but was actually a Mossad officer. An Israeli "unbuttoned" diplomat, American-born Bruce Kashdan, went after him. Dressing in the uniform of a Red Cross worker and driving a Red Cross car, Kashdan approached the kidnappers and convinced them that their hostage was a lowly driver for whom no one would pay ransom. The hostage was freed into Kashdan's custody.

The kidnapping campaign in Lebanon was primarily the work of Hezbollah and it proved quite successful, with of course, the Soviet exception. It had started with the hijacking of TWA flight 847 out of Athens on 14 June 1985. There were 139 passengers and 8 crew onboard and in the end, Hezbollah would humiliate the Reagan Administration.

The four hijackers were identified as Imad Mughniyah, Mohammed Ali Hamadi, Hassan Izz al Din, and Ali Atwa. The passengers were of mixed nationalities, but included no Israelis. After 17 days, three trips from Beirut to Algiers and back, the continual beating of passengers and the murder of an American sailor, the ordeal ended. The Reagan Administration prevailed upon Israel to give into to the hijackers' demands and release 735 Shiite terrorists-prisoners.

The four hijackers were later indicted in US Federal Court and placed on the FBI's Most Wanted list. Interestingly, Mohammed Ali Hamadi was arrested two years later in Germany, tried, convicted and sentenced to life without parole. But, after 19 years in prison, he was suddenly paroled and sent to Lebanon in 2005 even though the United States still wanted him. (It turns out that he was exchanged for a German ex-pat kidnapped in Iraq.)

Imad Fayez Mughniyah aka Hajj Rodwan rose in the ranks of Hezbollah and allegedly killed more American citizens than any one terrorist prior to Nine-Eleven. It was Mughniyah, having been successful with the TWA 847 hijacking, who was tasked with instituting the Hezbollah kidnapping program in Lebanon that ran for over a decade. It was later determined that he was also involved with the BLT and Drakkar bombings in 1983, two attacks on Israeli institutions in Buenos Aires in 1992 and 1994 and other assorted atrocities.

Imad Mughniyah

Although one of the most wanted terrorist in the world, he was living quietly in the up-scale Kafar Soussa district of Damascus when the Mossad caught up with him. On 12 February 2008, Mr. Mughniyah got into his car and died instantly when his seat's headrest detonated. The three surviving terrorists are living (apprehensively) in Lebanon today under the protection of Hezbollah.

ᛦ ᛏ

After the October attacks, everyone understood that the Americans would abandon Lebanon ... everyone except perhaps President Reagan and the guardians of his media image. George Shultz saw the writing on the wall and urged Amin Gemayel, then the "legitimate Lebanese authorities," to compromise with his political rivals and end the bloody chaos. Shortly thereafter, a "reconciliation conference" was held in Geneva where Gemayel met with the leaders of the warring factions, Franjieh, Chamoun, Jumblatt and Berri. Present in spirit if not in person was President Hafez Al-Assad of Syria.

Lebanese President Amin Gemayel meeting with George Schultz

The first order of business at the Geneva conference was the demand that the Gemayel Government abandon the 17 May Agreement with Israel. Gemayel agreed. Ironically, the Agreement was the only tangible accomplishment of the Shultz 3-Phase Peace Plan, and in the end, he contributed to its renunciation. But meanwhile, the fighting in Beirut continued.

Having learned the lessons from the bombing of their headquarters, the MNF contingents dug in as the war became something of an artillery duel between the Shia and Druze gunners and the NATO warships in the bay. The Moslems were unable to get at the MNF units, so they turned elsewhere to attack the Americans and the French.

On 12 December 1983, in a repeat of the October bombings, "Islamic Jihad" destroyed the French and American embassies in Kuwait.[102]

℃ ℠

The Palestine Liberation Organization, the perpetual bad-news boys of the Middle East did not fare well during the fall of 1983. They had been nothing but trouble for Lebanon since they arrived in 1970. They had triggered Lebanon's sectarian war in 1975 and baited the Israelis until they invaded in 1982. Over half of the PLO guerrillas had been driven out of Lebanon, but Arafat had returned to command those who had returned and the remaining 10,000.

The game in Lebanon had now changed, however, and Syria was calling the shots on the Moslem side of the equation. Arafat apparently did not understand this and soon he had a mutiny on his hands. A former lieutenant of Arafat's, Mahmoud Labadi, led the insurgency, but it was instigated, funded and directed by Damascus.

As the Moslems and Druze were attacking the Lebanese Christians and the MNF in Beirut, a fratricidal war-within-a-war broke out between the rival PLO factions in the Bekaa Valley. Only about 4,000 guerillas remained loyal to Arafat and they were quickly driven out of the mountains and into the northern city of Tripoli. There they were besieged and pounded into submission by Syrian artillery.

On 20 December 1983, Yasser Arafat and his surviving guerillas boarded chartered Greek vessels and departed Tripoli for Tunis under escort by French warships. As they left the harbor, a flight of jet fighter-bombers flew overhead in a menacing farewell, the sun flashing off the blue and white Star of David on their wings. It was a repeat of the Beirut evacuation 15 months before and as usual, the PLO left behind a destroyed Lebanese city. This time, however, Arafat would not return.

Tripoli burns during inter-Palestinian fighting (AP)

A little over a month of heavy sectarian fighting followed in Beirut before the Lebanese Army began to dissolve into its Christian and Moslem components. On 5 February 1984, the Lebanese Government resigned and its Army dissolved for all intents and purposes. Moslem militias quickly took over West Beirut, trapping the MNF "peacekeepers" with their backs to the sea.

The following morning, 6 February 1984, the Multi-National Forces no longer had a "legitimate Lebanese authority" to support and President Reagan pulled the plug, announcing that the Marines in *The Root* would be "re-deployed" back to their ships.

First went the foreign civilians ... airlifted out to Cyprus. Then the troops of the MNF evacuated to their ships. On 28 February 1984, the Marines' rear guard elements mounted their amphibious armored vehicles and drove into the Mediterranean. Then the *New Jersey* lumbered up to the shoreline, turned her big 16-inch guns toward the Shouf and opened fire on the Syrian artillery positions overlooking Beirut. The American Navy claimed the *New Jersey* had destroyed 20 Syrian artillery pieces, but in reality it damaged only one. Thus the Reagan Administration's ill-conceived and costly Lebanon adventure ended. The Lebanese quagmire was left to the Israelis and the Syrians to sort out.[103]

On 29 February 1984, just 24 hours after the Americans departed, Amin Gemayel, the Christian President of Lebanon, flew to Damascus to pay homage to the *real* President of Lebanon, Hafez Al-Assad. Four days later, Gemayel announced that the Lebanese-Israeli accord of 17 May 1983 was "null and void."

And so it came to pass after all the pain, after all the blood, after all the death, after all the destruction, the situation in Lebanon remained basically unchanged except the Christians were out and the Moslems were back in.

In a final gesture, the *USS New Jersey* unlimbered her big guns and fired on Syrian artillery positions in the Metn Hills before declaring a victory and sailing away. There was a spontaneous outbreak of celebrations that lasted for days as the Moslems rejoiced in their victory over the Americans. Only days later, upon learning of the American invasion of Grenada, one bone-tired Israeli officer shook his head, sighed, "I hope they can win there."

USS New Jersey unleashing her "big iron"

cx ᘓ

For all the incompetence, naiveté, ignorance of matters Middle Eastern and blind dogma in residence within the Reagan Administration, still we must defend them. After all, Lebanon is the clearest contemporary example of the way things work in *Brown Disneyland.* The "suits" of the Reagan Administration talked the talk, but did not walk the walk. *Lots of big hats, but no cattle.* Any nation, which decides to intervene in The Levant, had better bring friends … and lunch. Sadly for the United States, President Reagan's prancers and dancers learned no lessons, and as we shall see, continued to dabble in the Middle East with disastrous results learning and relearning that one cannot rely on Arab rationality.

There is yet another point to make. The idea that providing arms to the Arab states would "establish stronger ties" was taken as gospel in Washington. No one apparently gave any consideration to the effects it might have on the delicate military balance in the Middle East.

The baseline of this equation is that sooner or later, the balance will tilt off-center from the status quo and the Arabs will feel strong enough to wage war on the Jews. This is the rule, not the exception and is exactly what happened in Lebanon.

During the Israeli invasion massive quantities of PLO weapons were discovered in deep caves south of Beirut and in literally miles of tunnels beneath the Sabra and Shatila refugee camps. There were enough small arms there to equip ten infantry divisions, leading to speculation in various intelligence communities that the Soviets had pre-positioned the weapons to facilitate a quick invasion of the Middle East. The Israeli Army moved all of the captured weapons back into Israel and it took 500 trucks, running 24 hours a day, for six weeks to accomplish the task.[104]

A majority of the weapons found were Soviet Bloc in origin, but there were American, British and other Western countries represented as well. It had been an interesting military build-up, which included artillery and armored vehicles ... items no one would expect to find in the hands of a terrorist organization. It also exposed the complicity of the Arab States, including Saudi Arabia, in the clandestine arming of the PLO, a known terrorist organization. Yet Saudi Arabia would never end up on the Reagan Administration's list of nations supporting terrorism.

Several of the captured vehicles were V-150 Commando armored cars manufactured by Cadillac Gage in Warren, Michigan.[105] Israeli Intelligence traced the serial numbers and discovered that they were originally sold to the Saudi Arabia National Guard (SANG) with American government approval. When the vehicles arrived in Saudi Arabia, they were immediately placed aboard another ship ... the *Penelope* ... and delivered to the PLO in Lebanon. Apparently, American third-party transfer restrictions did not apply to Saudi Arabia.

The military build-up of the PLO had transformed the rag-tag international terrorist group into a powerful, organized force. It dominated the local Lebanese Army and various militia factions within Lebanon, gaining enough strength to finally challenge the Israelis. It tipped the military balance, which began the same old cycle that had led in the past to shooting wars in the Middle East and would lead to shooting wars in the future.

It can be further argued that the Lebanese fiasco did strengthen ties between the Reagan Administration and the Arab states. This new relationship certainly produced benefits for individual American businessmen, most especially for those in the petroleum industry, but it came at a price.

The Arab states supported the PLO and did their best to push Washington into closer ties with that terrorist organization. In the process, the rank-and-file American citizen suffered. During the first five years of the Reagan Administrations, as George Shultz searched for solutions to the "Palestinian problem," over 300 American civilians were killed by PLO terrorists.

Finally, Lebanon also saw the emergence of new Moslem terrorist groups that were not affiliated with the PLO. The Shia Moslems, for example, gave the world the religious suicide bomber and acted as surrogates for the Islamic Republic of Iran. These and other radical Moslem groups saw a great victory for Islam when the Americans withdrew from Lebanon. Although inspired by PLO terrorism, it was these groups who would eventually take their hatred and their war to the United States ... in the name of God.

Interestingly, Nabi Berri, head of Lebanon's Amal Militia and the man responsible for the hijacking of TWA 847, was fronting for the new Shia terrorist movement, Hizb Allah (Party of God). And, while Mr. Berri was thus busy, he was also on the payroll of the CIA. This did not sit well with the Israelis.

Cઠ 80

Bechtel's Folly

> *"Where there is a sea, there are pirates."*

> Old Greek Proverb

While not as publicly egregious as the Enron scandal, the relationship between the Reagan Administration's foreign policy in the Middle East and the oilmen in Washington is self-evident and lies at the heart of matters. It was petroleum that set the scene for their dealings with Iraq and its tin-pot dictator, Saddam Hussein. As has become evident with the passage of time, it led to a whole plethora of dire consequences, including but not limited to, the Gulf War and Iraq War.

Iraq was an important, oil-producing, Arab State and an influential player in the American petroleum industry in the 1980s. Iraq's oil money also supported its war with Iran, which was just as important to the Reagan Administration. It is therefore easy to understand why from 1984, when George Shultz reestablished diplomatic relations with Iraq, until the eve of the Gulf War in July of 1990, the importation of Iraqi crude oil into the United States rose from a low of 60,000 barrels a day to 1.6 million barrels a day.

Conversely, it is also easy to understand why the Reagan Administration took a dim view of anyone dealing in Iranian crude, which supported the Persians' war against Iraq. This view would produce some interesting consequences in the future.

In the spring of 1984, the Bechtel Corporation - the firm that provided employment to Caspar Weinberger and George Shultz when they were not in government - came to Washington with a new proposal. The company was seeking financial assistance for Iraq in order to build an oil pipeline from northwestern Iraq to the Jordanian port of Aqaba on the Red Sea.

This pipeline dovetailed neatly with the Reagan Administration's efforts to support Iraq, it was a $1 billion cash cow for Bechtel and it had none of the potential embarrassment involved in supplying weapons. Indeed, it diverted Iraq's crude oil away from the war zone making it more difficult for the Iranians to disrupt deliveries, which were so critical to Saddam Hussein. He could then afford more war material. All in all, it was a beautiful project.

There was only one problem, which the Iraqis were quick to point out. Portions of the pipeline would be located within small arms range of Jordan's border with Israel and the Israelis had not hesitated in the past to destroy Arab construction projects they deemed not in their best interest. At that point in time, the Israelis were supporting the Iranians, not the Iraqis in the Middle East *war du jour.*

Aside from the Israeli problem, there was a lack of funding. At the time, the American financial community did not share all the enthusiasm being generated by the White House over its newfound Iraqi ally in the Persian Gulf.

Saddam Hussein wanted his pipeline constructed, but he insisted on direct American involvement. The While House was willing to get involved at the behest of Bechtel and the project was sent to the Eximbank for American Government loan guarantees.

The Eximbank looked over the project, found Iraq to be a lousy credit risk and tuned the deal down flat. After months of trying, the bank had continued to rebuff the pipeline project and so George Shultz decided to bring up the big guns.

On 25 June 1984, William Draper, the chairman of the Eximbank, got a phone call from his old Yale classmate, Vice President George Bush. That same day, the Eximbank green-lighted the Iraq-Aqaba Pipeline to the tune of $500 million in American taxpayer-backed loan guarantees. We feel it incumbent to point out that in June of 1984, Iraq, which had been removed from the List of Terrorist Nations in 1982, still had no diplomatic relations with the United States.

In Israel, the Likud government had been replaced by Labor, which was viewed as and has been, more amenable to American overtures. The Israelis thought it over and gamed out what the pipeline might mean to the Middle East when real peace was established. Israeli Prime Minister Shimon Peres signed off on the project.

Everything looked good until it leaked to the press. The White House, more attuned to President Reagan's popularity polls than any pipeline project for Bechtel, let it hum for a while before declaring it dead.

Looking back on that time period, it is not surprising that the oilmen in Washington attempted to salvage Iraq as a supplier and a customer even though Saddam Hussein was a Soviet client and his behavior gave common barbarity a bad name.

಄ ೞ

Friends Like These

"Lord, please save us from our friends; our enemies we will handle on our own."

Old Hebrew Prayer

Contrary to popular opinion, the relationship between the American and Israeli Intelligence services has been rocky and inconsistent at best. Its history has always reflected traditions, suspicions, national interests and more acutely, time frames.

Over the years there have been numerous tactical instances where these two organizations or portions thereof, have clashed. In *The Trades* this is called "friendly friction" and the matter of Ali Hassan Salameh ... called by the Israelis, "The Red Prince" because he was a Soviet-trained, terrorist-playboy ... is a case in point.

Salameh was the operations chief of Black September and the planner of the 1972 Munich Olympics massacre, among other terrorist acts. As expected, the Israelis reacted biblically to the killing of their athletes under a program coded CAESAREA, which has been more commonly called by journalists "The Wrath of God."

Much has been written about this operation that targeted Palestinian terrorist leaders for assassination,[106] but it is usually couched in terms of revenge. And, while the revenge aspect was certainly enjoyed, in fact, it was a tried and true Israeli method for fighting and defeating Arab terrorism.

Salameh was on a list of a baker's dozen Arab terrorists who planned and supported the Munich operation and were slated by the Israelis for their just rewards. He proved, however, a hard quarry to corner and by 1975, some three years after Munich and the untimely deaths of almost a dozen of his cohorts, he had risen in political statue and was on the payroll of the CIA.

This was hard for the Israelis to understand. One of the Israeli athletes killed in Munich was David Mark Berger from Cleveland, Ohio. [107] A graduate of Tulane University with a Masters and a law degree from Columbia, Berger was engaged to an Israeli girl, which was how he ended up in Israel. He was an NCAA weightlifting champion in college and had been quickly accepted on the Israeli Olympic team. The CIA cozying up to his killers was, in Israeli eyes, inconceivable no matter what the perceived benefits, which in this case were none.

In addition, the Carter Administration had publically assured the Israelis that they would not deal with any Palestinian terrorist or organization. But, in 1977 when Salemeh married his second wife, Georgina Rizak, the CIA sent them on a honeymoon to Hawaii and threw in a trip to Disney World, all at the expense of the American taxpayer.

So, the Israelis approached Salameh's CIA Case Officer, Sam Wyman, and inquired as to the status of his agent. Wyman kicked it up to his boss, Robert Clayton Ames. Caught cold and embarrassed on the horns of a political dilemma with an expensive, non-productive agent, Ames disavowed Salemeh. The Israelis killed "The Red Prince" with a car bomb on 22 January 1979. Ironically, Bob Ames died in the truck bombing of the American Embassy in Beirut by Hizb Allah (Hezbollah) in 1983.

CB ED

The founding fathers of the State of Israel were by and large, East European Socialists. The new nation they envisioned was a democratic Jewish State that still provided its citizens with the benefits of socialism.

The United States was the first country to recognize the new nation, but the Soviet Union was a close second. As the Cold War developed, both nations initially vied for influence over the new Jewish State. Israel chose to align itself with the First World democracies rather than the Second World's socialist and communist regimes.

However, American politicians, influenced by people like Senator Joseph McCarthy, became wary of Israel's *social* democracy and this suspicion filtered down to the American Intelligence agencies. Throw in a little inherent anti-Semitism and this mixture initially crippled efforts by the CIA to exchange information with Israel's Intelligence services.

The CIA saw in the Israelis an ability to penetrate the Soviet Union far beyond its own capabilities and accordingly devised a plan. The legendary CIA counterintelligence chief, James Jesus Angleton, was assigned to liaise with the Israelis, instituting safeguards in the fledgling Jewish Intelligence services so the needed exchange of information could take place.

The most well-known safeguard instituted by Angleton - one that is still in practice today - was the prohibition against any Jewish immigrant from any Soviet-bloc country being allowed into Israeli Intelligence. There were many others, of course, and once these safeguards had been instituted, a somewhat restricted flow of intelligence began passing between the two communities.

Up until 1973, it proved a beneficial relationship to both parties. Under the Nixon Administrations, the Department of Defense had eroded the preeminence of the CIA. In October of 1973, the American Intelligence Community helped lull the Israelis into believing that the Arab Armies massed on their borders were merely on training exercises. It proved disastrous for Israel and no one has ever been able to definitively explain whether this was on purpose or was simply the normal incompetence of American Intelligence. In all fairness, it was Israel that wrongly decided there would be no attack.[108]

From 1973 until 1981, there was gradual erosion of the bilateral intelligence exchange between the two countries, due is no small measure to the politicizing of the American Intelligence Community. In 1981, all intelligence sharing was abruptly halted after Israel attacked the Iraqi nuclear complex at Al Tuwaitha.

Most like to blame Admiral Bobby Ray Inman, the brilliant, if very weird, Deputy Director of the CIA. On a political level, however, this would have been next to

William Casey and Bobby Ray Inman

impossible without the support of the DCI himself, Bill Casey. Casey, by all accounts, would never have supported an intelligence embargo, unless the President overruled him. It is now substantially clear that indeed he was overruled and that the man who influenced the President's decision was Caspar Weinberger, the Secretary of Defense. And so it stood until 1983, when the US Congress attempted to crank up intelligence exchanges between the two nations.

That year the United States and Israel signed an official agreement to share intelligence with each other. This agreement was actually a caveat attached by Congress to the Reagan Administration's large weapons sales to the Arab States. In formal terms, it was called the "U.S.-Israel Bilateral Intelligence Sharing Agreement of 1983" and through this agreement, fully evaluated intelligence reports were supposed to pass back and forth between the two respective intelligence communities. Its' purpose, as constituted, was to prevent an Arab military surprise of Israel with their new American weapons.

It was a binding, written agreement backed by an Executive Order and was not subject to the interpretation of lower-level facilitators. After all, people who are *elected* are supposed to set the policy, while people who are *appointed* are supposed to carry it out. Elements within the Reagan Administration's Department of Defense, however, felt an obligation to decide just what they wanted the Israelis to have ... and to have not ... in an obvious effort to protect the darker aspects of their "Level Battlefield Doctrine" and their Arab friends.

Beginning in late 1983, there were several meetings between American Intelligence officials and their Israeli counterparts to facilitate the exchange of information. One member of the American liaison team was a brilliant young intelligence analyst named Jonathan Jay Pollard. Assigned as a representative from Naval Intelligence, Pollard was an expert on Soviet weapon systems - especially those being shipped into the Arab States - surface ships and fleet operations in the Mediterranean.

Prior to the first liaison meeting, the American team was given its final negotiating instructions by staffers from the office of the Secretary of Defense,

Caspar Weinberger. As the Navy's representative, Jay Pollard later recalled,

"The material I was authorized to give them (the Israelis) had been so sanitized, redacted and distorted that it was essentially worthless."[109]

Pollard's superiors emphasized that the members of the liaison team "were only to pass on enough information to scare the hell out of the Israelis, but not enough to let them counter various Soviet-bloc equipment then flooding into the region," he recalled.

These instructions, Pollard also noted, "were in clear violation of the 1983 US-Israel Exchange of Intelligence Agreement in as much as they prevented us from passing anything of any real value on to the Israelis."[110]

In 1983, there was talk about the administration's pro-Arab leanings, but the "Level Battlefield Doctrine" was a still-secret policy. The liaison meetings between American Intelligence and its Israeli counterpart represented a threat that could not only trigger an Israeli military reaction, but might expose the administration's secret policy to Congress and the public. Had the American people known about it, there is no doubt that the military build-up of Iraq would have been stopped and more than likely, there would have been no Iraqi invasion of Kuwait and no Gulf War.

The proposition, proffered years later by Reagan Administration apologists, that Iran would have defeated Iraq in the Iran-Iraq War (1980-1988) is arguable, if not a non-starter. With a little American help and *without* the introduction of chemical and biological weapons, the Iraqis could have produced a stalemate just as they did in the end.

Every individual in the Reagan Administration with even remote knowledge of the clandestine Iraqi military build-up had to know that sooner or later, Israel would become the *target du jour* for Saddam Hussein's enhanced military capability. This was exactly what the former Secretary of State, Al Haig, had been screaming about until his forced resignation in 1982.

The national security of Israel, an official non-NATO ally of the United States, was of no concern to the Reagan Administration, to put it mildly, and apparently no one saw any threat to Kuwait and Saudi Arabia from their "Arab brothers" in Iraq. In retrospect, this is hard to understand when the White House is supposed to be staffed by our "best and brightest."

The White House "spin" on the Middle East in the early 1980s was expressed as a genuine concern over the Iran-Iraq War. It tilted toward Saddam Hussein, who was portrayed as a hero holding back the Iranian, Islamic-fundamentalist hordes. Never mind he started the whole thing by his ill-considered invasion of Iran. Not surprisingly, this was the same view tendered and promoted by the Arab states.

Whether or not the unilateral abrogation of the 1983 Intelligence Sharing Agreement by Caspar Weinberger was in violation of law is an issue that has been lost and now a matter for scholars of legal history.

This often-cited, legal footnote is thin at best, but the deed obviously stood against the stated public policy of the Reagan Administration and the wishes of Congress. It did, however, present a moral dilemma for Jay Pollard and the other American Intelligence representatives to the Israeli liaison meetings.

During the first intelligence-sharing meeting, the Israelis were completely forthcoming in their presentation as Pollard later recalled. Israel was interested in the Soviet weaponry being shipped into the Middle East. On a tactical level, they were concerned with the weapons being shipped into Syria, but on a strategic level they were carefully watching Iraq.

The Israelis were critically interested in what American Intelligence knew about the nuclear, biological and chemical (NBC) weapons being developed and manufactured in Iraq. Clearly, they felt that these weapons would be turned against them after the cessation of hostilities between Iran and Iraq and they said so.

The American delegates, under instructions, were not forthcoming. They fabricated, they denied and they ignored. This was completely evident to the Israeli representatives and soon tempers rose accordingly.

At one point during that first meeting, Jay Pollard spoke privately to his superiors about the wisdom of withholding information on the production of chemical weapons by the Iraqis, for which the Israeli delegation was pressing. Pollard's supervisors responded that the Israelis had no *need to know* about the chemical and biological weapons and once again it was made clear that the policy was set by the Reagan Administration, no matter what the implications might be. "You know how sensitive Jews are about poison gas," one laughingly commented.[111]

Jay Pollard came away from this first meeting astounded, but kept his fears to himself until he could check all his traps. In his position as an analyst at the Naval Intelligence Support Center (NISC) in Suitland, Maryland, he had the ability to procure the original "Top Secret" reports and compare them with the redacted versions that had been turned over to the Israelis. He did exactly that and what he found was even worse than he suspected. Not only was the intelligence turned over to the Israelis of little or no value, it had often been "cooked." Further, the American DOD denied the very existence of information on many specific subjects when the Israelis inquired.[112]

As part of his job at the Naval Intelligence Support Center, Pollard was tasked with monitoring and reporting shipments of sophisticated weaponry and "technology transfers"[113] to foreign countries. He was well aware of the questionable, if not illegal, American shipments to the Arab States, most of which were destined to support Iraq in its war with Iran.

The threat to Israel notwithstanding, it was evident that Iraq would be an even more serious threat to Kuwait and Saudi Arabia. After all, Iraq had attacked Iran over territorial grievances and Saddam Hussein openly harbored the same ambitions toward Kuwait. Should Iraq attack Kuwait and/or Saudi Arabia, the

United States would most certainly be dragged into a Middle East war. As we shall see, Pollard was not alone in this analysis.

The more Pollard looked at the situation, the more he became convinced that some secret American policy agenda was driving the play. Alarmingly, the apparent agenda was centered on the clandestine, military build-up of Iraq. Pollard reasoned correctly that if the underlying policy had been "kosher," the Reagan Administration would have implemented it in the open and with congressional approval. As it stood in 1984, only a few top American policy makers and selected intelligence officials knew anything about it. Pollard had pieced it together only because of his involvement with the Israelis in the intelligence sharing farce.

It did not take a rocket scientist to see that in spite of some (alleged) positive foreign policy benefits lingering in front of the effort, it was a half-witted approach that could only lead to another Middle East war. Whoever fashioned the policy had no basic understanding of Middle East history or the Arab-Israeli conflict.

Operationally, such a policy could be carried out only in the shadows, far away from public view. The only way for the Reagan Administration to do this was to cloak it in "National Security" and turn over its execution to the spooks.

Much has been made of Jonathan Pollard's frustration over his analysis of the clandestine, Iraqi military build-up and the secret American policy agenda driving it, given his subsequent actions.

In the argument over his motives, most journalists and intelligence aficionados always seem to miss the "trigger," that one event that acted as the catalyst. That event came as a direct result of the clandestine military build-up of Iraq just a few months after the first US-Israel intelligence-sharing meeting. It happened at a place called Majnoon, which translates as "crazy" in Farsi, the language of the Persians.

ଔ ଚ

Here Be Dragons

"And you shall be driven mad by the sight of what you see."

Deuteronomy 28:34

Northeast of the Iraqi city of Basra, on the Iran-Iraq border, there is a trackless, swampy wasteland called in Arabic "Hawr Al Hammar." Somewhere out there, in a place antiquated cartographers would have left blank except for the caution "Here Be Dragons," lie two thin strips of dry land known as the Majnoon Islands.

Early in February 1984, Iranian commandos slipped through the Howeiza marshes and took the islands. By morning, they already laid a pontoon bridge and their combat engineers were surveying the approaches for an earthen causeway back to the Iranian mainland. Within days some 30,000 Iranian troops were dug in on the islands.

Iranian Revolutionary Guards

There were sporadic Iraqi counterattacks, which were easily defeated, but on 27 February 1984, Iraqi Republican Guard units mounted an all-out assault. The Iraqis opened the battle with air strikes and a heavy artillery bombardment. Along with high explosives, they fired "cocktail" rounds that burst in the air or on impact and spread deadly clouds of chemical and biological agents. Two of the chemicals were readily identifiable as the nerve gas, Sarin (GB), and the blister agent, Mustard gas (H). More agents, however, were in the Iraqi "cocktail" rounds than were immediately apparent.

The Iranians died en masse, but when the wind shifted, the deadly soup was blown back into the ranks of the attacking Iraqis. A small tear in protective clothing, a scratch and the individual soldier went down with the ineffable horror, Gas Gangrene. Most died hard and ugly, expending their last strength "dancing the kickin' chicken." And when it was over, the dead were left where they fell on the permanently poisoned ground. It was said that the few, terminally ill survivors went insane.[114]

Apparently there had been American military advisors and "spooks" with the attacking Iraqi forces[115] so American Intelligence had a quick read on what actually happened at Majnoon where, unbelievably, the Iranians prevailed.

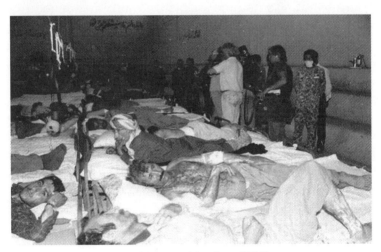

Iranian casualties from CBW

Additionally, a Belgian toxicologist, Dr. Aubin Heyndrickx, fed information to the West from Teheran where he was attempting to save the surviving Iranian casualties.

Dr. Heyndrickx promptly identified the most apparent chemical weapons as the nerve agent Sarin and the blister agent Mustard gas. He also identified Gas Gangrene - caused by a weaponized bacterium, Clostridium Perfringens - Pulmonary Anthrax and the carcinogenic Mycotoxin, T-2. [116] He isolated other pathogens, but could not readily identify them. Heyndrickx proffered that they had been genetically altered. His information was passed to the United Nations.[117]

As the Iranian casualty figures became known, Israeli Military Intelligence (AMAN) became keenly aware that something sinister had happened at Majnoon. The Israelis were not the only ones watching the developments. Other Western intelligence organizations, including the British, were focused on those far-away islands in the middle of nowhere.[118]

Slowly, the word came out of Iran from Heyndrickx and Iranian sources that the Iraqis had employed "cocktails." It took a few weeks for Israeli human intelligence (HUMINT) assets in the Persian capital to confirm it, but it was almost immediately clear that the biological terror-genie had escaped from its bottle at the Majnoon Islands.

In the past, there had been two instances of the reported use of Soviet-made biological weapons - Laos and Afghanistan - but nothing had ever been proven. Those previously identified "cocktail" rounds customarily use a burster charge to disperse the agents in aerosol form and blanket the target area with a fine, light mist. This mist, which is slightly oily in nature, has a yellow hue. Hence, the name given to it by its victims: "Yellow Rain."

It was clear that the Iraqis had employed "Yellow Rain" at Majnoon. The biological agent readily identified and normally associated with "Yellow Rain" is a Mycotoxin.

Mycotoxins are a broad class of naturally occurring fungal poisons which are associated with serious illness and death in human beings. [119] While strictly speaking, Mycotoxins are chemicals not pathogens, they are classified as bioagents because they are carcinogenic, biologically produced poisons.

Initially, the Israelis suspected the Iraqi Mycotoxins were from the Aflatoxin[120] family, but when a soil sample was obtained from Majnoon, it was clear that the Iraqi bioagent was from the family of Trichothecenes. United Nations inspectors later confirmed this when they visited the Majnoon battlefield and took samples.

Scientists at the super-secret Institute for Biological Research, located in the Israeli town of Ness Ziona, isolated one culprit. It is called simply "T-2," a particularly nasty Trichothecene described as a "blister agent-like toxin" which immediately attacks the eyes, skin and respiratory system and is about 40 times more toxic than Lewisite or Mustard gas. This Trichothecene, like most Mycotoxins, is considered carcinogenic ... cancer causing. Additionally, there were rumors that the Israeli scientists found other biological agents, some genetically altered, but if they did, they are not talking.

Iraqi sources later confirmed to UN inspectors that the deadly pathogen, Clostridium Perfringens, was also employed at Majnoon. The results, however, were less than satisfactory, for apparently as many Iraqi soldiers died from Gas Gangrene as did Iranians.

Shortly after the battle, the Israeli Intelligence services issued a new priority collection emphasis. It specified a requirement to ascertain any and all information on shipments of biological agents and associated manufacturing equipment going from any country to Iraq.

At the next US - Israel intelligence sharing meeting in the spring of 1984, Israeli representatives submitted a report on the use of T-2 in the Majnoon attack along with a request for information from the Americans. Once again, the American delegates were not very helpful about the probable source(s) of the biological toxin, and further assured the Israelis that there was no credible evidence to support their contention that Iraq was building CBW manufacturing facilities with European help.

In point of fact, however, American Intelligence knew all about the giant Iraqi complex near the town of Samarra and had known about it since an American firm, the Pfaulder Corporation of Rochester, New York, designed it in 1978.

When the Americans lied to the Israelis on orders from the Secretary of Defense once again, we have been told that it had a disastrous psychological effect on the US Navy's representative, Jonathan Pollard. He was the only person attending that meeting who knew all about biological toxins like T-2 and pathogens like Clostridium Perfringens. It is most likely that he also knew who supplied these materials to Iraq.

The Israeli fears expressed at the previous meeting in 1983 had been confirmed at Majnoon in 1984. Their report on the attack revealed to American Intelligence that Israel knew Iraq was in possession of weaponized biological agents. Moreover, it was clear that the Israelis suspected Iraq was *manufacturing* chemical and biological weapons since they found no indications of any large-scale shipments to the Iraqis from outside, source countries. Israel suspected the Germans were assisting the Iraqis and for the American Intelligence Community, it was a giant red flag.

Drawing on the Israeli information, the CIA became convinced that the Iraqi CBW manufacturing capability presented such a *clear and present danger* to the Jewish State that a unilateral attack on those facilities could be expected in short order. They even gamed out the expected attack in a study for President Reagan. A copy of this CIA study eventually found its way to Israeli Intelligence through Jonathan Pollard. Another copy went to the Saudis, courtesy of the US Defense Secretary, and from the Saudis to the Iraqis.[121]

In mid-April 1984, Israeli agents tracked the T-2 back to a West German company, Josef Kuhn GmbH, located in Neustadt am Rubenberge. A "prayer meeting" was held with the German owners, who shortly thereafter dismantled their business and sought other career challenges.

This did not stop the Germans supplying the Iraqis with Trichothecene Mycotoxins. In 1986, the Munich subsidiary of Sigma-Chemie, an American biochemical company based in St. Louis, Missouri, delivered a DM 30,000 order to the Iraqis, consisting of T-2, TH-2, Verrocarol, and Diacetyoxyscirpenol (DAS).

There are those among the Israelis who believe with a certainty that God has vested the German people with a character flaw. This belief is based not only on the Herero and Namaqua genocide in Southwest Africa (1904-1907), the Holocaust of the Second World War (1939-1945), but reinforced by several post-war incidents that found individual Germans working for the destruction of the Jews of Israel. The discovery that Josef Kuhn GmbH and Sigma-Chemie had sold Trichothecene Mycotoxins to the Iraqis hit a sensitive nerve with the Israelis and inflamed their long-held prejudice against the Germans.

ог ഔ

CHAPTER 5

PICKING SIDES

"Until you have fought the Israelis, you have not fought a real Middle East War."

Hafez Al-Assad
President of Syria

The White Pipeline

"For there is nothing hid, which shall not be manifested; neither was anything kept secret, but that it should come abroad."

Mark 4:22

In September 1980, Iraqi forces attacked Iran across their mutual border and triggered the eight-year Iran-Iraq War. It also triggered an arms bazaar that attracted most of the known world's purveyors.

The clandestine sales of weapons, spare parts and munitions to belligerents in the Iran-Iraq War would come to be called in Hebrew slang, "Import-Export-Rappaport" and cannot be described without the liberal use of the word "cluster". It evolved into a strange, geopolitical theater that featured the Israelis supporting Iran with the help of the CIA while the National Security Council supported Iraq, also with the help of the CIA.

The Israelis, taking the Iranian side against their Arab enemy, secretly agreed to immediately provide Iran with $200 million worth of war material for which they received covert American approval. After this initial shipment ... tires for F-4 aircraft ... Israel began delivering weapons and spare parts by air on regular basis by the summer of 1981.[122]

Civilian transport aircraft, chartered from the small Argentinean airline, Transporte Aereo Rioplatense (TAR), normally flew from Israel out over Cyprus, then swung east over northern Turkey and finally south into Teheran to deliver these goods.

In early July, TAR dispatched a Canadair CL-44 turboprop transport to Israel from its European base in Basel, Switzerland. On 18 July 1981, this aircraft, designated Yankee Romeo 224, was on its third trip back to Israel when its navigation systems malfunctioned. Somewhere over northern Turkey, YR-224 inadvertently crossed the border into Soviet airspace.

The Soviets had been monitoring the Israeli flights since they began and had been watching YR-224 from the moment it left Teheran on its return leg. MiG interceptors hailed the errant transport on the radio and ordered it to land at a nearby Soviet airbase. The turboprop never had a chance, but true to the calling of *The Trades,* the transport's pilots decided to evade and make for the Turkish border at all possible speed. They paid for the attempt with their lives.

Since YR-224 was a European-registered aircraft shot down by Soviet interceptors, the Swiss Civil Aeronautics Board opened an immediate investigation.

A Canadair CL- 44 Turboprop like YR-224

The Israelis and the Iranians kept quiet while TAR had to divulge the fact that the plane had been chartered by a French company, which just happened to be owned by Israeli businessmen. [123] Furthermore, the Soviets, whose client Iraq was locked down in a war with Iran, had no reason to remain silent. The incident was all over the media within a matter of days, with details that could have only come from Soviet Intelligence.

From the outset, the shoot down of Yankee Romeo 224 appeared to be much like the proverbial case of the armed jaywalker. There just had to be more to the story and, of course, there was.

The fall of the Shah of Iran in 1979 had stranded over 30,000 Iranian Jews under an Islamic Revolutionary regime. While seemingly a footnote to the vast arms deliveries, their fate was of major concern to the Israelis. The Israelis, siding with their former friend over their traditional enemy, offered an opportunity to rescue some of the Iranian Jews, and they took immediate advantage.

Every time an aircraft clandestinely flew arms from Israel to Iran, it returned with Iranian Jews. The number of Persian Jews who died in the crash of Yankee Romeo 224, if any, remains a mystery to this day. It did not, however, close the clandestine Israeli-Iranian pipeline, [124] which continued to deliver weapons, munitions and supplies in massive quantities throughout the eight-year, Iran-Iraq War.

There was never any argument over American approval of these Israeli arms shipments to Iran. When the Israelis sold items to the Iranians, they were allowed to replenish their inventories from American suppliers. Thus, it was an acute embarrassment for some of President Reagan's top people who had been promising the Arabs US support for Iraq in its war with Iran. The downing of Yankee Romeo 224 and the subsequent media exposure was, most likely a partial reason the Reagan Administration began clamping down on Israeli support of Iran.

Secondarily, the President's advisors had been chafing at the bit since their arrival in Washington as they watched the British and others take commercial advantage of the expanding Middle East war. Naturally, they wanted into the play.

However, any efforts to sell military materials directly to Iraq were immediately vetoed by General Alexander Haig, Reagan's Secretary of State. Haig perceived the war in a long view and was concerned about what the consequences of arming Saddam Hussein might mean in the post-war Middle East. In the end, Haig was right. As is now clearly evident in 20/20 hindsight the Western military build-up of Iraq resulted in the invasion of Kuwait and the First Gulf War.

The Israeli-Iranian arms trade would prove to be a thorny "wait-a-minute" vine for the Reagan Administration in the political jungle of the Middle East. Having decided to circumvent the Israeli-Iranian WHITE PIPELINE or CHANNEL ONE, the Reagan Administration turned loose a group of inexperienced cowboys from the National Security Council. This effort came to be called CHANNEL TWO and would include such now-well-known players as Adnan Khashoggi, Manucher Ghorbanifar, Amiram Nir, Oliver North and John Poindexter.

On 4 September 1985, another exposure occurred during what was loosely coded the COFFEE operations. During a CHANNEL TWO operation on a return flight from Tabriz, Iran, an American-owned DC-8 aircraft ran afoul of Turkish air controllers. The Turks identified the plane as being owned by International Airlines Support Group out of Miami, but a spokesman stated that the aircraft had been sold to International Air Tourism of Nigeria (Smoke).[125]

It was the second flight in a CHANNEL TWO operation, but apparently the proper "arrangements" were not in place for the plane's over flight of Turkey and it was immediately challenged. When the intruder's cover story did not hold, Turkish Air Force units were

A DC-8 Cargo Plane

scrambled to intercept.

This time the pilots were successful in their evasion, and once out over the Mediterranean, they declared an emergency. They were immediately instructed to land in Tel Aviv.

When the aircraft touched down at David Ben-Gurion International Airport, it was quickly rolled into a secured hangar. According to some sources, over 60 Iranian Jews disembarked along with the flight crew.

The following morning, the "emergency landing" of a plane coming out of Iran was on the front page of the Israeli newspapers. The military censors went to work immediately and there was not a single mention of the event again. The incident, however, would come back to haunt a great number of people.

The DC-8 aircraft had delivered a number of American-made TOW anti-tank missiles to Tabriz on 30 August 1985. It was the first of a number of flights that would deliver a total of 504 TOW missiles to the Iranians. The first two cargo flights were coded EXPRESSO and CAPPUCCINO and just over a year later, these COFFEE operations would become the first acknowledged weapons shipments in the Iran-Contra Affair.

TOW Missile   *Benjamin Weir*

In spite of the exposure of the EXPRESSO flight on 4 September 1985, the CAPPUCCINO flight delivered additional TOW missiles on 14 September 1985. The following day, the Reverend Benjamin Weir, an American ex-pat held hostage in Lebanon, was released.

Marine Lieutenant Colonel Oliver L. North, then working at the National Security Council, later acknowledged his participation in the COFFEE operations in his book *UNDER FIRE.* [126] According to North, his government support came from the CIA Directorate of Operations' Near East Division. It should be noted that these "bad boys across the river" were supporting the WHITE PIPELINE at the same time.

While it was "dark" to most CIA case officers, an FBI agent-in-place spotted the shipment being unloaded in Tabriz and identified the weapons as American-made TOW missiles. This he reported back to the FBI, which then queried the CIA. The Agency, in typical inter-agency one-up-man-ship, denied it and pushed for the termination of this extremely valuable agent as a "fabricator." [127]

In later operations, the National Security Council through its CHANNEL TWO was partially successful in securing the release of a few American hostages from Lebanon, but by and large, they were operating outside their element in *Brown Disneyland,* for there are few real secrets in *The Trades.* In the end, they would learn that clandestinely dancing to Middle Eastern tunes was a game for serious players only ... much akin to juggling hand grenades.

C ൽ

Overhead

"This wasn't an intelligence relationship, it was an intelligence dump."

Howard Teicher
National Security Council Staff

When the Shah of Iran got into trouble, the Carter Administration stood back apparently atoning for our (imagined) colonial past by non-intervention and after the fall of the Peacock Throne in February 1979 and the subsequent takeover of the American embassy by Iranian militants, the conventional wisdom within the American Intelligence Community held that fundamentalist Iran presented the major threat to American interests in the Middle East. Several "Young Turks" within the community disagreed.

One of them was a young Pentagon analyst named Howard Teicher. In 1979, Teicher helped author a 50-page analysis of the situation in which was claimed that Iraq, not Iran, posed the greatest danger in the Middle East. It went on to predict that Iraq would attack Iran "within 9 months" and that sometime in the future, Saddam Hussein

Howard Teicher

197

would confront the United States. His paper was not well received and dismissed by most of his superiors as being politically "too pro-Israel."

As events have a way of doing, Teicher's analysis and predictions were proven correct in the autumn of 1980 when Iraq attacked Iran. With his star on the rise, Teicher went to the National Security Counsel staff in the White House. There he found two like-minded true-believers in Donald Fortier and Oliver North.

The Reagan Administration's pro-Arab worldview took time to filter down and permeate the American Intelligence Community. But in February 1982, the Director of Central Intelligence, Bill Casey, took the first step in an effort to ingratiate the United States with Saddam Hussein. He secretly flew to Amman, Jordan where he met with Barzan Ibrahim Hassan al-Tikriti, head of Iraq's General Intelligence Directorate and Saddam Hussein's half brother.

Casey's message to Tikriti was simple: the United States was worried that Iraq was on the verge of military defeat. He suggested an agreement to cooperate and share intelligence on Iran between their two nations. Further, he told Tikriti that he would dispatch a group of experts to Baghdad to help in the war effort. Tikriti agreed.

Bill Casey and Barzan Al-Tikriti

As news of Casey's success made the rounds within the Intelligence Community, the "Young Turks" of the pro-Israel camp were horrified. They were convinced that the United States was playing with fire, but the Reagan Administration's plan went forward sheltered under the umbrella its pro-Arab "Level Battlefield Doctrine" and secured in the notion that Iraq would replace Iran as America's "best friend" in the Middle East.

During the summer of 1982 with world media attention focused on besieged Beirut, battles in the Iran-Iraq War reached new levels of horror. At the front just north of the Iraqi town of Basra, the Iraqi Army slaughtered Iranian soldiers at the rate of 7,000 a day for three solid weeks. No one realized at the time that it was clandestine American help that had turned the tactical tide of battle.

In 1984, President Reagan finally signed a National Security Directive (NSD), which *legalized* a great deal of the clandestine, illegal activity being carried out by the American spooks for the Iraqis. Additionally, the United States publicly emphasized Iran on the State Department's list of terrorism-sponsoring nations and instituted Operation STAUNCH at US Customs in an attempt to cut off war materiel going to the Iranian military.

When the United States re-established diplomatic relations with Iraq and reopened the American embassy in Baghdad, the largest contingent of American "diplomats" was from the CIA. STATION BAGHDAD became the operational base for the CIA's mission of insuring Saddam Hussein's survival.

One of the more sinister aspects of this effort came to light in the wake of the 1991 Gulf War. The American Department of Defense and the CIA were authorized under the previously mentioned NSD to share intelligence with the Iraqi Mukhabarat. It was this "intelligence sharing" in which some American intelligence professionals took great umbrage.

Electronic intercepts (SIGINT) were provided to the Iraqis on almost a "real time" basis. "Overhead" - spy-satellite surveillance photographs from the Key Hole 11 system - was also turned over to the Iraqi Mukhabarat. And, while the KH-11 system had already been compromised to the Soviets by a "mole," it did reveal to the Iraqis American "sources and methods" of intelligence collection and reporting.

"Sources and methods" are the secret of secrets, the holy of holies for any intelligence organization. Most American intelligence professionals screamed bloody murder for this type of information was not even provided to allies, much less to a Soviet client-state like Iraq. The upper management of the Reagan Administration apparently felt it was a case of expediency necessary for them to push their secret agenda. As it turned out, it proved to be expediency over common sense.

The provision of SIGINT and particularly Overhead to the Iraqi Army had the short-term effect of giving them a tactical advantage over the Iranians on the battlefield and saved them from military defeat. Long term, it gave the Iraqis a working knowledge of American "sources and methods," particularly the Key

Hole 11 imaging satellite system and the methods used in its deployment. [128] Understanding American satellite utilization greatly aided the Iraqis during the First Gulf War. This was the principle reason they set the Kuwaiti oil wells ablaze, helping to mask their tactical movements from satellite observation.

CB ED

Bloody Friday

"I was shocked by the devastating effects of these weapons, which have caused problems such as cancers, blindness and congenital malformations."

Dr. Christine Gosden
Senate Testimony
22 April 1998

Most of us have to consult a map to find Kurdistan and even then, most maps do not indicate its boundaries. The home range of the Kurdish people is located within the national boundaries of Turkey, Syria, Iraq, Iran and edges over into the former Soviet Union. In the past seventy years, most of these countries have, at one time or another attempted to suppress the Kurds' national aspirations. In most instances, this suppression has taken the form of outright genocide.

Iraq has been hell-bent on destroying its Kurdish population for quite some time and these efforts are important in the context of America's historical efforts in Iraq.[129] The Balasan valley in Iraq's Arbil province was the scene of some of the first attacks against the Kurds by Iraqi forces employing "cocktail" weapons.

On 16 April 1987, in the midst of the Iran-Iraq War, Iraqi Air Force units attacked 24 Kurdish villages in the Balasan valley. No one has been able to verify the number of Kurds killed outright, but some 286 men, women and children who were wounded in the attack, made their way to the city of Abril seeking medical help. After arriving in Abril, these wounded survivors were rounded up, arrested and then executed by Iraqi forces. Because they were then hastily buried in a mass grave, there is little or no information on the specific Iraqi weapons, which wounded them in the first place.

Halabja was a Kurdish town of about 80,000 inhabitants located in the Iran-Iraq frontier zone, northeast of Baghdad. The town's inhabitants have never made a secret of their hostility toward Saddam Hussein and their frontier town was a hotbed in the struggle for Kurdish Independence. The term "Bloody Friday" refers to Friday, 17 March 1988, when Iraqi Air Force units attacked Halabja.

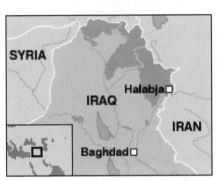

The attacks began on the afternoon of the 16th when "cocktail" weapons were dropped on the approaches to Halabja in an apparent attempt to seal the population inside the town. Before dawn on "Bloody Friday," Iraqi air units began systematic attacks on the town itself, which continued into the following day.

The population of Halabja was completely unprepared. Thousands died in the poisonous clouds of Mustard gas, Soman, Tabun and Sarin. Bodies littered the streets where they fell with no visible marks of injury, their faces appallingly distorted in asphyxiation. Those who survived were horribly burned by the Mustard gas.

Halabja, March 1988

Little would have been known of the reprehensible carnage if it were not for Western journalists, who with the assistance of the Iranians and the Kurdish Resistance, managed to get into Halabja shortly after the attack. Among the first journalists to arrive was Gwynne Roberts, a British television producer, who documented the attack on film. Stills from Roberts' film were published throughout the world the following week.

In spite of the public outrage, Western governments refused to condemn Iraq. The diplomatic reasoning held that negotiations between Iran and Iraq to end their 8-year war were in a delicate phase and

Kurdish dead in the village of Halabja, March 1988

could not be threatened. Not surprisingly, the Arab states stood firmly behind Saddam Hussein and when a Kurdish delegation approached the Government of Kuwait, it was generally ignored. Upon explaining to the Kuwaitis that innocent civilians were sprayed with poison gas, a Kuwaiti official reportedly commented, "What did you expect to be sprayed with, rose water?"[130]

We are reminded that it was during this time frame that American military advisors and intelligence officers were working with the Iraqi forces. This would only come out later, but it is reasonable to assume that those Americans and their bosses in Washington were well aware of what took place at Halabja.

Six weeks after the attack and after Gwynne Roberts' horrific photos had been published, the United Nations issued a report on the incident. Colonel Manuel Dominguez Carmona, a Spanish military doctor, authored the report, which concluded that responsibility for the attack could not be ascribed to either Iraq or Iran. Since Halabja was located in the battle zone, Carmona even suggested both nations might have been responsible.[131]

In January 1998, Dr. Christine Gosden, the chief of Medical Genetics at Liverpool University,[132] went to Halabja to assess the ongoing effects of the Iraqi attack ten years later. She was accompanied by the British journalist Gwynne Roberts, who filmed her journey for a television documentary.[133]

Not surprisingly, Dr. Gosden found the surviving Halabja villagers suffering from bizarre health problems similar to those associated with the sick American veterans of the Gulf War.[134] "It's the same collection of predictable problems and abnormalities..." she stated.[135]

On her return visit, Dr. Gosden noted that "Still...many people suffer skin irritations, eruptions, scarring, terrible itching and burning sensations." Comparing the birth defects in the population of Halabja to those in the population of the nearby town of Sulaimaniyah, which is ten times its size, Gosden noted:

"The incidence of harelips and cleft palates, spina bifida, congenital heart defects, Downs syndrome and other major chromosomal disorders were all over three times higher in Halabja. The same ratios were found in cases of miscarriages and unexplained infant deaths... mostly due to undiagnosed heart defects."[136]

In the area around Halabja, the flora and fauna had taken on the aspects of some mad scientific experiment from a 1950's monster movie:

"It's not just the people who have been affected... the plants and animals have also mutated. Snakes have become bigger, more aggressive and more venomous and deaths from snakebites have increased. The locusts are much bigger and eat through leather and PVC. Grain and fruit yields are all down."[137]

In March of 1998, Christine Gosden completed her report on her findings in Halabja and began speaking to the press. In April, she traveled to Washington where she testified on the effects of "cocktail" weapons before the combined Senate subcommittees on Technology, Terrorism, Government and Intelligence.

On her personal reactions to her findings in Halabja, she told the Senators:

"This journey and the horrifying findings have shocked and devastated me to an extent which I had not believed possible. It is the deliberate use of weapons of this ferocity, which have the power to kill or maim in perpetuity, which I find so terrible."[138]

It was, of course, the business end of the Level Battlefield Doctrine … with *the power to kill or maim in perpetuity.*

Halabja: Dr. Christine Gosden and Gwynne Roberts

ଔ ଓ

CHAPTER 6

A CLEAR AND PRESENT DANGER

"On a bleak island in the Aral Sea, one hundred monkeys are tethered to posts set in parallel rows stretching out toward the horizon. A muffled thud breaks the stillness. Far in the distance, a small metal sphere lifts into the sky then hurtles downward, rotating, until it shatters in a second explosion. Some seventy-five feet above the ground, a cloud the color of dark mustard begins to unfurl, gently dissolving as it glides down toward the monkeys. They pull at their chains and begin to cry. A few cover their mouths or noses, but it is too late: they have already begun to die."

Ken Alibek
BIOHAZARD

Samara and Salman Pak

"Denial is much more than a river in Egypt.

Mark Twain

By March 1984, elements within the CIA were becoming increasingly alarmed by the Iraqi manufacture of chemical and biological weapons, those infamous "weapons of mass destruction." The completion of the enormous chemical complex near the Iraqi town of Samara, some 120 kilometers north of Baghdad, was hard to ignore. The complex encompassed 25 square kilometers and was supervised by Dr. Abdullah Montaser Al Ani,[139] the Managing Director of the State Enterprise for Pesticide Production (SEPP). The conventional wisdom in intelligence estimates held that SEEP could produce enough pesticide at Samara to eradicate the entire insect population of the earth.

The Samara facility had been built by a consortium of West German companies led by Karl Kolb GmbH of Drieich. In 1981, the year the project started, Kolb was managed by Helmut Maier while his "man in Baghdad" was another German named Franzl. An Iraqi national named Nazar Al Khadhi, the Baghdad representative of Preussag AG and Water Engineering Trading (WET), was Franczl's deputy for the project. Connecting the dots, it was easy to discern that both German companies, Preussag and WET, were major subcontractors in Samara.[140]

Since the attack on the Majnoon Islands in February 1984, which has been covered previously in some detail, and other suspected deployments of chemical weapons by the Iraqis, the Reagan State Department had become increasingly nervous, obviously fearing an exposure and began quietly trying to rein in the West Germans. They began sending the first of literally hundreds of "non-papers," that is non-binding, official statements of policy, to the West German Foreign Ministry expressing American displeasure. It was a duplicitous effort at best and the Germans knew it, so they politely ignored the Americans.

Finally on 30 March 1984, *The New York Times* published an article detailing the Samara Chemical

Complex and naming some of the West German contractors and suppliers. It was clear in *The Trades* that the story had been planted by either individual CIA officers who had *gone off the reservation* or by some hostile spooks ... Israeli or perhaps even Iranian. Whichever, it was certainly not in the best interests of the Reagan Administration's still-secret

"Level Battlefield Doctrine," although it immediately got the attention of the Germans, which was probably the primary objective.

There was of course, "official" consternation on the part of the Israelis, coming so close on the heels of the American denial to their inquiries on Iraqi CBW manufacturing capabilities. At that point, it was clear that Iraq *was* manufacturing its chemical weapons at Samara. And, there were also heavy indications that disgruntled American intelligence officers were not happy campers.

Something else was bothering Israeli Intelligence much beyond what they perceived as this American duplicity. Lost in and among the vast Samara complex was a small building that housed a Security Level 4 biological laboratory for the handling of infectious diseases. According to later media reports, Water Engineering Trading (WET) of Hamburg built the lab. WET turned out to be a shell company owned by Preussag AG, the German chemical giant in Hanover, and was managed by another German, Peter Leifer. In this small lab, the Iraqis were testing viruses and bacterial bioagents on beagles. The Israelis knew that the testing of chemical agents on live animals would not require the tightly controlled environment of a Bio-security Level 4 laboratory.

The leaking of the Samara story to *The New York Times* helped the Israelis a great deal, but it illuminated only part of the Iraqi threat.

As noted previously, Karl Kolb GmbH of Drieich began working on the chemical complex at Samara at the same time another German firm, Thyssen AG, started working on a separate biological facility. The Thyssen plant was located 17 kilometers south of Baghdad near the tomb of Salman Farsi, a close companion of the Prophet Mohammed. Three other important companions of the Prophet are buried there and the site is called Salman Pak.

In many ways, Salman Pak was even more frightening than Samara, for it was a dedicated biological weapons complex run by the Iraqi Center for Technological Research. It was the first such Iraqi biological facility and as previously mentioned, it was where shipments of Trichothecene Mycotoxins from Josef Kuhn GmbH of Germany and West Nile Fever virus cultures from the CDC in Atlanta ended up. And, it was at Salman Pak that the Iraqis tested biological agents on large primates, quite possibly human beings.[141]

The simultaneous construction of the massive facilities at Samara and Salman Pak led Israeli Intelligence to believe that Saddam Hussein had an overall blueprint from which he was working far beyond the original APD study. Rumors had been circulating within the scientific community for some time and

Israelis began to take them seriously. Finding that new blueprint, if it indeed existed, would short cut Israel's collection efforts and Israeli Intelligence was into short cuts.

cg ɛͻ

The Father of All Fears

"Allah made three mistakes...
He created Persians, Jews and flies."

Saddam Hussein

Convinced by the APD study that the path to his military domination of the Middle East lay in weapons of mass destruction, Saddam Hussein's efforts to acquire chemical and biological weapons (CBW) bumped along in the decade from 1972 until 1982. In 1980, when Iraq invaded Iran, the program became somewhat revitalized. Then in 1982, under pressure to offset Iraqi military reverses, Iraq's prominent microbiologist, Dr. Abdul Hindawi, was assigned to further investigate bioweapons as a possible source of military salvation.

Abdul Nassir Hindawi received his PhD in microbiology from Mississippi State University at Starkville in 1969. In the scientific community Hindawi enjoyed the reputation of an Anthrax expert; in intelligence communities he is considered the father of Saddam Hussein's Biowarfare program and all that implies.

Hindawi completed his investigation and authored a report on his findings in 1983.[142] In it he outlined the methodology for the acquisition, cultivation and mass production of biological weapons for the immediate practical application against Iranian forces. He further surmised that bioweapons were far more cost effective than chemical weapons. Copies of his report were circulated to the top officials of Iraq's Baath Party and within a short period of time, Saddam Hussein assigned a "presidential priority" to Hindawi's program.

In February 1984, Dr. Hindawi and his colleagues were able to cobble together enough mixed agent weapons for a practical field test against the Iranian Army at Majnoon. The CBWs were horrendously effective, but Iraqi inexperience with their deployment led to a tactical disaster.

Sometime between March and May of 1984, Israeli Intelligence managed to procure a copy of the Hindawi Report.[143] Their efforts were obviously triggered by the Iraqi attacks at Majnoon the previous February, the continuing spate of rumors from the scientific community and information from their American agent-in-place, Jonathan Pollard. Thus by mid-1984, they were "in the loop" so to speak insofar as Iraq's bioweapons were concerned.

By 1985, Hindawi was the head of Hussein's bioweapons development program at the Al Muthannas State Establishment and working on his first love, Bacillus Anthracis, the ubiquitous old biowarfare standby, Anthrax.

Perhaps sometime before, but at least by 1985, Hindawi began sourcing various biological cultures from outside suppliers, particularly from American Type Culture Collection in Rockville, Maryland and from the Centers for Disease Control in Atlanta.[144]

Hindawi started slowly in February 1985, ordering only two plant pathogens from ATCC, one for the Iraqi Atomic Energy Agency and the second for the Ministry of Higher Education.[145] Interestingly, the Iraqi Ministry of Defense paid for both cultures, but the United States Department of Commerce (read: the CIA) approved the transactions prior to shipment.

In April and again in May 1985, Hindawi ordered more pathogens from the United States, but this time from the Centers for Disease Control in Atlanta. Again, the shipments were ordered through two different "customers," the Iraqi Ministry of Health and the University of Basra. In the latter shipment, the CDC sent cultures of West Nile Fever virus.[146] This was followed by another purchase from the CDC in June and yet another from ATCC in July.

In March and April 1986, Hindawi ordered cultures of Botulism Toxin (Botulinum Toxoid) from the CDC with Al Muthannas State Establishment, Officers City, Al Muthannas as the buyer. Utilizing these cultures as seed stock, the Iraqis were eventually able to weaponize Botulism.[147]

In May 1986, Hindawi used the Iraqi Ministry of Higher Education to order 24 different cultures from American Type Culture Collection. Among them were the germs that cause Brucellosis, Anthrax, Botulism, Gas Gangrene and Rabbit Fever (Tularemia). Once again, the US Department of Commerce approved the shipment and no objections surfaced. Still, for reasons unknown, the Iraqis stood down and abstained from ordering more biological cultures for over a year, at least from American suppliers.

Then in August 1987, another ten cultures were ordered and shipped from ATCC, this time to the Iraqi State Establishment for Drug Industries. Iraq's war with Iran was still in full swing, the "Level Battlefield Doctrine" was in place and American military advisors were with the Iraqi Army. While the United States Government played the accomplice or at the very least was unconcerned with the shipment of deadly pathogens to a tin-pot crazy like Saddam Hussein, the Israelis took a much dimmer view.

The 10-culture shipment in August 1987 triggered a passing interest from the United States Senate. By January 1988, Senator John McCain (R-AZ) wanted to know what exactly an American supplier (ATCC) was doing shipping the old bioweapon standby, Tularemia, to Iraq. He formally quizzed the State Department, which gave ATCC a clean bill of health, so to speak, on their Iraqi transaction. McCain was apparently unaware of the Reagan Administration's "Level Battlefield Doctrine" and more likely, his interest was only peaked by the ongoing Iran-Contra investigations.

Hard on the heels of the State Department inquiry, the Iraqi bioweapons program was consolidated at a new research and production facility, Al Hakim, then the largest in Iraq. Dr. Hindawi became the Managing Director, a post he held from 1989 until 1991. Production was overseen by General Amer Saadi and Dr. Rihab Taha, [148] the infamous "Dr. Germs." Ahmed Murthada coordinated procurement and the entire project fell under the responsibility of General Hussein Kamel Majid, Saddam Hussein's son-in-law.

In hindsight, it should have been patently obvious that Iraq was moving from experimentation to production of bioweapons. In 1987 and again in 1988, Dr. Hindawi and his team ordered a total of 39 tons of biological growth media from two European firms, Oxoid in Bedford, England and Fluka Chemie Ag in Buchs, Switzerland. There is absolutely no doubt that the United States, along with the rest of the world, knew what was going on in Iraq at the time, but once again it seemed political agendas overrode common sense.

In February 1988, someone in the American government began leaking stories to the media, which explained that Iraq had acquired CBW from the Russians. It is, of course, possible that American Intelligence knew what was coming and was shoring up their bets in case it might go public. Looking at these articles in retrospect, that may have been or in a "best case" perhaps it was simply some worried Spook going "off the reservation" playing a little CYA. [149]

In the midst of moving into his new facility, Hindawi and his colleagues conducted a series of field tests with their biological agents. These were live-animal tests conducted at the Muthannas weapons testing range in Muhammadiyat in early March 1988. The agents employed were Botulism toxin (Clostridium Botulinum) and Bacillus Subtilis, an Anthrax simulant. The delivery vectors for the weapons were R200 aerial bombs and the tests were successful. [150] We will later address these trials in a different context, but for the moment, the significance of these experiments became apparent short weeks later.

On 28 March 1988, Iraqi Air Force units attacked several Kurdish villages with these mixed-agent "cocktails." As noted previously, over 5000 Kurds were killed in the "Bloody Friday" attack on the village of Halabja. On the black scorecard of such grisly matters, Dr. Hindawi is generally credited with this "success."

In April 1988, ATCC shipped three more cultures to Iraq in spite of the notoriety of the Halabja attacks. As before, the Commerce Department approved and while this purchase drew no particular attention, one shipment attempted in August would come back to haunt the United States.

That June, Iran and Iraq signed a ceasefire ending their 8-year war. With the ceasefire came the departure of the American military advisors and the intelligence on Hussein's weapons of mass destruction dried up. In fact, during the First Gulf War, American Intelligence did not know that the massive CBW production facility at Al Hakim even existed. Consequently, the complex survived the war unscathed. Its existence and significance were not generally known until the defection of the Iraqi General, Hussein Kamal Majid, to Jordan in 1995.

In August 1988, Dr. Hindawi and his colleague, Dr. Abdul Rahman Thamer, attended a scientific conference in Winchester, England. The conference sponsor was the British Biodefense Institute at Porton Down and the two Iraqis presented credentials from Iraq's Technical and Scientific Materials, Importation Division in Baghdad.

Shortly after the conference, Dr. Hindawi telexed an order to Porton Down requesting a Pulmonary Anthrax culture.[151] The one he requested was the rare and particularly virulent Ames strain. [152] The British, however, were not as cavalier with their pathogens as their American cousins and turned down Hindawi's request.

Information developed later indicated that Dr. Hindawi was able to obtain his cultures of the Ames strain from the University of Birmingham. It only became important after the post-Nine Eleven biological attacks in the United States which employed weaponized Pulmonary Anthrax ... the Ames strain.

In September 1997, Iraqi officials told UNSCOM inspectors that the Hindawi Report had a huge impact and as a result a "presidential priority" had been given to biological weapons development. One perceived objective was to produce "a viable deterrent to a possible attack by Israel using nuclear weapons," the Iraqis stated in justification. This, of course, echoed the base-line concept espoused in the APD study and the Reagan Administration's "Level Battlefield Doctrine."

In 1991, Dr. Hindawi was relieved of his duties at Al Hakim and sent back to the University of Baghdad to teach. Then on 9 March 1998, the Iraqi Government announced the arrest of the then 70-year-old Hindawi. According to the government, he was about to leave the country on a false passport. If true, it suggests that Hindawi may have been in touch with some friendly spooks.

Since the Iraqi regime fell to American forces in 2003, nothing has been heard from or about Dr. Abdul Nassir Hindawi.

C3 80

CONDOR

"It was going to be one hell of a missile, and it was going to change everything."

CIA Officer
Directorate of Operations
Near East Division

The fight over the CONDOR missile was typical of the skirmishes in the *Spook War* and involved the activities of numerous individuals in different parts of the world over a span of several years. Tracking it is confusing, because of the necessity to tie diverse, singular events together in order to form a coherent, overall picture. Bear with us.

The CONDOR ballistic missile program figured

American Pershing II, Israeli Jericho II, Egyptian-Iraqi Condor II

prominently in the military build-up of Iraq and thereby became a focus of Israeli clandestine efforts. Obviously, the introduction of this new missile into the arsenals of Egypt and Iraq would greatly upset the military balance in the Middle East.

American Pershing II, Israeli Jericho II, Egyptian-Iraqi Condor II

The original project began in 1982 as a result of the Falklands War when Argentina started developing a rocket for weather research purposes called CONDOR. By late 1982, the Argentineans were running out of development funds for their program. Enter the Arabs. The moribund rocket project began to evolve into a weapons project - CONDOR II - with the addition of two partners, Egypt and Iraq, who had been shopping for a weapons delivery vector similar to Israel's American-made Pershing II missile and its' indigenous variant, the Jericho II. Iraq restarted the CONDOR II development with an infusion of $3.2 billion.

In Egypt, the project was coded BADR 2000 while the Iraqis called it SAAD 16, after their development facility of the same name near Mosul. The Argentineans and Americans referred to the missile as CONDOR or CONDOR II, but for simplicity's sake, we shall call the military version CONDOR.

Initially, Egyptian agents reached out to the German aerospace giant Messerschmitt-Boelkow-Blohm (MBB) [153] for the overall technical guidance of the CONDOR project. For their participation, MBB earned more than $250 million, most of it through its wholly owned subsidiary, Transtechina.

In 1985, at the insistence of MBB, the participating Western vendors formed an entity called the Cosen Group to run the project. Cosen was then retained by the ultimate customers, Iraq and Egypt. The Cosen entity was a consortium of European designers, engineers and businessmen, who then established a network of front companies to hide their role as the directors of the CONDOR project for their Arab clients. [154]

Other European vendors soon joined the project. Two notable firms were Fiat of Italy (through its' SNIA-BPD subsidiary) and CFF Thompson of France.

The Argentine side involved several subcontractors, among which were Aerotec and Conseltec SA of Buenos Aires and Instesa SA of Cordoba. The project's center was located at a remote Argentinean Air Force base near Cordoba where the German, Egyptian and Italian technicians worked with their Argentine counterparts in the development effort. This facility, known as Falda del Carmen, produced rocket engines for the CONDOR. In the wake of the Gulf War, UN inspectors found three plants in Iraq that were identical clones of the Falda del Carmen plant. To the Israelis, it was in step with the original ADP blueprint.

In Egypt, their part of the project (BADR 2000) was based at a top-secret, secured facility outside Cairo known simply as FACTORY 17. (One should note the similarities between the BADR 2000 project and the Helwan project of the late 1950s and early 1960s, which included some of the same European vendors.)

The new missile was a two-stage, solid-fuel vehicle with a 500-kg payload. It had chemical, biological and nuclear warhead capability with good accuracy and a range of 1000 kilometers.

CONDOR triggered the interest of British Intelligence, most especially after it shifted from a weather research rocket to a ballistic missile. The Falkland Islands were, after all, well within the new missile's range and the Falkland War had only recently been concluded with a British victory.

The funding for the development of this new missile system came mainly from Iraq, but by late 1984, the United States was lending clandestine financial support through its CCC loan guarantees as part of the "Level Battlefield Doctrine."[155]

At the time all of these activities were secret and in fact, there was an on-going, public endeavor in the West to stop the proliferation of missile technology into Third World countries.[156] CIA officers in the Near East and National Collections Divisions were feeding information on the CONDOR missile development into the White House. For its part, the Reagan Administration trumpeted its' public embrace of this non-proliferation effort, while maintaining clandestine funding and support for the CONDOR development in Egypt and Iraq. Had Congress known, it would have never allowed the funding of the missile's development, but since the Reagan Administration was clandestinely providing money through the CCC loan guarantees, the legislative branch was kept in the dark.[157]

The United States also had a legal obligation under the Camp David Peace Agreement to inform Israel about the BADR 2000 project in Egypt. The Reagan Administration did not inform the Israelis nor did it inform Congress.

One can only speculate whether or not President Reagan knew and approved of this action or lack of it, because the White House "troika." was running the day-to-day business of the government. It is clear, however, that Caspar Weinberger and George Shultz did know. Further, in keeping with Weinberger's intelligence embargo, the Americans lied to the Israelis when they inquired about the CONDOR missile's development.

Of course, the Israelis knew about the CONDOR program[158] and by late 1984, could readily check on what the Americans were telling them. Through the liaison meetings under the intelligence sharing agreement they would submit an official report on an item of interest and request information in return. Then, LAKAM would task Jonathan Pollard to find out the truth. The Israeli experience showed that 75 percent of the time, American Intelligence lied to them about the very existence of the requested information. Such was the case in the matter of the CONDOR missile, a weapon system that would have changed the entire military balance in the Middle East.

On a tactical basis, we now move to the particulars. When the Israelis tasked Pollard to research the CONDOR missile in early 1985, he opened an official technology transfer investigation[159] to cover his efforts. To all outward appearances, Pollard was anticipating the possibility that Egypt and/or Iraq would attempt to recruit American engineers to spy for their missile programs. For Pollard, this counterintelligence investigation was possibly significant so he went through the drill with his usual thoroughness.

In listing his potential targets for Arab penetration, Pollard noted in his paperwork the Aerojet-General Corporation of Sacramento, California.[160] What he did not know at the time was that Aerojet employed a certain Abdelkader Helmy, an Egyptian-born American citizen, as a senior propulsion engineer at its Rancho Cordova facility. In one of those ironic twists that are so common in *The Trades,* Helmy was an Egyptian spy stealing American technology for the BADR 2000 / CONDOR missile project.

Aerojet Brochures

Pollard dutifully filed his technology transfer investigation memo with US Customs Intelligence and forgot about it. That memo then lay dormant in the computerized files for the next few months before Customs opened an investigation.

Customs agents ran a quick check of security clearances at Aerojet which produced Egyptian-born Dr. Abdelkader Helmy and he was immediately placed under full surveillance.

Surprisingly, Helmy spoke openly on the phone to his co-conspirator, James Huffman, in Lexington, Ohio. Huffman was a marketing representative for the Teledyne Corporation, which begged further questions that were never teased out.

By June of 1986, US Customs asked for the assistance of technical experts from the DIA in order to flesh out their investigation. By then it was relatively clear that Helmy and his co-conspirators were stealing technology, chemicals and other materials supporting the development of the CONDOR missile.[161]

Then in late March of 1988, almost two years later, Swiss Intelligence (UNO) sent the CIA an Alert Notice. Swiss sources indicated that the Egyptians were shipping large amounts of restricted materials out of the United States via diplomatic pouches on board weekly Egyptian Air Force flights out of the Washington-Baltimore Airport. The material, such as carbon-carbon fiber, was destined for FACTORY 17 in Egypt, where the CONDOR missiles were then being fabricated. The CIA notified US Customs.

How the Swiss happened upon this information has never been noodled out and when compared to the scenario around the Babylon Gun (to be covered shortly), one divines an interesting pattern of coincidences ...if there be such in *The Trades.* Be that as it may, US Customs was on the case and through their wiretaps learned that most of the restricted material was being purchased through a California front company, which in turned shipped it to the Egyptian embassy in Washington.

Coverage of Helmy's garbage produced an additional windfall of evidence, including tasking for the purchase of specific materials from his handler, Colonel Hussam Yossef, who worked out of the Egyptian embassy in Vienna, Austria. This information was turned over to the Defense Intelligence Agency for assessment and it concluded, "The list of items/materials being sought by Dr. Helmy is entirely consistent with items necessary to support the manufacture of a ballistic missile."[162]

So proficient were the Customs agents and so sloppy were the Egyptian spooks that the whole case was quickly wrapped up and presented to the US Attorney for the Eastern District of California in Sacramento. Customs had the whole ring, including Egyptian Admiral El Gohary at the Egyptian embassy in Washington and his boss, Field Marshal Abd el-Halim Abu Ghazala, the Egyptian Minister of Defense.

The Customs agents filed their criminal complaint in US District Court in Sacramento on 23 June 1988. Then they waited 24 hours, to catch the Egyptians in *flagrante delicto.* The occasion was a shipment of 195 kilograms of carbon-carbon fiber being loaded aboard an Egyptian Air Force plane in Baltimore. Simultaneously, they arrested Helmy, his wife and the Teledyne representative, James Huffman.

Federal court documents in the Helmy case show that he passed to Egyptian Intelligence use-technology on carbon-carbon fiber material for rocket nose cones, instructions on building rocket engine nozzles, and a complete package needed to upgrade an existing tactical missile system. Helmy's main tasking, however, concerned developmental problems the Arabs were having with the BADR 2000 / SAAD 16 / CONDOR missile. Most of his collection requirements emanated out of FACTORY 17 and had been passed to him through his handler in Vienna as the evidence showed. Without the efforts of Helmy and his co-conspirators, the completion of development of the CONDOR was at best doubtful.

At the direction of Egypt, Helmy plea bargained as is the norm for cases of "friendly espionage" and cooperated in the American damage assessment. More information then surfaced in his debriefing.

Within one year of their arrival in the United States, Helmy and his wife were naturalized citizens. This is unheard of in the complex citizenship labyrinth of the US Immigration and Naturalization Service (INS). Even more interesting, Helmy received his security clearances during his second year in the United States.

Federal agents discovered one possible explanation for Helmy's apparent smooth sailing past American safeguards during his debriefing. Abdelkader Helmy operated under the authority of Field Marshal Abd el-Halim Abu Ghazala, the Egyptian Minister of Defense, who was a close personal friend of the American Secretary of Defense, Caspar Weinberger. In fact,

Weinberger's office made sure that Ghazala was not indicted in the case, being named only as an un-indicted co-conspirator. How this friendship impacted Helmy's breeze to citizenship is not known, but it certainly does "walk like a duck."

After the public exposure of the affair, American pressure was brought on Egyptian President Hosni Mubarak and General Ghazala was dismissed from the Defense Ministry.

In his plea bargain, Helmy was sentenced to forty-five months in prison with the charges against his wife being dropped after he cooperated in the American damage assessment. His prison sentence was later reduced to two years. It was, after all, a case of "friendly espionage."

Helmy's efforts enabled the Arabs to solve their major development problems with the CONDOR missile. In fact, they could not have done it without him. But, the Iranians first felt the practical effects of Helmy's espionage when Soviet-supplied Scud B missiles, modified in part according to information he supplied, began falling on Teheran during the "War of the Cities." In 1991 during the First Gulf War, the same modified Scud B's were fired on Saudi Arabia and Israel. It was a modified Scud B that destroyed the makeshift barracks in Khobar on 25 February 1991, killing 28 Americans in a classic rendezvous between American soldiers and the business end of the "Level Battlefield Doctrine."

The event that apparently first triggered the original Swiss inquiry ... never mind the source ... was the shipment of 16 CONDOR prototypes out of FACTORY 17 in Egypt to Iraq for testing and evaluation under wartime conditions.[163] These missiles were successfully launched with stunning accuracy against the Iranians during 1988 in the so-called "War of the Cities."

The missile attacks had a devastating psychological effect on the Iranians and helped push them toward a negotiated peace with Iraq in June of 1988. The CONDOR missile and its use against Iran also fed the growing concern within the British and Israeli Intelligence services which in turn, trickled down to the Americans.

The British with their own view of the Third World saw the proliferation of this missile technology not only as a threat to the Falkland Islands, but to Israel and the rest of the Middle East as well. Aware of the impact CONDOR would have on the military balance, the Brits decided to act and approached it on the diplomatic level. The Egyptians manufacturing the missiles was at the core, so they quietly applied the pressure there to cut off the program at FACTORY 17. Ultimately, they were partially successful in Egypt, but the Iraqis then undertook the manufacturing of the CONDOR themselves.

With the British success in Egypt, the Israelis took on the responsibility of negating the program in Iraq, but diplomacy was not an option for them. At that moment, Iraq was gearing up to manufacture the missile and its components, so the Israelis laid their traps looking for that critical component and waited patiently for the right opportunity to strike. As we shall see, that opportunity finally came in August of 1989.

Still another aspect of the CONDOR project was evolving during this same time frame. The CIA's National Collections Division had been keeping an eye on a new Egyptian pharmaceutical facility in the Cairo suburb of Abu Zabal. The Swiss firm of Krebs AG had supplied chemicals and equipment for the facility and CIA analysts felt that chemical munitions for the CONDOR missile could be manufactured there. In some quarters of the American Intelligence Community, the proliferation of weapons of mass destruction was a growing concern.

Throughout 1988, Iraq continued to progress with the development of its biological weapons and was soon mating them to delivery vectors, one of which was the CONDOR missile.

Two Iraqi development programs, which concluded that spring, were particularly significant to Israeli Intelligence. The first was the successful launch of CONDOR missiles against Iran, confirming its viability as an operational weapon system under wartime conditions.

The second occurred in March 1988 when the Iraqis conducted a series of tests with two of their biological agents at the Muthannas weapons test range in Muhammadiyat. [164] The bioagents tested were Botulinum toxin, derived from Clostridium Botulinum cultures, and Bacillus Subtilis, an Anthrax simulant. An American supplier with US government approval had sold both agents to the Iraqis. [165] The tests were conducted on live animals surrounded by Petri dishes and the delivery vector employed was an R200 aerial bomb. The tests were successful.

Apparently, the Israelis were not particularly impressed with the Iraqi Air Force's ability to deliver biological agents in aerial bombs on Israel. They were, however, concerned about the CONDOR IRBM, which had a nuclear, chemical and biological capability and had already been tested on Iranian cities. On a tactical level then, it was simply a matter of targeting the proper component manufacturing facility to set back the entire program. That target soon presented itself.

Part of Iraq's overall SAAD 16 project was a sub-program coded simply PROJECT 96. This was the manufacturing facility at Al-Hillah, which had been designed and constructed under the supervision of the German firm, Messerschmitt-Boelkow-Blohm (MBB). This plant manufactured solid fuel rocket propellant used in the CONDOR missile. The plant at Al-Hillah exploded on 18 August 1989.

The first, small explosion was followed almost instantaneously by secondary, "sympathetic" detonations that destroyed the entire factory. It came during working hours and when the smoke cleared, over 700 workers, including many Egyptian technicians, were dead. There would be no rocket propellant for the CONDOR coming out of Al-Hillah.

The Iraqi government was very quiet about the disaster and little was publicly known until the arrest of a British journalist on 15 September 1989 at Saddam International Airport where he was about to board a plane for London. Farzad Bazoft of the *London Observer* was charged as an Israeli spy in connection with the Al-Hillah explosion.

ය ෨

CHAPTER 7

MEETING ENGAGEMENTS

*"You may fly over a land forever; you may bomb it,
atomize it, pulverize it and wipe it clean of life—but if
you desire to defend it, protect it and keep it for
civilization, you must do this on the ground, the way
the Roman legions did, by putting your young men in
the mud."*

T.R. Fehrenbach

Rumors of War

"And ye shall hear of wars and rumors of wars ..."

Matthew 24:6

With the departure of Alexander Haig from the Reagan Administration in 1982, the Israelis began to believe they had lost their last friend in White House. The Reagan Administration's shift toward the Arabs had been evident from the beginning, but by late 1982, the indicators were solid and in context, more ominous.

In general, the American public and their representatives in Congress supported the Israelis over Arab interests so naturally the Reagan Administration, which took the opposite view, felt it necessary to keep the "Level Battlefield Doctrine" dark, especially from the mainstream media.

It can be argued that any reasonable American would have foreseen that bringing the Arab States into military parity with Israel was a formula for disaster on its face as it had been every time it was previously attempted. Arming a lunatic dictator like Saddam Hussein with weapons of mass destruction - for whatever reason - was another matter entirely. That was insanity.

As implied, the Israelis are generally intolerant of wild, political schemes propagated by outsiders in the Middle East, which may or may not go sour and threaten their existence. In fact, they have a substantial history that supports their position.

And, all factors considered, the "Level Battlefield Doctrine" was a psychotic policy that was certain to produce *a clear and present danger* to the survival of the Jewish State. In the process, it was absolutely certain to tip the scales of the Middle East military balance, thereby triggering a shooting war.

It is perhaps unfair to single out the Reagan Administration, for other administrations have naively played in the Middle East attempting, as it were, to apply their own political agenda, their own "fairness," with no clue as to the likely consequences.

Later, during the second Reagan Administration and into the Bush (41) Administration, with their secret agenda fully committed to Iraq, the American foreign policy goal was even stated as "bringing Saddam

Hussein back into the family of nations." [166] James Baker, the Secretary of State under George Bush, actually promoted the concept that Iraq would become the new American partner in the Persian Gulf, filling the void left by the fall of the Shah of Iran. (Baker was also the Bush Administration official who told the American people in 1990 they were going to war in the Middle East *to protect American jobs.*)

The entire political leadership of the Jewish State diametrically opposed the "Level Battlefield Doctrine," in all its manifestations. In short, there was a big-time clash of agendas. (Like all political matters, this is not completely accurate. There was a point in 1984 when Prime Minister Yitzchak Shamir of Israel became alarmed at the rising strength of Shia Iran and played with offering Israeli assistance to Iraq. The idea, however, was still born and the Iraqis would entertain nothing of the sort.)

On balance the Israelis were determined to intercede into the secret activities surrounding the military build-up of Iraq. They continued to cooperate with the American Intelligence Community where there were mutual agendas in play, but they quietly opposed the "Level Battlefield Doctrine" from the shadows and attempted to negate it. [167]

Retrospectively, one can readily discern the events of the resultant "Spook War." Intelligence and weapons embargoes, publicly trumpeted arrests of "arms dealers," public scandals and the real biggie, the Iran-Contra Affair, to mention just a few targets of opportunity that were exploited by one side or the other.

Unlike the traditional fights over turf rules, it was not business, it was personal.

As a general rule, the US employed its justice system and played the media to embarrass the Israelis and their American political supporters, subtly threatening their American aid. The Israelis went about matters differently. First they defined the problem project and its various parts then attacked a critical component, the loss of which crippled the whole. It was the Jewish variation of the old principle of warfare, Economy of Force.

Both sides employed certain restraints in the fight when it came to "wet work,"[168] only venturing over that line in a few instances. Occasionally, there would be a brief period of *low intensity* conflict followed by some "payback," that literally left bodies in the streets before one side or the other backed down. The consummate example of this was the "March Massacre" in 1990, which we will discuss in some detail later. Taken in total, these events clearly illustrate the shadow war over the "Level Battlefield Doctrine."

On a macro basis, the Americans enjoyed the strength of overwhelming size and resources while the Israelis had the home-court advantage. Most Reagan Administration operatives were *true believers,* driven by the certitude that it was in American interests to somehow make the Iraqi tiger change its stripes. The Israelis, who lived at Ground Zero and knew the Iraqis, could not afford the luxury of such illusions.

On balance, it was a fairly even match, but if we had to call a winner in the contest, it would certainly be Israel, hands down. While the Reagan and Bush Administrations managed to build up the Iraqi military enough to hold off the Iranians and satisfy the Saudis before the First Gulf War was finally triggered, the undisputed final score is that the Americans suffered massive casualties in that war and the Israelis did not.[169]

The American government has been employing a cover-up ever since the "Level Battlefield Doctrine" went sour, while the Israelis smugly scold them with, "This is your own doing and we warned you this would happen." One could look upon the American invasion of Iraq in 2003 as an effort to rectify this mistake.

This American-Israeli Spook War was a nasty affair on balance in which governments were embarrassed and people died. In the end, there was no right or wrong and we are left with retrospectively weighing the effects on both nations. It is clear that Israel survived in tact and that the United States ended up paying the price for their bad judgment and naiveté with the finest American Army ever fielded.

While certainly not the definitive account of this *Spook War*, we set the scene with some of the machination on the political level and believe it is now important to memorialize a few of the isolated tactical incidents that took place in the shadows. Most agree that the conflict opened in 1983 in Manhattan, the Federal Southern District of New York.

Cʒ ʁɔ

Operation STAUNCH

*"No enemy is so insignificant as to be despised and
neglected by any power, however formidable"*

Antoine-Henri, the Baron Jomini
THE ART OF WAR

It all started in October 1983 when the Reagan
Administration was hell-bent on normalizing relations
with Saddam Hussein's Iraq. Much has been written
about the reasons, but it is no longer disputed that it
happened.

That October Iraq's Foreign Minister, Tarek Aziz,
went to New York seeking approval of the UN Security
Council's Resolution 540, which condemned Iran for
continuing the war. Although Iraq had started the
conflict by its invasion in 1980, by 1982, the Iranians
had turned the tide and were fighting on Iraqi territory.
Saddam Hussein wanted to call it quits, but the
Ayatollah Khomeini was bound and determined to
hammer the Iraqis. Hence, Security Council Resolution
540.

While in New York, Aziz met with Secretary of
State George Shultz who was pushing for the
reestablishment of diplomatic relations between the two
countries at the behest of the Saudis. Having expelled
the Palestinian terrorist, Abu Nidal, and his Black June
Organization from Iraq as the Americans had requested,

Aziz was now acting coy, as if Iraq did not care one way or the other about diplomatic relations with the US. In fact, Aziz suggested that Shultz meet with Hussein in Baghdad to discuss certain matters the Iraqis would want as pre-conditions to any reestablishment of relations.

Iraq's main concern turned out to be the American-made arms and spare parts being supplied to Iran by Israel.[170] Aziz was convinced that Israel could not be acting on her own without American direction and he said so. Shultz tried to deny knowledge, but Aziz was ready. He gave Shultz a long list of shipments and Israeli operatives obviously collected by Iraqi Intelligence and suggested that the US cut off this operation as a gesture of good faith. Shultz promised to look into it. [171]

Operation STAUNCH was the State Department's answer to Iraq's request. This program turned loose US Customs on the Israelis and quickly resulted in numerous criminal cases in US Courts, always accompanied by a media blitz the Iraqis were bound to see. Most of the cases were tried in New York or Los Angeles where a high media profile was assured.

 C3 80

First Blood

"Our army depended entirely on oil revenues for literally everything, from the purchase of weapons to the salaries of foreign experts and the soldiers' pay."

Abol Hassan Bani-Sadr
President of Iran
MY TURN TO SPEAK

Before he became "America's Mayor," before he was selected as *Time* magazine's "Man of the Year," Rudolph W. Giuliani was a lawyer, a dedicated Democrat-turned-Republican and generally viewed as an ambitious political yuppie whose party loyalty superseded his sense of justice. He served in the Justice Department under the short presidency of Gerald Ford and during the Carter Administration, he returned to private practice in his native New York. Then when Ronald Reagan went to Washington in 1981, Giuliani was rewarded with the number three job at the Department of Justice. He served as an Associate Attorney General until 1983 when his political ambitions and some argue, *the Spook War*, took him back home as the US Attorney for the Southern District of New York.

Rudy Giuliani never concealed his aspirations and saw himself as a latter-day Thomas Dewey, who once held the same government office in Manhattan before running unsuccessfully for president in 1944 and 1948. Giuliani's visions would elude him until Nine-Eleven.

Some observers are quick to point out that Giuliani's return to New York in 1983 coincided with the

Reagan Administration's escalation of the Spook War. With Jerusalem secretly supporting Iran and Washington secretly supporting Iraq, the key area of conflict became the oil trade. It was oil revenues that supported both nations' war efforts and Washington was not only increasing American consumption of Iraqi crude, but was seeking ways to curtail Iran's oil production and its exports as well.

Arriving in Manhattan, Giuliani hit the ground running. Some believe that he brought from Washington a "target list" of Israelis. For your humble servant, that's a bit thin since the infamous "Iraqi List" would only be delivered to the Americans in October 1983, after Giuliani arrived in New York. Of course, there could have been other lists. Be that as it may, his first prosecution was of a man named Marc David Rich, who coincidentally happened to be a key trader of "Iranian Light" crude oil.[172]

But Rich was more than that, a great deal more. Marc Rich was a Belgian Jew fluent in three languages and a naturalized American citizen. [173] He was a successful international commodities broker who practically invented the "spot market" for crude oil and owned companies, offices and homes all over the world. Rich also secretly held Israeli citizenship, and was a political – level, clandestine operative for Jerusalem.

Shortly after taking office in Manhattan, Giuliani began to openly threaten Rich. Rich sent his attorneys to discuss the potential charges with the US Attorney's office and these negotiations ground on for a period of months. The alleged offenses committed by Rich and his companies had taken place during the Carter Administration and while the Justice Department was aware of his business dealings at the time, it saw no misdeeds. Why the Reagan Justice Department regurgitated these matters in 1983 and divined criminal activity in them suggests more sinister reasons may well have been in play.

By the summer of 1983, with the negotiations going nowhere, Rich tired of the game and along with his partner, Pincus "Pinky" Green, left for Europe. Upset with what he characterized as a "political persecution," Rich renounced his American citizenship.

On 19 September 1983, a Federal Grand Jury in New York returned a 56-count indictment against Rich, Green and their assorted companies. They were charged with Tax Evasion, Wire Fraud, Racketeering (RICO) and Dealing with the Enemy (Iran).

In what would become a self-promoting pattern, Giuliani held a press conference to announce the indictment, which he characterized as the "largest tax evasion case in US history." It was the first time Giuliani used the RICO statues in what was essentially a civil case and it was a very questionable application of his prosecutorial prerogatives. [174] That being said, if Giuliani had won convictions in trial, Rich faced the seizure of his companies and his assets, $48 million in alleged back taxes, plus a 300-year prison term.

By the time he was indicted, Rich was living in Zug, Switzerland and was no longer an American citizen. While legally he had no obligation to return to New York to face the indictment, he was quickly placed on the Justice Department's international fugitive list.

Because of the threat of seizure under the RICO statues, two of Rich's companies entered into a plea agreement with the government, plead guilty to lesser charges and paid fines in excess of $200 million in March 1984. As is the way of these matters, they saved legal expenses and survived to continue doing business in the United States. Giuliani was able to boast that they were "guilty" thus justifying his prosecution. Everyone walked away from this horse trade semi-happy.

Rich continued his commodities trading and traveled extensively throughout the world. From the late 1970s through the early 1990s, he was secretly involved in securing the release and airlifting thousands of persecuted Falasha Jews from Ethiopia to Israel. He also continued his business relations with Iran, and became, in essence, a deniable contact point between the Israeli and Iranian governments.

Rich was involved with other clandestine projects as well, one of which was his ongoing effort to secure the release of three Israeli prisoners being held by Shia Moslem terrorist groups.[175] The disclosure of his efforts to free these Israelis was a dead giveaway of his connections to Israeli Intelligence. Ironically, the effort to release these soldiers would surface again in 1986, during another case Giuliani brought against Israeli defendants.

From 1983 to 2000, the US Marshal Service hatched several plots to arrest Rich and later bragged that they "almost" captured him in various locations. The charges, however, were not extraditable from most countries and more often than not, the Marshals themselves were threatened with arrest as they plotted and skulked all over Europe. Additionally, Israeli bodyguards always protected the fugitive businessman. The Marshals did approach Israeli officials who promised to cooperate, but then candidly told the Americans that Rich would never be caught.[176] One effect it did have on Rich, however, was it precluded him from visiting his 27-year-old daughter, Gabrielle, who was dying of Leukemia in New York in 1996. After her passing, Rich arranged to have her grave moved to Israel.

One of the charges leveled against Marc Rich came back to haunt the US Government in 1986, three years after his indictment. At every opportunity, Rudy Giuliani publicly proclaimed that Rich was trading with Iran while American diplomats were being held hostage in Tehran. This was true. Iran was using its' oil revenues to purchase weapons and munitions from Israel and other countries. It was also true that in 1980, when Rich's alleged offense took place, the Carter Administration was allowing Israel to supply Iran with American-made military spare parts. The Israelis would then purchase replacements from American manufacturers. This policy continued during the two successive Reagan Administrations.[177]

Among the Israelis there was confusion over the duplicity in the Rich indictment. Still, the decision was made not to come to his rescue publicly and expose his sensitive connections to Jerusalem. Subsequently,

Israeli officials and Rich's defense lawyers made quiet overtures to the American government, but nothing came of them. Giuliani had been too publicly vocal to compromise and settle the matter quietly. In Switzerland, Rich was out of harm's way and continued operating clandestinely for Israel. It is said that he was instrumental in helping establish the Peace Agreement by and between Israel and Egypt.[178]

With the Marc Rich case, Rudy Giuliani was just getting started. Between 1983 and 1986, he brought a number of federal cases against Israeli operatives usually in the guise of illegal arms dealing with Iran. Finally in April of 1986, he brought a case against ten European and Middle East businessmen, four of whom were Israelis. As we shall see, when Giuliani publicly touted this case as "the largest arms smuggling case in American history," Israel stuck back with a vengeance.

The case against Marc Rich sat there and hummed for more than 17 years. Then on 20 January 2001, in one of his last acts as President, Bill Clinton pardoned Marc Rich and Pinky Green.[179] Although there was absolutely nothing they could do about the President's constitutional ability to grant these pardons, Clinton-hating Congressional Republicans screamed bloody murder and called hearings to "get to the bottom of this."

Rudy Giuliani was one of the first of the Republican Party faithful to testify in this new congressional inquiry. After reiterating that the Rich case was the "largest tax evasion case in American history," he opined, "You just don't pardon fugitives."[180]

(President Carter pardoned hundreds of Vietnam-era draft dodgers, all of whom were fugitives, but never mind.)

Rudy Giuliani   Marc Rich

And thus, years after the Spook War, the bitterness remained between the antagonists. In August of 2001, the Israelis passed on general warnings of a terrorist attack against the United States, but in order to be taken seriously, they were forced to do it through two friendly intelligence services, one of which was the French SDECE. Still, the warnings were ignored.

og &o

An Expendable Asset

> *Spymaster: And if you are caught,*
> *we will deny all knowledge of the affair.*
>
> *Spy: Naturally.*
>
> *Spymaster: And then we'll betray you and we'll let you*
> *rot in a foreign prison and not lift a finger to help you.*
>
> *Spy: Hey! Isn't that a little extreme?*
>
> *Spymaster: Not really. It's the Jonathan Pollard clause.*
>
> "Dry Bones"
> The Jerusalem Post
> 17 August 1997

The phone call that came into his Santiago headquarters that February morning in 1986 did not bode well for the Chilean industrialist Carlos Cardoen. There had been an explosion at the Industrias Cardoen plant in Iquique, the great duty-free commercial port more than 1100 miles from the capital, on the Pacific coast. Carlos Remigio Cornejo Cardoen, the American-educated owner, [181] enjoyed not only close ties with Saddam Hussein, but also with the Central Intelligence Agency. He was most certainly aware that his business dealings and dangerous liaisons might well provoke an angry response - like an explosion in his plant – carried out by interested parties of the Jewish persuasion. In fact, he had been personally warned according to some sources. [182]

Carlos Cardoen and Sadam Hussein

Few people knew that the Cardoen plant, which employed over 700 workers in Iquique, manufactured cluster bombs. Few had seen the Iraqi cargo aircraft land weekly at the Iquique airport and taxi over to the non-descript plant to be loaded. But, the Israelis had and they were about their usual mischief. The explosion, later deemed to be sabotage, killed 29 people and set loose an angry outrage against Cardoen by the local inhabitants of Iquique.

Cardoen Industries was part of the Chilean effort to develop an indigenous arms manufacturing capability in the wake of President Carter's military embargo over human rights issues. Cardoen began by manufacturing a line of Swiss-designed Mowag armored vehicles, later expanding to land mines and hand grenades, and by 1981, had produced his first cluster bomb unit.

In 1982, Cardoen met Nasser Beyodoun in Miami and signed him on as the representative of Industrias Cardoen in Iraq. In early 1983, Beyodoun secured the first Iraqi trial order for 3000 cluster bomb units. Cardoen hastily set up manufacturing facilities at Iquique and delivered his first order, $21 million worth, in early 1984.

It was immediately apparent to Cardoen that as the Iraqi orders grew, he had an urgent need to expand his manufacturing capability. To this end, his agents found two old bomb factories, complete with their production machinery, in the United States and purchased them as "scrap metal" in 1984. With the Reagan Administration in power, the Carter Administration's arms embargo of Chile meant nothing. The American bomb-making machinery was imported into Chile and immediately set up in the Cardoen plant at Iquique.

In the summer of 1984, James Guerin, president of International Signal and Control (ISC)[183] in Lancaster, Pennsylvania purchased the Marquardt Corporation of California for $43 million. Marquardt was the première American manufacturer of cluster bomb units for the Department of Defense. Guerin was a veteran CIA facilitator and part of the clandestine American effort to arm Iraq.[184]

Shortly after ISC took over Marquardt, blueprints and technical specifications for the company's Mk 20 "Rockeye" cluster bomb unit illegally found their way to Industrias Cardoen in Chile. Some sources state that

Alan Sanders, a CIA operative delivered them to Cardoen.

The plant in Iquique began producing "knock-offs" of the "Rockeye" in short order, complete with fuses covertly supplied by ISC – possibly through the CIA cut-out, Gamma Corporation – from its plant in Lancaster, Pennsylvania.

MK 20 "Rockeye" Cluster Bomb Unit (CBU)

Carlos Cardoen still had one more problem, which he overcame that year with the help of the Reagan Administration. He needed large amounts of the metal zirconium to improve the efficiency of his cluster bomb units. In 1984, he managed to import over 30 tons of this strategic metal in spite of the fact that it was on the State Department's munitions control list.

Cardoen's secret facilitator in these purchases was the American Ambassador to Chile, James Daniel Theberge. It was Theberge's staff, which officially signed off on the caveats that the State and Commerce Departments, as a matter of course, attached to these restricted sales. While all three of these 1984 transactions were patently illegal under American Law, someone had to take the bureaucratic responsibility and "paper the file" to expedite their completion.

In 1985 when a Commerce Department official complained that the shipments of zirconium to Cardoen Industries - they rose to 37 tons that year - were "irregular," Ambassador Theberge delivered his assurances that quelled the protests.

The fact that Cardoen's cluster bomb units, enhanced with American zirconium, were going to Iraq was an open secret. Everyone and their brother monitored Iraqi and Iranian aircraft and ships that might be carrying war materials. And, while Ambassador Theberge handled the "policy issues" that accommodated these Cardoen transactions, the intelligence operatives stationed at the American embassy in Santiago still dutifully reported in detail to their "home offices" in Langley and the Pentagon.

Back in Washington, these intelligence reports were evaluated, folded, stapled, mutilated and published within the Intelligence Community. A special copy, along with supporting documents, was automatically sent to those agencies specifically tasked with monitoring technology transfers. One of those agencies was the Naval Intelligence Support Center in Suitland, Maryland, where Jonathan Pollard was employed.

The issue of cluster bomb units was a particularly sensitive one with the Israelis. In 1982, the Reagan Administration had publicly screamed bloody murder when the Israelis used them against Syrian Army units during the Lebanon invasion. [185] Two years later, the same screamers were supplying the same weapons to the Iraqis for use against the Iranians, with little or no regard for their potential use against Israel or Iraq's Arab neighbors.

James Theberge completed his ambassadorship in late 1985 and returned to Washington. He was soon employed part-time at the CIA and had also signed on as a consultant for Cardoen Industries. [186]

There is strong circumstantial evidence to indicate that Israeli Intelligence was responsible for the 1986 "accident" at the Cardoen plant in Iquique. Many knowledgeable sources agree that it was a warning shot. "Had they been determined to destroy the entire facility," one American source told us, "they could have done so like (they did) at Al-Hillah. Cardoen's cluster bombs were not that much of a threat. The message was for the Americans." *Spook War.*

Ari Ben-Menashe, a former Israeli spook, contends in his 1992 book, *PROFITS OF WAR,* that Cardoen was also involved in the production of precursor chemicals for the manufacture of chemical weapons. These chemicals were also being supplied to Iraq in cooperation with the CIA.

On 18 January 1991, as the Iraqi missiles were falling on Israel and Washington was in the throes of cardiac arrest, US Customs agents descended on Cardoen's Miami offices to serve a search warrant. They carted away truckloads of documents and effectively closed down the operations of Industrias Cardoen in the United States. They later seized Cardoen's Miami home, which he had purchased from one of Florida's US Senators, Bob Graham. Thus ended Carlos Cardoen's romance with the Reagan Administration.

In the aftermath of the Gulf War, with the public exposure of the "Level Battlefield Doctrine" and all its disastrous consequences, the "Iraqgate" scandal broke. US Customs, which had been patiently waiting for a political policy change, indicted Cardoen in May of 1993 for defrauding the government in the zirconium purchases.

James Theberge, who died in 1988, was spared any accountability, but he was most certainly the primary "cut-out" between the CIA and Carlos Cardoen. After his indictment, the CIA found Cardoen expendable and threw him to the wolves.

Cardoen, with some naive sense of honor, agreed to return to Miami to stand trial if the judge would allow him to introduce evidence showing that his part in the arming of Iraq had the full support and backing of the United States government. [187] The federal trial judge, Shelby Highsmith, refused to allow it. [188]

In 1995, the trial went forward without Cardoen. Carlos Cardoen was tried in absentia, convicted in absentia, sentenced in absentia and went on to serve his prison term ... in absentia. [189]

All his former sponsors, the United States Government, could do was seize his house in Florida. It is said that Cardoen now resides in Cuba.

ᑢ ᔑ

The Bank on Peachtree Street

"BNL-Atlanta was reported to have helped finance large parts of the Condor II missile program, a joint program of Iraq, Egypt and Argentina."

Senior Judge Marvin H. Shoob
United States District Court
Northern District of Georgia
Court Order in 1:CR-91-78-MHS
23 August 1993

In 1980, when Saddam Hussein sent his Republican Guard divisions crashing across the Iranian border, Iraq's oil income was $28 billion a year. By 1983, he was in *deep shit* - not to put too fine a point on it - both militarily and financially. His oil income for that year had shrunk down to $8 billion. The Arab states, the Arabists in the US State Department and emissaries from Iraq were begging assistance from the United States, although no diplomatic relations existed between the two countries in 1983.

So, George Shultz discussed using the Export-Import Bank to guarantee loans that would enable American manufacturers to participate in the clandestine military build-up of Iraq. The State Department did not press that approach because Iraq could not provide "a reasonable assurance of payment" and the Eximbank would have to decide for itself whether or not the Iraqi government still had ties to international terrorists. Although the Reagan Administration had informed Congress on 26 February 1982 that Iraq was no longer on its list of "Terrorist Nations," no one was willing to push that particular issue.[190]

Instead, they came up with a scheme whereby the Commodity Credit Corporation (CCC) of the Department of Agriculture would guarantee bank loans to finance American farmers' exports to Iraq. Throwing out the new program into the American banking community generated no great enthusiasm, even though the US government was guaranteeing 98 percent of the Iraqi loans. Then, Morgan Guaranty Trust of New York stepped up to the plate and signed on with a first loan to Saddam Hussein. Morgan's participation in the Reagan Administration's scheme gave it credibility.

The way matters developed, an Italian state bank with branches in the United States would become Iraq's primary lender utilizing the American CCC loan guarantee program. The Banca Nazionale del Lavoro (BNL or National Labor Bank) was owned by the Italian Treasury. BNL was the largest Italian bank and had been a prime financier of a 1980 weapons deal between Italy and Iraq.[191] They also financed a $225 million deal whereby the Italian company Valsella of Brescia supplied Iraq with nine million land mines.[192]

In 1983, Christopher P. Drogoul[193] became BNL's branch manager in Atlanta and in 1984, made his first loan to Iraq. That deal, a $13 million wheat and flour sale under the CCC program, was "kosher." In early 1985, Drogoul opened a $100 million line of credit for Iraq utilizing the CCC loan guarantees. Then in December of that year, Drogoul opened a further line of credit for the Iraqis in the amount of $556 million, but this one was not "kosher" and soon went "off the books." At that point, BNL's loans to Iraq went "illegal," although the American government, through the CCC program, still guaranteed them. It would

later be brought out in US District Court in Atlanta that BNL's home office in Rome was completely aware and approved of the "off-the books" loans to Iraq.[194]

From 1985 until 1989, the "illegality" of the BNL loans to Iraq was known to the Reagan Administration, the Bush Administration and the rest of the world. Foreign intelligence agencies were well aware and kept their governments fully informed. Additionally, it was clear to everyone that Iraq was not using the American taxpayer-guaranteed loans to import American farm commodities. By 1989, some $5.5 billion worth of loans had gone to Iraq through BNL, a majority of the funds being used to finance Saddam Hussein's military, including the development of the CONDOR missile. Since the illegalities of BNL's dealings were an open secret, the entire operation was vulnerable to anyone wanting to bring it down. One nation that would benefit from stopping Saddam Hussein's cash flow was, of course, Israel.

Had he given it more than cursory thought, FBI Special Agent William Hinshaw might have noticed the unusual timing of the phone call his Atlanta office received at the end of June 1989. Two lawyers representing Mela Maggi and Jean Ivey from the BNL's Atlanta branch wanted to discuss certain irregularities in a loan portfolio being handled by their bank.

In many subsequent discussions held with the two women, that resulted in an immunity-from-prosecution agreement on 29 July 1989, it was clear to the FBI that intense outside pressure was being exerted on the two BNL employees.

In later years, Hinshaw, who then was the Special-Agent-in-Charge of the FBI's Atlanta field office,[195] and others involved with the BNL investigation, would recall a persistent rumor at the time. It was all speculation, mind you, but it surfaced over and over and laid a frightening chill on the two BNL employees-turned-informants whenever it was mentioned. It was so out-of-place on Atlanta's Peachtree Street that it turned many serious researchers skeptical, yet it never went away. It was the Hebrew word for Institute: Mossad.[196]

On Friday afternoon, 4 August 1989, hoards of FBI agents and Federal Bank examiners simultaneously descended on the BNL branches in Atlanta, New York, Chicago, Los Angeles and Miami.[197] In a matter of minutes, Saddam Hussein's cash spigot in the United States was turned off.

As the federal investigation of the BNL proceeded, it became an open threat to the "Level Battlefield Doctrine." When the FBI turned over the case to the Justice Department for prosecution, the Bush Administration applied the brakes. "We had the horse in the gate, but they wouldn't open the gate," commented Bill Hinshaw in 1992.[198]

Federal Judge Marvin Shoob, who sat as the trial judge in the BNL case, had a similar view in 1993:

"I think the government entered into an effort early on to support Iraq as a matter of national policy. They used the CIA and Italy to effectuate that purpose. Many of the things that were done were in violation of acts of Congress and US arms export laws. They were aware of the law, and they skirted it. It was an effort to arm Iraq, and then, when things got out of hand, they didn't want the information to come out."[199]

But by 1989 when BNL was closed down, it was too late anyway. The war that Jonathan Pollard, Howard Teicher and others had predicted and tried to stop was less than a year away, and the ghostly specter of weapons of mass destruction ... aslihatul dammar ashammel ... was rising to cast its long shadow over the Middle East.

CŚ Šͻ

The HUNTING HORSE

"A well placed spy is worth two divisions."

Napoleon Bonaparte

The first time the two men met was 24 May 1984, at the lobby bar of the Washington Hilton Hotel. The two could not have been more contrasted, yet they were both brilliant in their respective fields. Neither could have known at the time, but their meeting would eventually end their careers.[200]

Aviem Sella was not an experienced *Katza*[201] - spy handler - and he was meeting the first real-life spy he had ever encountered. Sella was a computer whiz kid, completing his Ph.D. in the United States. He was also a Colonel in the Israeli Air Force, a fighter pilot who planned and organized the 1981 attack on Iraq's nuclear reactor, and one of Israel's most brilliant tactical air operations planners.

At this clandestine meeting, Sella was operating with the approval of his boss, the chief of the Israeli Air Force, Major General Amos Lapidot. Once Israeli Military Intelligence, AMAN, decided to accept the American "walk-in," the agent was turned over to the Scientific Liaison Bureau, the Technical and Scientific intelligence agency of the Israeli Ministry of Defense. In *The Trades,* this low-profile intelligence organization was known by the acronym, LAKAM.

Jonathan J. Pollard, the younger of the two men, was well educated, well read, got by in five languages, and was a rising star in the American Intelligence Community. An analyst at the Naval Intelligence Support Center (NISC) in Suitland, Maryland, Pollard, at 29-years-old had received high recognition for his work and was on the fast track for promotion.

In his position at the NISC, Pollard was not only tasked with tracking Soviet weapons then pouring into the Middle East, but also with "technology transfers" ... cases of illegal American dealings in weapons and weapons technology, and industrial espionage. Not only did he know *who* was shipping *what* into the Middle East, but to facilitate his job, he enjoyed access to a great deal of the American Intelligence Community's classified information, its library.

Before he even met with Sella, Pollard, who had been assigned as a Naval Intelligence representative to the US-Israel intelligence sharing effort, had determined that the secret military build-up of Iraq presented a *clear and present danger* not only to Israel, but to Kuwait and Saudi Arabia as well. He reasoned that the Israelis were the only people who would take some sort of action to negate this on-going, officially sanctioned, insanity.[202] But, like Sella, he was not experienced in the ways of espionage; he was just an overly bright kid with a library card about to play the *Great Game*[203] on a far more serious level.

Sella   Pollard

By meeting with Sella in May, Jonathan Pollard knew he was *crossing the Rubicon*; that he was "walking in" as a source for Israeli Intelligence. He had tried working through his own superiors with the alarming information he had uncovered, but he had been continually rebuffed because of the still-secret policy agenda. Now, in his own mind, he had no alternative.

There was something else about Pollard that intrigued the Israelis beyond his access to American intelligence on the Arabs, the Soviets and the shipments of Western material and technology into the Middle East. Since the Battle of Majnoon earlier that year, they were desperately interested in what he wanted to talk about: Iraq's nuclear, chemical and biological weapons of mass destruction.

Moreover, Jay Pollard was the son of the eminent microbiologist, Dr. Morris Pollard, head of the Lobund Laboratory at Notre Dame University, in South Bend, Indiana. The young spook, who drank coffee with Colonel Sella that morning, knew exactly what Class III

Pathogens were, and was one of the few American intelligence professionals who did. Information on the shipments of pathogens from the United States to Iraq, which Pollard's Intel shop monitored, was a priority collection requirement at that point in time for Israeli Intelligence.

The first classified documents Jay Pollard subsequently turned over to the Israelis concerned the Samara chemical complex. In retrospect, it is likely that the Israelis were by then reasonably up to speed on Iraq's capability to manufacture chemical weapons. They did not know about the small, Biosecurity Level 4 lab within the Samara complex, nor did they know about the "Level Battlefield Doctrine" and the scope of the associated American duplicity in their intelligence sharing. To some Israelis, it was the Yom Kippur War all over again.[204]

Jonathan Pollard was a closely held secret within Israeli Intelligence. Very few knew who he was or even his code name and his information was classified JUMBO, meaning no foreign dissemination.[205] But, the idea that AMAN never knew they had an agent-in-place within American Intelligence - floated after Pollard's arrest - is utterly preposterous. With the flow of Pollard's work product into its analytical branch it was all too evident and by the late summer of 1994, AMAN officers were calling their unknown American benefactor, THE HUNTING HORSE.[206]

Cʒ ℬɔ

Sidestep

*"I can't say I was ever lost, but I was
bewildered once for three days."*

Daniel Boone

In July 1984, the Reagan Administration was hit with another potentially ominous exposure. A *Washington Post* correspondent, Rod Norland, managed to get an interview with Lieutenant General Maher Abdul Rashid, an Iraqi field commander. In describing a recent battle with the Iranians, Rashid noted that, "When you are faced with insects, you use insecticide."[207] This was almost identical to the statement made some two years earlier on Baghdad Radio. The Israelis were worried that they might have misread the previous statement and began thinking they might be looking directly at a colossal intelligence failure.

In Washington, the Reagan Administration, sensitive to the media flap, called in the Saudis to discuss the publicity over the Iraqi CBW matter. The Saudis candidly told the Americans that the use of poison gas was the only way the Iraqis could stop Iran's Revolutionary Guard units from driving through the defenses and turning south for Kuwait City. They also agreed to speak to the Iraqis about limiting press access.[208]

For its part, the Reagan White House deflected media inquiries by stating it was possible that Iraq had obtained chemical weapons from either the Soviet Union or Egypt. Biological agents were not mentioned in the press statements and neither was the fact that the Administration was well aware that the Iraqis were already *manufacturing* their own chemical weapons.

As events would prove out, the Iraqis were not only manufacturing weapons of mass destruction, but Western businesses were supplying them the technology, materials and equipment to do so. By the end of the Iran-Iraq War in 1988, this commercial trade was widespread.

First the Reagan Administrations and later the Bush Administration frustrated American law enforcement agencies in their pursuit of American companies that were secretly selling "dual-use" materials and technology to Iraq. It can be argued that Class III Pathogens have a "dual-use" appearance under the premise that they were used in "research," which no doubt, they were. The application of the end product of that research is the question that begs. After all, how often does one see a natural outbreak of Gas Gangrene or Pulmonary Anthrax?

Simply because the Administration thwarted law enforcement efforts on this export trade, these transactions were not rendered legal. In some cases, the legality of a transaction may never have been in question, but the ethical implications certainly were. To illustrate this, we point to the example of the Iraqi petrochemical complex known as PC2.

In the summer of 1988, Lieutenant General Amer Hamoudi al Saadi,[209] a German-trained chemist who headed Iraq's chemical weapons and ballistic missile programs, asked the Bechtel Corporation to consult on the planning and construction of one of Iraq's most ambitious petrochemical complexes. Located about 70 kilometers south of Baghdad, PC2 would produce ethylene oxide – used in fuel-air explosives – as its principal product. Additionally, it was planned to produce chemical precursors such as thiodiglycol, one of the principle ingredients in the blister agent, Mustard gas.

Bechtel was paid for this contract by letters of credit issued by the Atlanta branch of Banco Nazionale del Lavoro (BNL). The Commodity Credit Corporation of the US Department of Agriculture in turn guaranteed these letters of credit. At the time, George Shultz, the former president of Bechtel, was the American Secretary of State. He had engineered the re-establishment of diplomatic relations with Iraq and put in place the financing scheme through the Department of Agriculture. Shultz, as well as his Bechtel colleague and fellow stockholder, Caspar Weinberger, would later claim that they had no knowledge of the PC2 contract.

03 80

CHAPTER 8

LOOSE FILES AND AMERICAN SCRAMBLE

"The plan was conceived in ignorance of facts and error of judgment and apparently executed in the spirit of its conceptions."

The Evening Transcript
Boston
12 June 1861

SIREN

"He was sentenced on the basis of things whispered in the ear of a complaint judge ...The Pollard case is just another test of whether we Americans, Republicans or Democrats, care more about the truth or more about protecting the prerogatives of powerful people."

Angelo Codevilla
Senior Staffer
Senate Intelligence Committee

The year 1985 was memorable for American Intelligence. As a matter of fact, the media dubbed it the "Year of the Spy." The Reagan Administration was rudely awakened to the fact that the Soviet Intelligence services, both the KGB and the GRU, had successfully penetrated American Intelligence ... big time.

The catastrophe started with the disappearance of two American agents-in-place as has been described previously, which started a virtual hemorrhage of revelations on Soviet penetrations. By the end of that memorable year, there would be 17 espionage indictments before American federal courts and one of them would be the Jonathan Pollard case.

There had been a lulling of the American Intelligence Community during this period, partially because the White House was preoccupied with Lebanon and the American citizens who had been taken hostage there,[210] which was getting most of the media play.

The National Security Council was busy with its secret efforts to influence the Iranians with arms-for-hostages deals, the co-called "Second Channel," while the Pentagon's Defense Intelligence Agency was beefing up the Iraqi military efforts against the Iranians.

In the midst of this "cluster" was CHANNEL ONE, the unbridled and massive Israeli effort to support Iran with the approval and cooperation of the CIA.

The Contras were lighting up Central America with the assistance of the CIA while the American Congress, at the time in the hands of liberal politicians, was bound and determined not to finance anything to do with that.

Finally, there was the largest CIA war ever mounted to hammer the Soviet 40th Shock Army then

LOOSE FILES AND AMERICAN SCRAMBLE

occupying Afghanistan. It was fought using a surrogate guerrilla army of fundamentalist Mujahedin groups. One group - Al Qaeda (The Base) - was under the leadership of a wealthy, Saudi-born "holy warrior" named Osama bin Laden. [211] Other guerrilla leaders like Jalaluddin Haqani and Gulbuddin Hekmatyar would also be branded "terrorists" in the wake of Nine-Eleven.[212]

By November 1985, Jonathan Pollard was working what amounted to two jobs, one for American Intelligence while "moonlighting" for the Israelis. In order to maintain his high, personal standards in his "work product" for both masters, he abandoned some of the basic tenets of security or so it would seem.

As of mid-November, he had already fallen under suspicion and had been targeted by American counterintelligence. Not only had the "Year of the Spy" heightened counterintelligence activities within the American Intelligence Community, but Pollard had been a player in the seizure of the *Achille Lauro* hijackers by the US Navy in September ... an operation that seemed a glaring success in the media, but actually resulted in the death of a highly placed Israeli agent within the Egyptian Army's General Staff.[213]

The Achille Lauro

The Israeli air raid on the PLO headquarters at Hammam Lif, outside Tunis, on 1 October 1985,[214] had not gone unnoticed. It was clear that the Israeli tactical planners [215] had extremely accurate information, including precise radar frequencies of the Arab air defenses along the entire North African coast.

Tunisia was normally not a collection target[216] for the rather small and thinly stretched Israeli Intelligence services, yet their Air Force units flew the 1,500 miles from Israel and arrived over their target completely undetected by either the Arabs or US Naval units in the Mediterranean. It was another signpost that pointed to an Israeli "mole" somewhere within either Soviet Military Intelligence or American Military Intelligence. Since Naval Intelligence had the responsibility for coverage of the North African coastal defenses, naturally suspicion fell there.

All of these incidents heightened the atmosphere of suspicion within the Intelligence Community, especially Naval Intelligence. In retrospect, Jonathan Pollard seemed oblivious to the character of the threat against him.

Having explained these factors, it is now incumbent upon us to briefly discuss how, in all likelihood, Jay Pollard was exposed. There is perhaps a ninety-five percent chance that an American agent inside Israel fingered him, or at least alerted his American handlers that there was a "mole" in play. This is generally the way of these matters and those who argue that good sleuthing by counter-intelligence or exposure by a co-worker was responsible are way off the mark ... possibly out of ignorance but more than likely on purpose. Such a false story is standard in *The Trades* and is called "smoke."

In 2001, the truth came out. The agent who exposed Pollard was a politician ... a member of the Likud Central Committee in Israel. He was recruited by Tommy Votz, ostensibly the Second Secretary in the US Embassy in Tel Aviv, but in reality a CIA case officer working under a State Department "legal" cover. The agent's name was Andrzej Kielczynski (aka Josef Barak) and he was recruited in June of 1985.

To our knowledge, it has never been openly discussed before and the reasons are obvious: First ... sources and methods. Secondly, how would it look if the media discovered that the US had an agent with access to Israeli Intelligence when the Reagan Administration was having such a wonderful time Jew-bashing? This exact scenario went "loud" when it was discovered through the purloined Snowden documents given to

WikiLeaks, that US Intelligence was electronically monitoring the Israeli leadership.

Pollard himself may have contributed to his own downfall. In *The Trades,* when an officer decides to sell out to the opposition, the first thing he does is finger agents within his "new" sponsor's service ... the so-called "Nasty Circle." In this manner, he is protecting himself from exposure. Pollard, on the other hand, refused to expose any American agents inside Israeli Intelligence, as a matter of principle. It is doubtful if he knew of any in the first place, because he had no *need to know* and was not high enough in the food chain to have access to them. (The same can be said for the Strategic Bombing Index and the RASIN manual ... both to be covered later.)

While we can argue it round or flat, the method of his exposure is anybody's guess at this point. But, once his superiors picked up on him, the full power of counterintelligence locked onto him like a homing missile. Slowly but surely, the Naval Investigative Service and the FBI built their case as they surreptitiously watched him remove classified material from his office.

Still, there were several puzzling questions that seemed to haunt American investigators. That Pollard was removing classified material in an unauthorized manner was not one of them, but for what reason and for whom?

Most of the pilfered information they were able to track in the case dealt with Soviet weapons capabilities and weapons shipments to the Arab countries. It was also clear that Pollard had collected every scrap of information on chemical and biological warfare in the Middle Eastern countries, including evaluations of Israeli capabilities in this arena.

An FBI source that worked on the original investigation told us in 1997 that they could not "structure a theory" that made Pollard "walk like a duck."[217] It was, the agent insisted, "One hell of a problem. The Soviets washed out early (as sponsors) since it was obvious they would not be interested in collecting and paying for information on their own weapons capabilities and shipments." While the chemical and biological information was extremely sensitive, it appeared that no country in the Middle East would sponsor Pollard's efforts for the same reasons that excluded the Soviets."

"There was even a point," our source told us, "when the ideas floated that he (Pollard) was using the material to work on an academic paper, or was working on a newspaper article, or was working for some non-proliferation, environmental outfit like Greenpeace."

Late Monday afternoon, 18 November 1985, Pollard called his wife, Anne, to tell her he was en route home. Moments before, under the watchful eye of a surveillance camera, he had loaded up some Top Secret documents for the Israelis. As he got into his automobile, shotgun-wielding FBI and NIS agents immediately surrounded the car. Obviously, the counterintelligence folks wanted to have a serious talk with him.[218]

It was clear to Pollard, after several hours of interrogation that the counterintelligence investigators were "fishing" for his sponsor so he decided to turn that to his advantage. Like any good spy, he began to "dissemble" in an effort to buy some breathing space. His discovery and detention could not have come at a worse time. Avi Sella and his wife, Judith, were in the United States traveling without diplomatic cover. The two Israelis were what is called in *The Trades,* "illegal" and subject to immediate arrest.[219]

After two hours of interrogation, about 7 PM, Pollard knew he had to warn his wife. He was allowed to call Anne to tell her he would be delayed. During that phone conversation, Jonathan gave his wife the pre-arranged "burn code" that alerted her to his discovery by the authorities. Anne Pollard called Avi Sella and arranged an immediate meeting.[220] Within 12 hours of Anne's warning to Sella, all of the Israelis who had ever been in contact with Jonathan Pollard were out of the United States and safely back in Israel. Pollard went home that night knowing full well that it was only a matter of time before the FBI arrested him.

Israeli Intelligence knew that they had the potential for a major problem as soon as Sella passed back the word. Pollard had been a closely held asset of LAKAM, and as such, was not known to the mainstream Israeli Intelligence Community. While his identity had not been known, mid-level Israeli Military Intelligence officers had surmised his existence from the flow of his work product and had even nicknamed him the "HUNTING HORSE." [221]

For reasons unexplained to this day, LAKAM had made no safety net provisions for the Pollards and at the last moment, with the predator sharks circling their prey, a small group of AMAN operatives from Unit 504 attempted to rescue the threatened Israeli spy.

Meanwhile, Pollard was maintaining his freedom one day at a time by dissembling to the FBI, while hoping for an opportunity to be extracted by the Israelis. His efforts to contact his handlers were unsuccessful. Finally in desperation, he called the Israeli Embassy in Washington. This was what the AMAN rescue effort had counted on and Pollard was told that he was to come to the embassy.

On the morning of 21 November 1985 after his wife's appointment with her doctor, Jonathan and Anne drove onto International Drive and, as instructed, fell in behind an Israeli embassy car with diplomatic plates, which they followed into the embassy grounds. Several cars full of FBI agents ground to a halt in front of the embassy.

Inside the embassy grounds, the Pollards were greeted by Shin Bet[222] agents. The Israeli Ambassador, Meir Rosenne, was away on business that fateful day and the man in charge was Elyakim Rubinstein. [223] "Eddy" Rubinstein, a Jerusalem lawyer, was not aware of the rescue effort and seeing the FBI agents gathered outside the embassy grounds, ordered the Pollards expelled.[224]

Outside the embassy gates, the FBI arrested the Pollards and drove them away. Upon observing the arrests and watching the FBI agents pouring over the Pollards' car, a Shin Bet officer wrote a brief message to his superiors in Tel Aviv. He took it to the communications section for encoding and transmission. It read: "Hunting Horse down hard."

In Tel Aviv, the message from the embassy in Washington was received at the Kirya, Israel's Pentagon. The last-ditch effort to save the Pollards had failed and the small group of AMAN officers suspected there would be hell to pay. At the direction of Yitzhak Rabin, the Minister of Defense, a new signal was sent from IDF headquarters to the office of the Cabinet Secretary instructing him to alert the Cabinet. This message read: "Siren"

There are several postscripts to the story of the Pollard matter. Almost immediately after the spectacular arrests, a most bizarre event occurred. Jonathan Pollard was in the process of being released from the DC jail when his father, Dr. Morris Pollard, arrived for a visit. Dr. Pollard, fearing for his son's life, quashed the release. To this day, it is not clear if Jonathan's release was the work of AMAN, an American set-up or simply a mistake on the part of his jailers.[225]

As is standard in matters of "Friendly Espionage," the two intelligence services involved met to see if things could be quietly worked out. In the Pollard matter, this meeting took place in Washington at the end of November 1985, after Jonathan's arrest. Major General Ehud Barak, IDF, Chief of AMAN, headed the

Israeli delegation. Lieutenant General Leonard H. Perroots, USAF, Director of DIA, headed the American delegation. William Casey, Director of Central Intelligence, refereed.

In general terms, the Israelis wanted Jonathan and Anne quietly released. They argued that the Pollard situation compared to their release (after debriefing and damage assessment) of an American immigrant to Israel who worked for the CIA and was arrested by the Shin Bet in 1982. They were against Jonathan being debriefed prior to his release (naturally), but agreed to the Pollards voluntarily giving up their American citizenship and being deported to Israel.

The DIA, representing Weinberger's position, was opposed to the release. They argued that they were unwilling to commit to a release prior to Pollard's debriefing and damage assessment, which they felt was fair.

William Casey, seeing that the two positions were irreconcilable, cast his vote in favor of the Israeli position. He presented his recommendation to President Reagan, but by then, Weinberger and Schultz had cranked up the media and the President sided with State and Defense over Central Intelligence.

The one sticking point was the debriefing of Pollard. The Israelis knew that should the full scope of his activities be exposed to the Americans, it would cause irreparable, political damage to the Reagan Administration, which it ultimately did.

Israel's reaction to this decision was ill advised as well. A committee was formed by Shimon Peres, Yitzhak Shamir and Yitzhak Rabin, who returned from a visit to New York, to handle the Pollard matter. It consisted of six wise men, three affiliated with the Likud party, and three affiliated with Labor. When this committee, which was coded SIREN, came into being they were fully empowered by the government to settle the entire matter on the political level and Israeli Intelligence was no longer in the loop.

With the entire Intelligence Community counseling the Government of Israel to "stonewall" the Americans, the SIREN committee decided on a different approach. It was this political committee that generated the "rogue operation" scenario and endorsed returning a few purloined American documents to show "good faith," but in the process sealed the Pollards' fate.

Jonathan Pollard, on the advice of the SIREN committee, and seeking a lighter prison sentence for himself and no prison time his wife, Anne, entered into a plea agreement on 23 May 1986. It is the way things are normally done in matters of "friendly espionage."

The busted spy tells the government what classified information he has turned over to his "sponsor," the US Department of Justice does its damage assessment, and the American Intelligence Community makes its internal adjustments to cover any exposures. The convicted spy usually goes to prison for a couple of years to satisfy the government's outrage and more often than not, is deported after completing his prison term.

It is understood by both parties that friendly nations always spy on one another and when an operative is caught, the matter is handled in a quiet, civilized manner so as not to interfere with the relationship between the party countries. Thus, the world remains safe for diplomatic cocktail-parties.

In the Pollard case, however, the Reagan Administration changed the rules after the Secretary of Defense reviewed the results of Pollard's debriefing.

As is customary, Pollard was questioned while attached to a polygraph. The examination is in two parts. The first part consists of the interview where the questions are asked, answered and recorded. Then the subject is hooked up to the machine and the questions are asked a second time to check his truthfulness. In Pollard's case, it took a total of 140 hours hooked up to the polygraph before his inquisitors were content they had everything. In *The Trades,* this is called "fluttering."

When the Department of Justice was satisfied that it had the whole story from Pollard, Assistant US Attorneys Charles Leeper and David Geneson prepared a "Damage Assessment" for submission to the sentencing judge.

In this assessment, formally known as the "Victim Impact Statement," the Justice Department set out the damage Pollard had caused the United States. It was clear that he had not compromised any American agents, facilities or programs, but Leeper and Geneson explained that Pollard had "threatened the U.S. relations with numerous Middle East Arab allies (sic)" and (ironically) "skewed the balance of power in the Middle East."[226]

What is more interesting is the treatment given to Weinberger's intelligence embargo:

"Moreover, because Mr. Pollard provided the Israelisvirtually any classified document requested by Mr. Pollard's coconspirators, the U.S. has been deprived of the quid pro quo routinely received during authorized and official intelligence exchanges with Israel and Israel has received information classified at a level far in excess of that ever contemplated by the National Security Council. The obvious result of Mr. Pollard's largesse is that U.S. bargaining leverage with the Israeli government in any such further intelligence exchanges has been undermined."[227]

Finally, Leeper and Geneson stated that Pollard's actions caused the Anti-Terrorist Alert Center to expend "untold hours" with the FBI and NIS, disrupting the normal flow of work. The entire episode, they concluded, had "emotionally traumatized" Pollard's fellow workers. And that was it.

Given the amount of damage outlined in the assessment, a reasonable person might conclude that Jonathan Pollard had not caused all that much of a problem. It was, after all, a case of "friendly espionage." One might have expected that Pollard would have been sentenced to a few years and deported to Israel at the completion of his sentence, but that was not to be for two reasons. The first was because he worked for the Israelis, who were at the time the bane of the Reagan

Administration. Secondly, he had exposed some of Caspar Weinberger's more serious peccadilloes as the Secretary of Defense.

Pollard's "fluttering" revealed that he was a little more active than the Justice Department first suspected. It seemed that the young analyst had reached out and recruited a sub-agent named Ahmed Tashkandi, who was a member of the Saudi Arabian diplomatic mission to Washington.

Tashkandi had provided Pollard with, among other things, the minutes and memoranda of four 1985 meetings between Caspar Weinberger, Prince Bandar, the Saudi Ambassador to the United States, and Prince Sultan, the Saudi Defense Minister. The subject of these meetings, according to the documentation, was "The Israeli Threat." Further, it was established that Weinberger passed along American Intelligence studies on the "Israeli Military Establishment" to the Saudi Arabians. In essence, this made Weinberger guilty of the same offense for which Pollard was arrested ... "friendly espionage."

The documentation of these meetings established the Reagan Administration's "Level Battlefield Doctrine" beyond doubt and brightly illuminated its hostility toward Israel in spite of its continued public posturing. It was sordid behavior and not the sort of thing one might expect from the Secretary of Defense of the United States, most especially since Israel was officially a non-NATO ally.

Additional information provided by Tashkandi to Pollard showed the inner workings of an emergency arms transfer to Saudi Arabia by the Reagan Administration over Labor Day weekend in 1985. This involved the shipment of 400 "Stinger," shoulder-held, anti-aircraft missiles, when Congress was in holiday recess and unable to object or approve. Sometime later, one of these missiles was used to shoot down an American Marine helicopter in the Persian Gulf, resulting in the death of the crew. In 2001, Taliban troops fighting in Afghanistan used several of these same missiles against US Air Force planes supporting the Northern Alliance forces.

Far more threatening was the fact that Saudi Arabia allowed Syrian pilots to fly their American-made F-15 fighter planes. In 1985, Syria was a client of the Soviet Union and this action on the part of Saudi Arabia compromised America's top-line, air superiority fighter to the Soviets. This was certainly known to the Department of Defense since Jonathan Pollard was in daily contact about the matter with the American Air Force attaché in Riyadh, Saudi Arabia.

When the Justice Department lawyers submitted their damage assessment to the court, they let it be known that the Secretary of Defense would submit additional memoranda in camera. It was at this point that the Pollard matter became the most controversial espionage case in American history.

Weinberger took a personal affront to the Tashkandi revelations and submitted a still secret, sentencing memorandum to the Pollards' trial judge,

Aubrey E. Robinson, on 3 March 1987. In this, his second pre-sentencing declaration, the American Secretary of Defense characterized Jonathan Pollard as the "worst spy since Benedict Arnold" and outlined a litany of damages and alleged treasonous acts committed against the United States. Weinberger finished by suggesting:

"...there can be no doubt that he can, and will, continue to disclose U.S. secrets without regard to the impact it may have on U.S. national defense or foreign policy. Only a period of incarceration commensurate with the enduring quality of the national defense information he can yet impart, will provide a measure of protection against further damage to the national security."[228]

Weinberger's allegations turned out to be patently false, but Pollard's defense attorney, Richard Hibey, did not take the opportunity to answer them for reasons unknown.[229]

Just for good measure, the Office of Naval Intelligence claimed that Pollard had broken his plea agreement by consenting to two interviews by journalist Wolf Blitzer. This was awfully thin, for as we shall see, these two interviews took place with the consent of the Intelligence Community, the Department of Justice, prison officials and with NIS agents present.

On 4 March 1987, Judge Robinson[230] "threw the book" at the Pollards, giving Jonathan and Anne the maximum sentences allowable under law in spite of the fact that their convictions were obtained under a plea agreement and they had cooperated fully with investigators in the Justice Department's damage assessment.

On 10 September 1991, the US Court of Appeals heard the Pollard case on appeal. That something very unusual happened in the case is evident and one of the court's questions was telling:

"How in Lord's name can that be justified? How can it be justified that the Secretary of Defense uses the term 'treason' and that the government lawyer used the term 'treason' in a case in which the government could not and did not charge treason?"[231]

In a split decision, the US Court of Appeals turned down Pollard's request for a new trial. It is interesting to note that the two Jewish judges voted against, while the Christian judge voted for Pollard. One of those two Jewish judges was Ruth Bader Ginsberg, who was later named to the Supreme Court.

With the "special treatment" given to the Pollards, Weinberger openly declared war on Israel. By the spring of 1986, it was "open season" on Israeli agents as Attorney General Edwin Meese began pushing hard for more criminal prosecutions of alleged Israeli "arms dealers." This effort was geared toward cutting off the Israeli-Iranian "White Pipeline" (aka CHANNEL ONE) while publicly embarrassing the Jewish State and thereby diminishing its' influence with the US Congress.

The Spook War was in full swing, but like most of the Reagan Administration's secret agendas, especially those originating with Caspar Weinberger, this one also backfired. Israel, after all, had teeth. The Jewish State was neither Grenada nor Panama and bad luck seemed to be the Reagan Administration's best friend.

In April 1986, the US Attorney in the Southern District of New York, Rudolph Giuliani, targeting still more Israelis, went a case too far.

ርሪ 8ට

The Passover Plot

> "...Lest we forget:
> Our four lonely Jews in Bermuda ...
> No Mama, No Papa, No Uncle Yehuda."

> The Jerusalem Post
> Passover
> April 1986

This matter was one of the most damaging events in the *Spook War*. It began as a simple tactical effort, but quickly got out of hand and almost brought down the President of the United States.

There is speculation, even among those involved, as to its genesis, but one fact is absolutely clear: It triggered the greatest scandal the Reagan Administration faced during its two terms in Washington.

Some believe it was a simple attempt by the US National Security Council running CHANNEL TWO to displace and even supplant the Israeli-CIA CHANNEL ONE in supplying arms to Iran. Others proffer that it was simply another attempt by the administration ... under persistent Arab pressure ... to curtail the supply of weapons and munitions sustaining the Islamic Republic's war effort against Iraq. Or it may have been only an individual in trouble trying to trade his way out. And, as is common in *The Trades,* there are complete sets of unambiguous facts to support each supposition. One thing is clear, however, there were Israeli spooks who believed with a certainty that other Jews were persecuted because Israel did not defend Pollard.

The Spook War was then at full boom. That was clear enough. In a meeting in the White House on 21 April 1986, the Director of Central Intelligence, Bill Casey tried to warn President Reagan that the arrests of Israelis, combined with the media frenzy surrounding the Pollard Affair, did not bode well. "This war is getting out of hand," he told the President. Unfortunately for all concerned, he was overruled.

On 22 April 1986, the US Attorney for the Southern District of New York, Rudolph Giuliani, and the Commissioner of US Customs, William Von Raab, announced to the media the arrests of ten individuals, four of whom were Israeli, in what became known as the "Brokers of Death" case.[232]

A week before Passover, five of the individuals were arrested at the Hamilton Airport in Bermuda after arriving on a British Airways flight from London. The other five were arrested after arriving in New York. The so-called "Bermuda Five," which included the four

Israelis, fought extradition to the States and won their case. There was talk that Israel would send a jet to Bermuda to pick up its accused nationals, but the defendants were turned over to US Customs agents at the Hamilton Airport and accompanied to a Pan-Am plane bound for London, as proscribed by International Law. There was, of course, a stop-over in New York enroute. *An old trick.*

The 10 "Brokers of Death" were charged with attempting to sell weapons to Iran for use in their war against Iraq. Keeping in mind that the US Government was engaged in the exact same thing at the exact same time utilizing some of the same players in CHANNEL TWO, was a small detail that would only come out later. (The so-called WHITE PIPELINE or CHANNEL ONE never went "loud," although it may have been the ultimate target.)

There was briefly a sixth defendant ... one Manucher Ghorbanifar ... arrested in New York, but he was soon released.[233] And, contrary to the government's press releases, the defendants were not your ordinary, garden-variety gunrunners. When the media began to dig into the individuals' backgrounds, they found one was an Israeli Brigadier General, another was a London-based American attorney who had only two clients - J. Paul Getty and Adnan Khashoggi - and a third was, according to the US Government, "a high ranking Israeli Intelligence officer who was known to travel on 11 different passports."[234]

While initially Giuliani explained that government agents had "penetrated" a large arms-smuggling ring, the case turned out to be a US Customs "sting" operation directed against the Israelis.

Bill Casey's advice to President Reagan may well have been driven by other circumstances. Casey, as would later be revealed in government documents, was in monthly contact with one of the defendants ... the "high ranking Israeli Intelligence officer" ... and both sides had embarrassingly taped those telephone conversations.[235]

Still another defendant, a Greek-American associate of Adnan Khashoggi, had discussed the entire operation in detail with a close friend, a New York attorney named Maxwell Rabb. At the time of those conversations, Rabb just happened to be the United States Ambassador to Italy.[236]

The man who set up the "sting" for the government was as interesting a character as the defendants themselves. His name was Cyrus Hashemi, a mysterious, expatriate Iranian banker and CIA operative, who was also an associate of the famous Saudi wheeler-dealer, Adnan Khashoggi.

Rabb and Khashoggi

Of course, the Israeli Government denied any connection to the "Brokers of Death," but it came out in government documents that one of the Israeli defendants had demanded of the putative Iranian buyers, a *quid pro quo* ... the release of three Israeli prisoners ... as a pre-condition to the deal. Few observers picked up on this strange footnote until much later, or its subtle connection to the Marc Rich case, but it was soon clear that Jerusalem was doing a slow burn over the entire affair.[237]

On 21 July 1986, only two months after the arrests were made, Cyrus Hashemi, the US Government's "sting" man and key witness against the "Brokers of Death," was taken suddenly dead in London.

"I passed on to him a warning from the Middle East that he would one day have to pay for what he had done," said Hashemi's brother, Djamshid, "but he laughed it off. I believe my brother was murdered."[238]

Some have speculated that Cyrus Hashemi's death was the work of the Israelis who were giving the Reagan Administration an easy way out.[239] If so, Washington did not get the message. In yet another speculative scenario, Hashemi may have turned on his American sponsors and paid the price for his disloyalty.

Throughout the summer and fall of 1986, Rudolph Giuliani continued to trumpet the case as "the most significant arms smuggling case in history," labeling the defendants "terrorists" for allegedly dealing with Iran. It became routine for the Reagan Administration to hammer Israel over the Jonathan Pollard matter and the Brokers of Death in the media. These attacks always came just before there was to be a vote in Congress over some arms package being sold to the Arabs, which supported the administration's "Level Battlefield Doctrine."

The Israelis once again quietly informed the Reagan Administration that they were "up to here" with the nonsense, but Weinberger, Shultz and Meese were on a roll and their arrogance apparently overrode their common sense.

While the US Attorney, Rudy Giuliani, continually bragged about his high conviction rate, an analysis of his cases showed that a vast majority of his convictions were plea bargains. Rarely did the US Attorney's office go to trial and during the early summer of 1986, the "Brokers of Death" dug in their heels and began fighting back. It suddenly became apparent that there would be no plea bargains and that the ten defendants intended to go to trial.

In his 1990 book, *ENGINES OF WAR,* James Adams, the Defense Correspondent and Associate Editor of the *Sunday Times of London,* wrote about the abrupt turnaround from the prosecution's point of view:

"It was without a doubt one the Customs Service's most successful operations and all involved were confident of getting convictions on every count. But then things began to go badly wrong."[240]

Defense lawyers were soon peppering the court with motions declaring that the United States was doing exactly what the defendants had be accused of doing ... selling arms to Iran. This was a new twist and Rudy

Giuliani stated that the defendants were "taking comfort in their fantasies."

In answering the Defense motions, Giuliani produced a pile of sworn affidavits from the Department of State, the Department of Defense, the CIA, and the National Security Council in which each entity swore under oath to the Federal Court that the US Government was not supplying weapons to Iran in any way, shape or form.

The defendants, who knew differently, were stunned. Officials of the United States had lied under oath to a Federal Court, subverting the very system they had sworn to uphold and defend. For the Israelis, it was the last straw.

Shortly thereafter, an Israeli agent named Ariel Ben-Menashe contacted a *Time* magazine reporter, Raji Samghabadi, and laid out a story revealing the Reagan Administration's secret dealings with Iran. *Time* verified the story, but the White House managed to "spike" it citing the lives of American hostages were at stake. [241] Being unsuccessful at *Time,* Ben-Menashe then took a run at *Newsday,* the Long Island daily, but the results were the same.

So in October 1986, Ben-Menashe flew back to the Middle East and through Iranian agents, planted the story in a small, Lebanese newsmagazine. [242] It was immediately picked up by the wire services and triggered the "Iran-Contra" affair, the largest scandal ever suffered by the Reagan Administration, which almost toppled the popular, American president. [243] It also exposed the government's duplicity in the "Brokers of Death" case as well as several others brought into court in *The Spook War.*

Ben-Menashe and Samghabadi

This began a virtual hemorrhage within the federal courts. Many other cases, particularly those brought by the US Customs Service under Operation STAUNCH, [244] were thrown out of court. Additionally, defense attorneys representing defendants already convicted of dealing with Iran rushed to file motions for new trials. It was a clear set-back for the American side in the *Spook War.*

In January of 1989, just before George Bush (41) assumed the Presidency, the government dropped all charges against the "Brokers of Death." In making the announcement, the US Attorney, Rudy Giuliani, cited a "lack of evidence."

During the subsequent investigation by the Independent Counsel for Iran-Contra Matters, Special Prosecutor Lawrence Walsh discovered that Caspar W.

Weinberger had lied to FBI investigators and Congress about his role in the affair. He was indicted[245] based on his own contemporaneous notes, when they were discovered, and only saved from felony convictions by a presidential pardon from George Bush (41) in December 1992. Interestingly, Weinberger's handwritten notes showed that George Bush was "in the loop" and pushed the clandestine exchange of arms for hostages, contrary to the Vice President's public statements.

Friday, 25 November 2011, was the 25th anniversary of the Iran-Contra scandal. On that date, the Independent Counsel on Iran-Contra publically released that portion of their report that found neither Ronald Reagan nor George H. W. Bush criminally liable in the affair.[246]

Finally, as is often the way of these matters and despite the best efforts of the Israelis, their three soldiers remain missing.

 C3 80

La Raison d'Etat

> "Behold, I tell you a mystery, we shall not all
> sleep, but we shall all be changed."

I Corinthians 15:51

In most Western militaries there is a doctrine of "no one left behind" on the battlefield. It is a sacred compact between the government and its soldiers. The

United States, however, has mixed report card when it comes to the matter of PoWs, although politicians may dispute this, declaring "all came home."

The American record goes back to its ill-fated intervention into the Bolshevik Revolution of 1917 when US troops were deployed in support of the White Russian forces at the behest of Great Britain. Post-war records indicate that sixty (60) some-odd missing US soldiers are still unaccounted for and reports of them being alive in Communist prison camps are rife.

The records from World War Two indicate that around three thousand (3000) US servicemen are still missing. The important aspect of these particular MIA soldiers is that they were prisoners of the Germans and were liberated by the Red Army, after which they disappeared.[247] The consensus among historians is that Joe Stalin wanted billions of dollars to help reconstruct the Soviet Union and a free hand in ruling Eastern Europe. At the time (1953) Allen Dulles was the Director of Central Intelligence and by all accounts knew about the missing Americans. This "hostage" situation was negated when the American Government declared the men dead. The Eisenhower Administration's refusal to be "black mailed" marked the beginning of the Cold War. One might conclude that this evolved into a question of "political expediency." At least that is the short version.

The Korean War produced still another group of unaccounted-for US Servicemen, some eight thousand (8000) in all. In May 1954, General Mark Clark, the last commander of United Nations Forces in Korea, made a speech in which he voiced his belief that 3000 US

Servicemen were still being held by the Chinese.[248] This opened the flood gates that ended in a lawsuit filed against the Administration by the mother of a missing soldier and apparently triggered a "black bag" burglary at her home in which all of her paperwork was stolen.[249]

The missing of the Vietnam War is more contentious, probably because it is more recent. The problem arose when the Nixon Administration, desperate for a peace deal with North Vietnam, promised them billions of dollars to rebuild their country. Unfortunately, the US Congress would not go along with the deal and thus, most observers believe, the North Vietnamese would not repatriate all of the American PoWs. Interestingly, in 1992, the Soviet Premier, Boris Yeltsin, confirmed that the Soviets were holding or at one time held American PoWs from the Vietnam War. A committee was established to look into the matter, but then the Clinton Administration normalized relations with the Communist Regime of North Vietnam and once again political expediency closed the opening. Yet again, this is the short version.

American adherence to the old axiom of "no one left behind" appears to be rather spotty. That is not the case with the State of Israel. In fact, in all their wars, the Israelis have only six soldiers unaccounted for. The Jews will move heaven and earth to get back a prisoner from their Arab enemies as the world witnessed when they ransomed 1027 convicted Arab terrorists to Hamas for one kidnapped Israeli soldier, Gilad Shalit, in 2011.[250] Viewed as both strength and weakness on the part of Israel, its fierce stance on "no one left behind" figured prominently in the *Spook War.*

On the fifth day of the Israeli invasion of Lebanon – Operation SHALOM GALIL (PEACE FOR GALILEE), an armored column from General Giora Lev's 90th Division was pushing northward up the Bekaa Valley toward Joub Jannine. Spearhead units of the 362nd and 363rd battalions pushed into the Lebanese village of Sultan Yaakov. Opposing them were two armored brigades of the Syrian 10th Division plus guerrillas from the Popular Front for the Liberation of Palestine – General Command (PFLP-GC).

In what turned out to be a devastating Syrian ambush, some of the forward elements were cut off from their column. The trapped Israelis fought it out during the night of Thursday 10 June 1982 while their main body massed artillery units to support a breakout the next morning.

The surrounded Israelis broke out as planned on Friday 11 June 1982 covered by an artillery box. As the Israelis left, the Syrians worked quickly, pulling bodies from still-serviceable Israeli tanks and replacing them with specially-trained Arab crews. The captured tanks were driven onto a waiting low-loader transports parked nearby, which rapidly departed with their prizes.

Palestinian irregulars scoured the battlefield, looting bodies, grabbing Hebrew documents from inside the tanks and policing up the shell-shocked survivors. It was over in a short while and as the hornet-mad Israelis of the follow-on units crashed onto the battlefield, they counted losses of eight M-48A3 (Magach-3) tanks and some 30 soldiers dead or missing. Three of the Israeli tanks were missing.

The Syrian ambush had been orchestrated by the GRU[251], the Soviet Military Intelligence "spooks" and chagrined Israeli intelligence officers knew it immediately. The Russians were after two innovative pieces of hardware on the Israeli tanks: the reactive "Blazer" armor coating the tanks' exterior and the new sabot "dart" anti-tank round for its 105mm gun. The missing crewmen, the most important loss for the Israelis, were simply collateral to the Soviet-Syrian mission and were turned over to the accompanying terrorists.

On their way out of the Bekaa Valley, the victorious Syrians held an ad-hoc little victory parade as they drove through the village of Ayta Al-Fawkhar. There, according to informants, a captured tank along with several Israeli prisoners was displayed to the locals.

Some hours later, when the victorious Arabs reached Damascus, one tank was unloaded and driven under its' own power through the wildly chanting crowds on Beirut Street. Chained to the back of the tank's turret were five Israeli soldiers. Dean Brelis of *Time* magazine along with other reporters witnessed the frenzied celebration and even asked the Syrian authorities for permission to interview the prisoners.[252] An Associated Press photographer took a picture of the spectacle.

*Captured Israeli tank and prisoners chained
on the back of the turret. - AP photo*

Of the six missing crewmen, two – Hezi Shai and
Aryeh Lieberman – were later returned to Israel in a
prisoner exchange and the body of Zohar Lipschitz was
recovered by the Red Cross from the Damascus Jewish
cemetery in September 1983. Zachary Baumel, Yehuda
Katz, and Tzvi Feldman have not been heard from since.
Israeli Intelligence began the painstaking task of trying
to track the missing soldiers, but other than an
occasional hint from the Arab World, it is as if the earth
has swallowed them.

Years later, few observers of the *Spook War*, media or US antagonists, made the connection between the three missing Israeli soldiers and machinations of the Jewish spooks. This thread was missed in the parade of events, but in hindsight, it clearly stands out.

Baumel, Feldman, Katz

The three missing Israelis made their first American, judicial appearance in the Marc Rich case in September 1983, but it was ignored by prosecutors. Again, in the "Brokers of Death" case in 1986, the Israelis made their recovery a quid pro quo for the deal. Still, nobody flashed to it even though the US prosecutors were the same office that worked the Rich case.

At this writing, the three Israeli soldiers have been missing for thirty-one (31) years with no letters, no confirmed sightings, no Red Cross visits, and no word at all on their dispositions. Still they, along with Ron Arad, an Israeli airman captured in 1986, have not been forgotten.

An M-48A3 captured at Sultan Yaakov on display in Damascus

The general consensus is that the three are dead, but if so, the Jews want the bodies. Various Arab governments and terrorists groups want the bodies also, which they can ransom for convicted colleagues currently in Israeli jails. Thus, the scene is set for the latest (known) manifestation of the story.

In 2007, the Mossad went out to recruit a Lebanese Arab by the name of Siad al-Homsi, a veteran of the Soviet Army and a participant in the Battle of Sultan Yaakov back in 1982. In an elaborate scheme of recruitment that lasted over a year and involved several trips to China and Thailand, al-Homsi finally found himself face-to-face with the Israelis spooks in Bangkok.

They wanted to know all about the 1982 battle and if al-Homsi would participate in helping them recover three bodies they believed were buried at the site. The Israelis had the exact coordinates of the graves and al-Homsi was to see to their disinterment, after which the remains would be picked up by others. Matters were agreed to in early 2009, but then in May, before the logistics could be arranged, al-Homsi was arrested by the Lebanese authorities.

Siad al-Homsi (coded INDIAN) was arrested along with Mustafa Ali Awadeh (coded ZUZI) and both were charged with espionage although they did not know each other. The Lebanese credited the superior work of their counter-intelligence as is always the case, but in reality the agents were fingered from the other side ... as is always the case.

Al-Homsi did not deny it. In fact, he gave a taped deposition with a full description of his contacts and their methods. He added, of course, that he fully intended to turn the information over to the authorities once matters developed. He was sentenced to fifteen (15) years in prison, but served only three (3) before being amnestied. Whether or not al-Homsi had the graves' location or if the Lebanese have retrieved the bodies of the missing Israeli youngsters remains unknown.

The Israelis, having lost two agents-in-place, quickly ascertained the source of the leak. It turned out to be a 32-year-old, Australian-born Mossad katza named Ben Zygier and little or nothing would have been known of him had he not committed suicide on 15 December 2010.

The Shin Bet, Israel's internal security agency, arrested Zygier sometime in the summer of 2010 and because of the severe implications of the case, he was confined to the high-security Unit 15 at the Ayalon Prison in Ramla, Israel under the unoriginal name, "Prisoner X." In June, an Israeli judge issued a strict gag order in the matter of Israel vs. John Doe. Even the gag order was classified and there matters stood until December when he was found hanging by a bed sheet in his cell. At that point, an unidentified prison official phoned a journalist friend at Ynet, the Israeli daily.

Ynet published a short piece about the death of "Prisoner X" and that he was Australian. The Shin Bet visited the reporter and clamped down on the story, but it was too late. Various European media began digging, which generated some speculative and downright bizarre coverage, along with some factual tidbits as is normal.

One story circulated that Zygier informed Australian Intelligence that the Israelis were utilizing forged Australian passports, which was indeed the case when the Mossad assassinated the Hamas operative, Mahmoud al-Mabhouh, in Dubai in January of 2010. In spite of the CCTV coverage of the alleged assassination that went viral on the internet, lack of Arab credibility plus several obvious discrepancies in the scenario, [253] rendered a cynical world-view to the accusations. However, four forged Australian passports were utilized, causing the Australians to eject an Israeli diplomat …

probably the Mossad's Chief of Station. Zygier was arrested shortly thereafter.

A variation of the same story had Zygier informing the police of Dubai of the entire plot in exchange for protection after allegedly participating in the al-Mabhouh assassination. Of course the idea that Dubai could protect anyone from the Israelis is a little thin at first or even second blush. In fact, the only seeming connection between Zygier and the al-Mabhouh assassination is the fact that he had four (4) Australian passports, all of them kosher.

Yet another speculated that "Prisoner X" was actually a missing Iranian general who is thought to have been kidnapped by the Mossad. So finally in 2012, the Australian Broadcasting Corporation assigned it to their "Foreign Correspondent" section, which is similar to the American "60 Minutes" and after almost a year of digging, they aired two programs in 2013. The first was entitled "Prisoner X: The Australian Connection" and the second, "Prisoner X: The Secret."

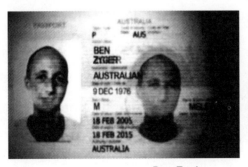 

Ben Zygier

It is alleged that Zygier attempted to double a Hezbollah (Hizb Allah – Party of God) Intelligence officer, but he was outclassed and played by the Arab. According to sources, Zygier fingered the two Lebanese Mossad agents, Ziad al Homsi (INDIAN) and Mustafa Ali Awadeh (ZUZI) in an attempt to establish his bone fides with his Hezbollah recruit. In their second program they interviewed al-Homsi, who flatly stated he had never met Ben Zygier.

To the casual observer, this story appears to be a typical Middle Eastern "goat grope." Awadeh and al Homsi ended up in jail. Zygier and al-Mabhouh ended up dead. The only winner in this story is Dubai Police Chief, LTG Dahi Khalfan Tamim who received his fifteen (15) minutes of fame and about a million hits on his You Tube video. And, the three missing soldiers are still missing.

03 80

The Bickel Papers

"Intelligence Collection Requirements"

(1). Technology Transfers
(2). Arms Trafficking
(3). Narcotics Trafficking
(4). Financial Transactions and Currency Movement
(5). Economic Activity - Commercial Fraud
(6). Fraudulent Passports
(7). Terrorism
(8). Organized Crime

Additional requirements, which address the exportation of reagents and precursor chemicals to foreign "straw" purchasers, is currently being developed and validated by the Regional Intelligence Divisions. "

Department of the Treasury
US Customs Service Memorandum
National Intelligence Collection Requirements
3 June 1989

By 1987, all the noise ... Iran-Contra, the Brokers of Death ... was centered on the National Security Council's CHANNEL TWO. The Israeli-CIA "White Pipeline" (CHANNEL ONE) was rolling right along while the Reagan Administration, independent of the NSC, was pumping arms into Iraq. And, it was this support of Saddam Hussein that had a number of folks worried.

Even Jonathan Pollard's radical actions in the face of this "Level Battlefield Doctrine" were based on his belief that Israel might be able to partially negate the threat. And, there were other Americans, some of whom were within Law Enforcement, who also saw the organized trade and technology transfers to Iraq as a threat and tried to do something to stop it. In the final analysis, they, like Jonathan Pollard, were right, but also paid an unconscionable price for their actions. One of the most hideous examples happened in the United States Customs field office in Houston, Texas.

Robert F. Bickel, Sr. was a Petroleum Engineer by training and a bit of a wildcatter by inclination. He started his "business career" as a commercial salvage

Bob Bickel

(hard hat) diver in Galveston, Texas after graduating from college.

While living and working in Galveston, Bickel met and befriended a young US Customs agent named Kenneth C. Brumfield. They ate and drank together in the early days and often exchanged information on the happenings around the port.

In the mid-1970s, Bickel decided to take an engineering job in Lima, Peru and Ken Brumfield dutifully introduced him to case officers from the Central Intelligence Agency. Bickel would neither confirm nor deny his relationship with the Agency, but official government documents carry him as a "contractor" handled out of the CIA's STATION LIMA. It was, after all, the time of the "troubles" with the "Shining Path" guerrillas in Peru.

It is said that Bickel was implicated in the mysterious deaths of several Cuban "advisors" to the Peruvian National Liberation Movement. While no formal accusations were ever made on the government level, he quietly left Peru after only a year or so in-country. He soon surfaced in Mexico City working as an Engineering Consultant to Pemex, the national oil company of Mexico.[254]

When he returned to Texas in the late 1970s, Bickel hooked back up with his old friend, Special Agent Ken Brumfield, who was by then a rising star in the US Customs Service based in Houston. As the years rolled by, Brumfield would contact Bickel from time to time, usually so he could review some bit of raw intelligence data and analyze it for the Customs Service. Bickel, as Brumfield well knew, was a talented analyst.

By 1981, Bickel seems to have been mixed up, through some old Agency contacts, with supplying the Contras. According to invoices that later surfaced in the Iran-Contra investigation, Bickel supplied electrical cables, transformers and related equipment needed for remote airstrips in Central America. During this time, he was also supporting his family with small, but financially lucrative deals in the "all bidness."

In 1985, Bob Bickel purchased a bankrupt former CIA proprietary called Commercial Helicopters, Inc. in Baton Rouge, Louisiana. He ran the company for almost a year, during which time CHI operated a remote Bell

Maintenance Station in Honduras. Unfortunately, Bell Textron decided shortly thereafter that it had waited too long for payment on its helicopters and closed him down.[255]

As noted above, his name did surface in the Iran-Contra investigations, but his role and that of CHI remains sketchy and unfocused. All he would say about his activities during this time period was "the Boland Amendment[256] made me nervous." Whatever the case may be, Bob Bickel took his licks, walked away and went back to work.

He returned to school in 1986 and began chipping away at an advanced degree in psychology, working toward his license in the State of Texas. He was still supporting himself and his family with small oil deals, one of which was destined to change his world.

In 1987, Bickel made a small purchase of North Sea, waste-crude from the bottom of an oil tanker at Texas City, the Port of Houston. When he arrived at the dock to pick up his purchase, he found that someone had pumped out his crude oil and absconded with it. Ever the anal retentive analyst, Bickel took a sample of his lost oil, looking for clues as to why someone might steal his oil-saltwater mixture.

Much to his surprise, his lab informed him that the oil was not North Sea crude at all, but rather Libyan light. It was at the time of the Rabta Chemical Plant embroilment with Libya and Bickel knew full well that no one was supposed to be importing Libyan crude oil.[257]

"A call to Ken Brumfield for lunch and a discussion was indicated," he explained.

At the time of Bickel's call, Ken Brumfield had risen to the position of Regional Director for Interdiction Programs. Brumfield confided in Bickel that while everyone was looking toward Libya as the arch-villain du jour, US Customs in Houston was worried about the amount of "dual-use" material and technology being shipped to Iraq. Customs is the law enforcement agency charged with the responsibility for policing illegal business dealings, including "technology transfers" and "dual-use" exports.

Over the next two years, Brumfield carefully documented the amount of trade between the United States and Iraq emanating from his region. He had many meetings with Bob Bickel, mostly concerning technical matters, which often required Bickel to provide a written analysis to US Customs. Bickel officially went on the Customs payroll in 1989 as a contract analyst, assigned specifically to the Iraqi "account."

It was during this time frame that Bickel began to circulate among the local Iraqi graduate students, who seemed particularly interested in open source literature on nuclear weapons. He deduced that their efforts might have been directed from Baghdad[258] and through these students, Bickel eventually sourced

a five-page shopping list of items the Iraqis were trying to purchase in the United States. The list included a variety of tactical radios and specialized testing equipment for applications in a physics laboratory. Bickel

311

also remembered that the Iraqis were interested in the radar of the Patriot SAM system (MIM-104).

US Customs technical specialists were called in to review the list and educate the field agents. "We had a lot of meetings with the tech agents," Bickel recalled. "When we opened communications with them (the Iraqis) we had to walk the walk and talk the talk."

Posing as arms dealers, the Customs agents began telexing the Iraqis. "It was all done through TRW," Bickel explained, "so you know the Agency (CIA) was in the loop."

"We could have taken 'em down big-time, but in the summer of 1990, the operation *went south*," Bickel told us.

In 1990, a group of former spooks, informally known as "The Brown Helmet Society," rallied around an ex-player named Richard Brenneke when he was indicted for perjury in Denver.[259] It was part and parcel of a then-blossoming scandal that would become known as the "October Surprise."[260] Bickel, whose analytical abilities were well known, was pressed into service by Brenneke's defense team[261] and he began to commute between Houston and Denver.

In March 1990, Bickel and Brumfield had one of their regular luncheon meetings. Ken Brumfield told Bickel that he was looking into the Welex Division of the Halliburton Corporation, one of the big Texas petroleum multinationals. [262] He passed a Customs Report of Investigation on Halliburton across the table to Bickel.

On the surface, Bickel admits that it made him "nervous" since the Bush Administration was made up of many former oil executives from Texas. Then Brumfield asked Bob Bickel a fateful question: "What is a pulse neutron generator and why would Halliburton be shipping so many to the Middle East?"

Bickel thought a minute before answering. "It's an electronic generator for sub-atomic particles, part of a thermal neutron detector. You use it in logging oil wells," he answered.

"Well, that makes sense," Brumfield said, "but, can you use it for anything else?"

Bob Bickel paused, took off his reading glasses and laid them down on the Halliburton Report. He looked Brumfield right in the eyes. "Yes, Kenny," he answered quietly, "You can also use a pulse neutron generator to trigger a nuclear bomb."

Brumfield quickly checked on the pulse neutron generator with a local physics professor at the University of Texas. The professor confirmed Bob Bickel's dual-use statement. Additionally, another report from the Customs Attaché in London confirmed both the Halliburton exports and the dual-use capability of the PNGs.[263]

Ken Brumfield was one of only four Regional Interdiction Directors in the US Customs Service. He was scheduled to present a plan to his three counterparts in Washington in late June 1990. It was a strategy for a nationwide interdiction effort that would be undertaken by Customs against the suppliers of dual-use materials and technologies, most of which seemed to be going to Iraq.

During this time, Bob Bickel was having personal problems. His ex-wife, Jerri, had been diagnosed with terminal cancer and he was sticking close to Houston. So, he began working in the Houston Customs office to prepare chronologies and flow charts for Brumfield's use at the Washington conference.

Taking a report from here and another from there, Bickel soon realized that there was organization to the Iraqi procurement effort, including, ironically, technology transfers for the CONDOR missile project.[264]

No one in the Houston Customs office was aware of the "Level Battlefield Doctrine;" they only knew there was a great deal of organized trade between the United States and Iraq that was at best, legally questionable.

Operating on the old spook maxim that "nothing happens by coincidence," Bickel decided to take out a little insurance. He made a copy of each and every scrap of paper that crossed his desk and squirreled them away for a rainy day. This collection of government documents would soon become known as "The Bickel Papers."[265]

When Brumfield left for the Washington conference on Technology Transfer Interdiction in late June 1990, Iraq was already threatening Kuwait. Brumfield's presentation ... slides, analyses, charts, graphs ... painted a fairly complete and alarming picture of the Iraqi procurement effort in the United States.

Brumfield also felt that his timing was perfect since many of his shipments could be tied into the illegal financing then being uncovered in the BNL investigation in Atlanta.

What Bickel and Brumfield did not know in June of 1990, was the Bush Administration was working hard to limit the damage being caused by American law enforcement agencies to the "Level Battlefield Doctrine." Two of the administration officials heavily involved in this "damage control" were the Attorney General, Richard Thornburgh, and the Secretary of the Treasury, Nicholas Brady ... Ken Brumfield's ultimate boss. The last thing these two men needed was to allow the US Customs field office in Houston to further feed the expanding BNL scandal.

Bickel's sixth sense kicked in the day Brumfield left for Washington and he prudently took his paperwork with him when he left the Customs office. That afternoon, he made several copies of "The Bickel Papers" at Kinko's, posted some to mail drops, sent copies to trusted friends, and secreted a few in and around the Houston area. He then went home and removed every scrap of paper that could be traced back to US Customs ... just as a precaution.

Ken Brumfield was busy setting up the slide projectors and arranging his display materials in the conference room at US Customs headquarters in Washington when he was called into an executive's office. He was told to immediately return to Houston and leave all of his material on the Technology Transfer Interdiction program there at headquarters. When

Brumfield asked why he was being sent back to Houston a mere two hours before the long-awaited conference was to begin, he was informed that a Federal Grand Jury had indicted him for Perjury.[266]

Brumfield managed to get in a call to his attorney to apprise him of the situation. His lawyer, Ron Tonkin, was a former Assistant United States Attorney, knew the drill and immediately called Bob Bickel to warn him. Several hours later, just as it was getting dark, US Customs agents, Harris County Sheriff's deputies and Houston Police showed up at Bickel's residence with arrest and search warrants. They wanted him on state charges of Defrauding an Innkeeper[267] and a search was evidently required to find the incriminating bills from the hotel. It was "almost embarrassing," an FBI agent would later tell us. "It didn't even have the panache of Mopery with Intent to Loon."

As the large entourage of federal and state law enforcement officials entered his residence to conduct their search, Bob Bickel watched from a vantage point across the street in a neighbor's home. He had no idea what the charges might be, but he knew he was going to jail. After the police officers left, Bickel slipped out and the old spook vanished into the night.

Robert Bickel went to ground in the only community he knew would never betray him, that loose grouping of old intelligence operatives mentioned above and generally referred to as "The Brown Helmet Society."[268]

Interestingly, the US Customs service considered Bob Bickel an employee who was *off the reservation,* and the manhunt for him was led by Special Agent Maxine Zacardy from the Internal Affairs division of the Houston field office. Zacardy concentrated her search for the *master defrauder of innkeepers* around the Houston area while Bickel looked on curiously from his refuge at the home of Richard Brenneke, outside Portland, Oregon.

When the American policy toward Iraq abruptly changed a week after the invasion of Kuwait, Bickel saw his opening. The US Customs service found out about "The Bickel Papers" in a front-page article in the *Houston Chronicle.* It was a shot through the heart and Customs Internal Affairs in Houston spun out beyond berserk.

Bickel, however, had only begun and he went after Customs with a vengeance. As one observer laughingly recalled to us, "He (Bickel) tortured them (Customs) so long, they thought it was a career." Soon, Congressional staffers picked up Bickel's planted media articles and he supplied crucial information that embarrassingly surfaced in hearings. [269] Lawsuits also began to emerge naming Iraqi suppliers and agents as defendants and were backed up with official government documents from "The Bickel Papers."

Always the proper gentleman, Bickel would occasionally call his ex-good friend, Special Agent Jack Bigler in the Houston Customs office, to discuss the problem. Bigler was in charge of Strategic Investigations and had worked closely with Bickel and Brumfield until the "big dump" hit them. Bigler, now eager to distance himself from his two former friends, often traced Bickel's calls attempting to locate him. Several times, he traced the call back to the switchboard of the General Accounting Office, the investigative arm of Congress, in Washington. Bigler dutifully reported this to Special Agent Mark Conrad, Chief of Internal Affairs and Maxine Zacardy's boss in Houston.

Everyone knew that Bickel could not stay beyond the clutches of the federal government forever, not with every federal agent on earth turning over every rock looking for him. Never mind that it was only a State of Texas charge, everyone in "The Brown Helmet Society" knew that it was only a matter of time if "Bick" would not leave the country. A false "shoe" (identity) was never the problem, but Bob Bickel's attitude was "screw it, nobody runs me out of my own country."

Early on, Bickel had given Jack Bigler the phone number of his attorney in Oklahoma City, in case US Customs ever needed to get in touch. That was a mistake. In December 1990, Maxine Zacardy and a group of US Customs agents traveled to Oklahoma City. In desperation, without a warrant and all that implies, the Customs agents simply tapped the attorney's phone lines and waited for Bickel to call.

On the afternoon of 19 December 1990, Bickel called his Oklahoma attorney, Mike Johnston. At 9:30 that night, 21 law enforcement officers led by US Customs agents kicked in all three doors of a nondescript house in North Houston and arrested Robert Bickel on the state charge of Defrauding an Innkeeper.

They then took the house apart in a search that went on for hours, but it turned out to be a dry hole.

Bickel got no trial, which is the way of these matters in *The Trades*. (*Why would he need a silly ol' trial that might have proved an embarrassment to the federal government?*) He was just quietly tucked away in the Harris County jail for the next ten months for his sins.

It was time that could have been completely lost, but Bickel, knowing that US Customs was really jonesing hard for his purloined documents, began to play that card. First, utilizing the "hide in plain sight" rule, he had a complete package of the "Bickel Papers" FedExed to himself at the Harris County jail. He had to re-familiarize himself with his trading goods, he told us.

He had more than twenty packages of documents stashed around the United States and could afford to lose a few as the price of some "field trips" out of jail. Maxine Zacardy of Customs was happy with the progress she was making retrieving Bickel's documents. She had no idea that there were over 20 copies.

So, the Customs agents would pick up Bob at the Harris County jail, take him to their air station where they kept a civilian wardrobe for him. He would change into a suit or sometimes blue jeans, they would all get into a US Customs airplane ... a King Air or a small jet ... fly off to pick up one of Bickel's packages and make a day of it.

Sometimes Bickel would take his two sons; sometimes he and the Customs agents would travel alone. They flew to Denver, New Orleans and

Washington among other cities on these "field trips." Bickel would sum it up by telling us simply, "It helped pass the time."

Meanwhile, Ken Brumfield was convicted of lying to a federal grand jury about three stolen parrots, sentenced to probation, fired from the Customs Service and the US Customs effort to halt the illegal arms shipments and technology transfers to Iraq came to an abrupt end. Never again before the Gulf War would US law enforcement attempt to enforce the export regulations and crack down on the Iraqi trade, for the Bush Administration had simply negated the Rule of Law, making it too risky for anyone to do their jobs.

The lessons of the Bickel-Brumfield matter are self-evident and double-edged. There were people in US law enforcement agencies that instinctively knew the dangers and cared enough to risk everything in trying to halt the illegal American exports to Iraq. There were just not enough of them.

C3 80

The BABYLON Gun

"A Canadian citizen with U.S. nationality came to Iraq. ... But nobody spoke of human rights of this Canadian citizen of U.S. nationality. After he came to Iraq, they killed him."

Saddam Hussein
March 1990

Dr. Gerald Bull had just returned to Belgium from a long business trip to the Middle East on 22 March 1990. His assistant had picked him up at the Brussels Airport and dropped him off at his apartment in the quiet suburb of Uccle so he could rest and clean up before going into his office. It had been a successful trip and he was carrying a $20,000 cash payment from his customer, the Government of Iraq.

Bull took the elevator to the sixth floor of his apartment building and walked down the hall carrying his luggage. He did not notice two men lurking in the hall's alcove beyond the elevator. As he reached the door to his apartment, Bull fumbled with his keys and the two men approached him from behind. As he inserted his key into the lock, the "shooter," raised a silenced .22 caliber automatic pistol and stitched Jerry with five rounds. Dr. Gerald Bull was dead before he collapsed on the floor in front of his apartment door. The second man, the "sweeper," had counted the shots and quickly picked up the expended cartridge casings.[270]

The two men then quietly walked down the back steps of the apartment building, exited through a rear garden area, and entered a waiting car.

Shortly thereafter, Jerry's body was discovered lying in a pool of blood, and the authorities were summoned. The Belgian Surete (Federal Police) soon ascertained through Interpol that Dr. Gerald Bull had a criminal record. He had served a short sentence in an American federal prison for violation of the Neutrality Act, read: arms smuggling. Jerry Bull, like Carlos

Cardoen, was a former CIA facilitator who had been thrown to the wolves.

They also discovered that Dr. Bull was a brilliant, if somewhat errant, Canadian ballistics engineer, who owned Space Research Corporation (SRC) and was involved with the military build-up of Iraq. Based on this, the Belgian authorities assumed that it was a case of political execution. They also noted that Jerry Bull's killers had not taken the $20,000 in cash he was carrying, indicating there was no motive other than his death.

Dr. Bull had apparently been warned in advance that his dealings with Saddam Hussein were not in his best interests. In the months before his death, several old friends in the arms trade who were known to have covert connections to Israel had visited Bull. In early 1990, a group of Israeli diplomats from their embassy in Paris visited Jerry at his apartment in Brussels. Michael Bull, Jerry's son, stated that his father had been "very nervous" after these visits.

Dr. Gerald Bull's journey to the rendezvous with his assassins began two years before when he signed a contract with Saddam Hussein's Iraq. It was known to the Iraqis as PROJECT 839 and involved the revamping of the Iraqi Army's artillery system after the Iran-Iraq War. Under this program, Bull arranged the purchase of some new G-5 155 mm artillery pieces through Cardoen Industries in Argentina and some of his special GC-45 "Base Bleed," long-range ammunition to go with them.

A byproduct of PROJECT 839 was the work Space Research Corporation received helping to modify Iraq's Scud-B missiles to increase their range. There is evidence to believe that Bull did the mathematical

SRC's BABYLON Gun set up at Jabal Hamran and a close up of the breech.

validation on the modified Scuds using the supercomputers at Aberdeen Proving Grounds in Maryland.[271]

The centerpiece of the PROJECT 839 contract, however, was the research, development and construction of a new, 600mm super gun by the Canadian ballistics genius. Later dubbed the "Doomsday Gun" by the press, SRC's BABYLON gun weighed 2,100 tons, was 512 feet long and could throw a two-ton, rocket-assisted shell more than 1,000 miles.

Dr. Christopher Cowley, SRC's chief engineer, later told the BBC's Panorama program in justification, "this was a very, very large cake that had to be cut up. We are talking not millions or hundreds of millions ... we are talking about billions of pounds. And every European government wanted their share of that cake." As is the way of these matters, the British indicted Cowley after the Gulf War when the affair became public.

The BABYLON gun project was near completion when Bull was killed, and only awaited the arrival of the last eight sections of the gun barrel. SRC had already completed a prototype gun, known as BABY BABYLON, which was successfully test-fired and later found in place by UN inspectors at Jabal Hamran in the Iraqi Mountains, 90 miles north of Baghdad. BABY BABYLON had an estimated range of 400 miles.

Sadly, the death of Jerry Bull deprived the world of one of the most inspired artillery geniuses, no matter who he was then serving. Brilliant and cagey, Bull carried most of his expertise to the grave. Because of this loss of knowledge, along with his ultimate failure and spectacular downfall, supergun artillery may have forever perished with him.

His death and the subsequent and timely confiscation of the last eight sections of the super gun barrel on 10 April 1990 in Teesport by British Customs,

Dr. Gerald Bul

strongly suggested a connection. The fact that British Customs knew the location and parts played by other European suppliers, is a clear indication that somebody's spooks had the matter clearly defined. Who supplied the information on Bull's supergun is a matter of conjecture, but in the end, it triggered the total collapse of the British effort to clandestinely arm the Iraqis.

One of the defendants in the government's rather obligatory prosecution in the supergun matter was Matrix Churchill Corp of Coventry. Three directors of the company, Paul Henderson, Peter Allen and Trevor Abraham were charged with violating Britain's Export Laws and the Embargo on weapons to the warring parties in the Iran-Iraq War.

In November of 1992, the trial opened in the Old Bailey, but matters *went south* rather quickly when it was discovered that one of the defendants, Paul Henderson, was acting as an agent of MI-6, reporting on

Iraqi capabilities and intentions. Henderson had been recruited into British Intelligence at the behest of Mark Gutteridge, the firm's export manager who left in 1988. As matters turned out, Gutteridge was an MI-5 agent working inside Matrix Churchill. Shortly after these disclosures in open court, the Crown's case collapsed.

It had all the earmarks of an Israeli operation. In many ways, it was reminiscent of Israel's pre-emptive strike on Iraq's nuclear reactor just before it went "hot" almost nine years before.

C3 80

CHAPTER 9

AGENTS OF INFLUENCE

"What happened is usually known to those who should know and whoever does not know should continue not knowing."

Shimon Peres
Prime Minister of Israel

Nice Jewish Boys

*"Those seeking full truth in news, alas,
Are drilling for oil but striking gas."*

Martin Hauan

It is a common myth that intelligence agencies never use journalists to do their bidding. It is also common myth that journalists are too ethical to get involved, that they will not violate the public trust, and slant their stories to the benefit of one side's agenda. According to Carl Bernstein, writing in *Rolling Stone,* over 400 American journalists have secretly carried out assignments for the CIA over the previous 25 years. The Church Committee found that in February 1976, fifty American journalists were still on the CIA payroll.[272]

The rewards for "cooperation" are too alluring for journalists to ignore on principle and center around access, which leads to career successes and celebrity. Unbiased reporting translates into "non-cooperation," which translates into "non-access." That is the way the game is played. During the *Spook War*, journalists were employed by all parties as agents of influence.

Two good examples of journalists used by the American side in the *Spook Wars* are Wolf Blitzer and Seymour Hersh. We are spotlighting these two individuals because they were both Jewish and they both rode the Jonathan Pollard case, advocating the position of the American Intelligence Community. Both then moved on to bigger and better things.

During the Reagan Administrations, Wolf Blitzer was a correspondent in Washington for the *Jerusalem Post,* Israel's only English-language daily. He was also a contributor to *Heritage,* the Southwest Jewish Press out of Los Angeles.

After Jonathan Pollard was arrested and began cooperating with the authorities, Blitzer wangled two interviews with him in order to write contemporaneous articles for *The Jerusalem Post* and a book on the case. [273] Pollard agreed to the interviews because of Blitzer's connection to Israel and because the spy had no other opportunity to present his position publicly.

On 20 November 1986, Blitzer arrived at the Federal Correctional Institute in Petersburg, Virginia with a camera and tape recorder. Federal authorities approved the interview and Naval Intelligence personnel were present, making sure Pollard revealed no classified information. Blitzer's article was published the following day in *The Jerusalem Post.*

Wolf Blitzer interviewed Jonathan Pollard a second time on 29 January 1987. Like in his first interview, Blitzer brought in a camera and a tape recorder with the permission of the federal authorities. One of the prison officials present during this second interview even took a picture of Blitzer with Pollard, which later appeared in his book.

When Pollard was sentenced on 4 March 1987, the government proffered to the sentencing judge, Aubrey E. Robinson, that the Blitzer interviews had been unauthorized and that Pollard had breached the plea agreement by allowing them. Pollard's behavior in the matter, the government stated, showed that he was arrogant, unwilling to yield to any authority and dangerous.[274] This was the public excuse the judge used to throw out Pollard's plea agreement and sentence him to life in prison.

Blitzer's book, *TERRITORY OF LIES*, was published in 1989. The Pollard camp was not happy with the book, which portrayed Jonathan as a bumbling "Sergeant Schultz" character. It was Blitzer's second book, but his unfamiliarity with *The Trades* was evident in many inaccurate details. These inaccuracies were set out by Pollard who subsequently hand-wrote a 103-page critique of *TERRITORY OF LIES*, on a page-by-page basis, for his attorney, Alan Dershowitz.

The American Intelligence Community, however, seemed fully satisfied with Wolf Blitzer's book, touting it as the "definitive" work on the case. Shortly thereafter, Blitzer left the *Jerusalem Post* and became a television reporter for CNN. Not surprisingly, he was assigned to cover the Pentagon. His fortunes have steadily risen from there.

The case of Seymour Hersh is far more complex and longer in duration. It is generally accepted in the Jewish community that Hersh is the Defense Department's "boy," since his attacks on Israel and Jonathan Pollard parrot the false accusations of the American Intelligence Community.

Interestingly, it is rather easy to associate the pronouncements of Caspar Weinberger and others with Seymour Hersh. And while it is a rather tedious recital of details, it was and is part and parcel of the *Spook War.*

It was a daisy chain of disinformation that can be traced back to the original 1987 proffering of then-Secretary of Defense, Caspar Weinberger. The first manifestation of anything unusual can be found in Weinberger's still-classified, ex-parte memorandum to Jonathan Pollard's sentencing judge.[275]

There was also the accusation that the US Attorney, Joseph diGenova, told the sentencing judge Pollard was also working as a spy for South Africa, which was rather convenient since the judge, Aubrey Robinson, was an African-American. This assertion conveniently faded away when it became public.

Another accusation was that Pollard turned over the National Security Agency's RASIN manual to Israeli Intelligence. A brief explanation is in order.

RASIN stands for Radio Signals and Intercept Notations and the NSA's manual is a multi-volume affair, which is never allowed anywhere in its entirety. Each volume is a loose-leaf notebook of sorts, which is updated constantly with the frequencies of every type of transmitter, radar, microwave relay, or the like in every country in the world. In this manner, it is easier for the signal spooks to eavesdrop on foreign communications and because that is what the National Security Agency is all about, RASIN is its "Holy of Holies."

RASIN is so highly classified that even NSA employees who use it daily are never allowed to work with more than one volume at a time. It is therefore necessary to believe that somehow Jonathan Pollard, a lowly GS-12, managed to get his hands on the entire manual, move it from NSA at Fort Meade to NISC at Suitland and then deliver it to the Israelis. Never mind that countries change their communications frequencies daily, which is why RASIN must be constantly updated.

For serious researchers, the RASIN accusation is a non-starter. For journalists like Seymour Hersh, it is nonsense that is written over and over as truth until some readers actually believe it, as we shall see.

Still another Weinberger allegation has been regurgitated each time the Pollard case has hit the media during the almost 30 years of his incarceration. This is the charge that Israel traded American intelligence secrets to the Iranians in exchange for Persian Jews. This allegation withered when the accuser, Caspar Weinberger, faded from the political scene with his reputation for honesty in tatters. It was however, too good a notion to simply toss out, so it was modified and refloated.

In December of 1987, two years after the Pollards were arrested, a United Press International (UPI) story appeared that put a new spin on the old Weinberger charge. Citing (unnamed) U.S. intelligence analysts, the story stated that Israel traded American intelligence secrets, sourced from Pollard, "to the Soviet Union in return for the promises to increase immigration of Soviet Jews." One is obliged to point out that these are the same intelligence analysts who have managed an almost perfect record for misjudging every major development in the post-World War II world, including, but not limited to, the collapse of the Soviet Union and Nine-Eleven.

This tidbit of information seems to have come originally from the head of counterintelligence of the CIA's Soviet Division, Aldrich Ames. The official US Justice Department damage assessment in the Pollard case never made mention of any information that would be even remotely useful to the Soviets, therefore most informed observers simply dismissed this bizarre allegation out of hand.

Adding to its disingenuous nature, the accusation came in the middle of the Iran-Contra investigation, which itself was a direct result of the *Spook War*. On balance, it was seen for exactly what it was, an attempt by elements within the American Intelligence Community to damage Israel by disinformation to the media.

Six years after Pollard's incarceration, this old allegation surfaced once again. There was a new, "clean" accuser, a new spin had been put to it, but it was the same old charge, warts and all.

Seymour Hersh was a free-lance journalist who broke the story of the massacre at My Lai 4 during the Vietnam War. He went on to win the Pulitzer Prize for it in 1970.

In 1972, he went to work for *The New York Times.* In 1986, Hersh was one of the first journalists to call Panamanian strongman, Manuel Noriega, a drug trafficker. His article appeared on the front page of *The New York Times* the day after Noriega arrived in the United States on an official visit.[276] The CIA eventually abandoned its erstwhile agent and he was later indicted, tried and jailed for drug trafficking.

By 1991, Hersh was the new agent for the prosecution in the ongoing battle over Jonathan Pollard. That October, Hersh published his book THE SAMSON OPTION, [277] which he intended to be an expose on Israel's nuclear weapons program. Since the subject of his book was nuclear weapons and Pollard was never accused of passing any sort of American nuclear secrets to Israel, it was a long stretch for Hersh to include the convicted Israeli spy in his story. In the end, however, it proved to be no hill for the stepper. To wit:

"Pollard indeed spied for Israel out of misguided loyalty - and for money - but none of the other widely held beliefs about the case are true. He was Israel's first nuclear spy." [278]

It is at this point that Hersh reveled in a little character assassination of Pollard, using fabricated and unattributed "facts," before he stated that Pollard provided Israel with American nuclear targeting information, which was exchanged by Israeli Prime Minister Yitzhak Shamir for Soviet Jews.

Like the RASIN manual accusation, it was a shocking "revelation" for the uninformed. And, like the RASIN matter, it does not bear up under scrutiny. For anyone who has even a nodding acquaintance with military affairs, the very idea that Jonathan Pollard would even have access to the US Strategic Library Bombing Index, as the target list is called, is beyond ludicrous ... it is moronic and bizarre ... even for Seymour Hersh.

We were also hard pressed to see any real value this might have to the Soviets, who after all, could find little use for this information. Suppose, for the sake of argument that Pollard passed on a list of Soviet cities targeted for American nuclear strikes, and that Shamir passed this to the Soviets. And suppose that the Soviets *did not* know that Moscow was a target. Could they move the city and hide it somewhere in the woods?

Yevgeni Primakov, alleged by Hersh to have been the Soviet receiver of the information called the story "utter nonsense." Yitzhak Shamir, through a spokesman called it "an outright lie" and the late Yitzhak Rabin stated that Israel never received any such information (from Pollard).[279] Then in December of 2000, Vladimir Karyoshkov, the head of KGB during the entire Pollard affair and beyond, stated:

"The KGB never received any information whatsoever from Israel or from the Israeli Mossad, whose source was Jonathan Pollard, or from any other source. It never happened."[280]

One can reasonably assume that this Weinberger-Hersh accusation is thus summarily dismissed, but Hersh had attempted to wrap his disingenuous scenario in whole cloth by pointing to an impact of this alleged Pollard-Shamir treachery:

"One senior American intelligence official confirmed that there have been distinct losses of human and technical intelligence collection ability inside the Soviet Union that have been attributed, after extensive analysis, to Pollard. 'The Israeli objective (in the handling of Pollard) was to gather what they could and let the Soviets know that they have a strategic capability - for their survival and to get their people out (of the Soviet Union),' one former CIA official said. 'Where it hurts us is our agents being rolled up and our ability to collect technical intelligence being shut down. When the Soviets found out what's being passed' - in the documents supplied by Pollard to the Israelis - 'they shut down the source.'" [281]

The teaser in play here is Aldrich Ames and while we do not know any of Hersh's sources, it is a good bet that Ames was one. The "former CIA official" quoted by Hersh may have believed this to be true. The CIA's agents were being rolled up in the Soviet Union at the time ... all of them ... but true to form, their "extensive analysis" was erroneous. Putting aside the fact that Pollard never even got close to these ill-fated, CIA agents' names, the chiseled-in-stone mindset against him and the Israelis ultimately protected the now-legendary, Soviet killer-spy known as NIGHTMOVER. In fact, CIA's analytical geniuses actually cost the lives of even more American operatives and in the end, the Director of Central Intelligence, James Woolsey, was forced to resign over the matter.

Not to belabor the point, but several of the CIA's Soviet operatives, who were exposed and executed, were not even recruited until *after* Pollard was incarcerated. Yet, up until 1994, nine years after his arrest, the Central Intelligence Agency was still pointing an accusatory finger at Jonathan Pollard. Perhaps it was a legacy from the *Spook War*, but we only learned the truth in 1994 when the FBI arrested Aldrich Ames. The infamous NIGHTMOVER turned out to be just another CIA official.[282]

As bad as the Agency's institutional anti-Semitism clouded its analytical judgment, there were those in Washington who knew the truth and were not afraid to inform the press, especially after Seymour Hersh's outrageous allegations in *THE SAMSON OPTION*.[283]

A certain "Washington official" familiar with the Pollard case told *Time* Magazine in 1991 "the spy did not provide such (Soviet targeting) data to Israel."[284] In 1995, on the occasion of a Pollard parole hearing, one of the investigators for the Naval Investigative Service, who originally worked on the Pollard matter, made a startling admission. "Ninety percent of the things we accused him of stealing," the NIS investigator told writer John Loftus, "he didn't even have access to."[285]

As to the bizarre accusations made in THE SAMSON OPTION, we agree with the comments by the Editorial Staff of The Jerusalem Post, which wrote, "Hersh's Israel-bashing is so egregious it gives yellow journalism a bad name."[286]

And finally, the arrest and conviction of the NIGHTMOVER,[287] Aldrich Ames, took a large bite out of Seymour Hersh's credibility in 1994. After that, the hits just kept on coming.

In 1997, he published THE DARK SIDE OF CAMELOT. Hersh, it seemed, had been initially suckered into this project by an enterprising former paralegal who peddled him a collection of bogus John F. Kennedy papers. While he did cut out the meat of this book, because it was based on these false papers, he valiantly attempted to recover his main thesis of scandalizing JFK. He drew serious and widespread criticism for his efforts.

During the American-sponsored Middle East Peace conference at the Wye Plantation in Queenstown, Maryland, in October 1998, the Israelis made a number of concessions to the Palestinians at the behest of the Clinton Administration. In return, the Israeli Prime Minister, Benjamin "Bibi" Netanyahu, asked the

337

American President to release Pollard and allow him to be taken back to Israel. The Israeli request for clemency came as no surprise to the Americans and the Palestinians, but the media, in its finest tabloid tradition, shrieked that it was "last minute" and an excuse for the Israelis not to implement the newly reached accords. This press manipulation was orchestrated by the American Intelligence Community and preempted any Israeli retaliation. It was a slick piece of work and illustrated the power of the intelligence bureaucracy to make foreign policy.

Under this media pressure, President Clinton reneged on his promise to release Pollard, but agreed to review the case. Jonathan Pollard, who had already been instructed to pack up his belongings, returned to his cell. The Israelis could not press the issue, which allowed the opposition to gather their forces.

Once again, Seymour Hersh jumped into the fray for the anti-Pollard faction of the American Intelligence Community in an all-too-apparent attempt to influence President Clinton's review of the case. On 18 January 1999, Hersh published an article in *The New Yorker* magazine entitled "The Traitor," which set the tone for his piece.

In this article, his attack was so vicious and so unfounded that he completely alienated the American Jewish community, not to mention the mainstream, non-Jewish public. There is neither room nor reason to counter Hersh's accusations point by point, although that can be easily done. His sources are as usual, vintage Hersh. There is the "retired Navy admiral, the well-placed, intelligence official, the high-ranking ho-hum and the former do-da." They never seem to have names, not even first names like a 1990's cocktail waitress. How then might one check Seymour's sources? The answer is clearly that they cannot be checked.

Hersh moves Jonathan Pollard all the way from a "misguided young man," through the underachiever who was always picked last for the ball team, to the crazed, drug addict depicted in his January article. It is an astounding transition.

Hersh states that Jonathan Pollard had a drug problem that we are to believe influenced his decision to spy for Israel. Forget for the moment that Pollard, as an employee of American Intelligence was subjected to continual drug testing, his only nodding acquaintance with drugs was the occasional smoking of marijuana during his college days ... exactly like the last three Presidents of the United States. This came out in his pre-employment interviews and polygraph examinations, yet he was still hired and given a Top Secret security clearance.

The new collection of Hersh allegations was soon embraced by others. A demi-enlightened congressman from the 11th district of Michigan, Fred Upton, was soon parroting them for his personal, political gain.[288] Their adoption, however, was not limited to no-name congressional wannabes. Paul Greenberg, a syndicated editorial writer, jumped right on the bandwagon in September 1999.[289]

In April of 2000, the public became aware of Hersh's latest (and final) disingenuous effort to reclaim the credibility that had eluded him since he wrote about the My Lai Massacre. It bears retelling because it concerns the First Gulf War.

Hersh began working on a new expose, a second My Lai Massacre, in an all-too-apparent attempt to finish his journalistic career with a bang. His new, alleged massacre took place just after the Gulf War cease-fire, when elements of the American 24th (Mechanized) Infantry Division were attacked by units of the Iraqi Republican Guard along Highway 8 between Basra and Baghdad.

The "24th ID" was under the command of General Barry McCaffrey, the most aggressive "ass-kicker" in CENTCOM, if not the entire US Army. Thinking that the American forces in front of them were just a screen, the Iraqis decided to attack in order to force their passage up Highway 8. *Big Mistake.*

Even though he was badly outnumbered, McCaffrey *saddled up, waded in amongst 'em, kicked their asses and took their names.* (The vaunted Republican Guard has always done better against unarmed civilians than against real soldiers.) After a fifteen-minute firefight, McCaffrey allowed the surviving Iraqis to flee into the surrounding desert. His troops then systematically destroyed the Iraqi vehicles, around 600 in total.

Because the engagement took place after the cease-fire, there was an official Army investigation of the incident, which cleared McCaffrey of any wrong doing. Nine years after this engagement, Seymour Hersh decided that American soldiers of the 24th ID had massacred unarmed, Iraqi prisoners on Highway 8.

A brief note is now in order about the nature of Arab soldiers in general and Iraqi soldiers in particular. The toughest Arab soldiers are the Jordanians, followed closely by the Egyptians and the Syrians. For the Iraqi Army, the rule of thumb is when you attack them, only about ten percent will fight, the rest will either run or surrender. During the Gulf War, the Iraqi Army surrendered en masse. They surrendered to helicopters, remotely piloted vehicles and commercial airliners flying overhead. They surrendered to television crews and Saudi street vendors. A lady got out of a taxi on 5th Avenue in New York and 14 Iraqi soldiers surrendered to her. That is their nature.

Lawrence of Arabia once noted that "the Arabs make war because the women are watching" and it is true. Many of the US casualties in the Gulf War came from "friendly fire" accidents and not from the hostile actions of the Iraqi Army. There it is. Generally speaking, they are a pitiful lot and not the sort of enemy prisoners that generate the frustration and anger necessary to shoot them down in cold blood.

Seymour Hersh, who was neither in the Gulf nor has he ever faced an Arab enemy, did not realize that his alleged massacre of POWs, made no sense on its face. It simply did not *walk like a duck* to any reasonable person who had even a nodding acquaintance with Middle East warfare. It certainly did not sit well with the Gulf War veterans, especially those from the 24th ID, who participated in the battle on Highway 8.

Hersh's target, the man he intended to scandalize, was Barry McCaffrey. Unlike the incarcerated Jonathan Pollard and the long-dead President Kennedy, McCaffrey, was not only alive and well, but loved a good fight.

When Hersh began interviewing McCaffrey's old "battle buddies," the retired soldiers turned on the journalist. "I really want to bury this guy," Hersh allegedly told retired Colonel Ken Koetz. According to General James Scott,

Hersh told him that McCaffrey "had destroyed the careers of many officers" and was "universally disliked." General Scott further stated that Hersh told him General John Van Alstyne implicated McCaffrey in military wrongdoing. But, Van Alstyne stated "This is very disturbing, since I have never spoken with Mr. Hersh on any subject."[290] Van Alstyne was clearly another source *that never was.*

In another nice piece of Hershesque "investigative reporting," retired Colonel Justin Hughes stated that Hersh had related a story that McCaffrey had stolen another boy's bicycle when he was eleven years old and living in Fort Leavenworth, Kansas.[291] To us, this had a ring reminiscent of the character assassination of Jonathan Pollard, and like the Pollard allegations, was not true. McCaffrey never lived in Fort Leavenworth.

When Hersh published his "investigative" article, "Overwhelming Force," nobody noticed. Thankfully, his star appears to have waned.

It is true that both Hersh and Blitzer enjoy celebrity that affords some protection from their fellow Jews ... the Israelis do not spill Jewish blood on whims, nor are journalists ever targeted for covert action unless their credentials are only covers for other activities. At worse, they are dismissed as "Judenrat" Jews, a most derogatory of labels. On the other hand, the "gunslingers" from the Iraqi Mukhabarat and their surrogates from the PLO, have no such inhibitions.

Blitzer and Hersh

We believe it is important, therefore to contrast the fate of Hersh and Blitzer, who operated on the side of the Americans, with two British journalists who were bent toward the Israeli view, if not working for Israel during the *Spook War*. Unlike the two American journalists, the two Brits paid with their lives ... part of events that would come to be called the "March Massacre."

C8 80

The March Massacre

"Nothing is ever done in this world until men are prepared to kill one another if it is not done. "

George Bernard Shaw
Major Barbara, Act III

The destruction of the German-built, rocket fuel manufacturing facility at Al-Hillah, Iraq came only short weeks after Iraq and Iran accepted UN Resolution 598, ending their 8-year war. As noted previously, the Al-Hillah plant, which was coded PROJECT 96, was part and parcel of Iraq's CONDOR missile program.

Iranian-born Farzad Bazoft, a British subject working as a journalist for the *London Observer*, and a British nurse, Daphne Parish, were arrested as they were attempting to board a plane for London on 15 September 1989.

Bazoft and Parish had visited the Al-Hillah industrial complex just prior to the explosion that destroyed the rocket fuel facility almost a month earlier. In Bazoft's luggage, Iraqi Mukhabarat agents discovered a test tube containing a soil sample from the Al-Hillah complex.

Interestingly, other British journalists had also visited Al-Hillah just prior to the explosion, including a television crew from Independent Television News in London. Why the Mukhabarat zeroed in on Bazoft and Parish, leaving the other journalists unmolested, has never been definitively ascertained. It may have been because Bazoft was Iranian-born, but a more obvious reason seems to be that one or both of them may have indeed worked for Israeli or British Intelligence. It should be remembered that these two services were working together on the CONDOR matter.

Bazoft and Parish were detained for six months before being brought to trial in March of 1990. Parish was evidently treated humanely, while Bazoft was subjected to strenuous interrogation, which resulted in his "confession" as "a British spy working for Israel," which makes no sense on its face.

The trial of the two Britons took place on 10 March 1990, and Daphne Parish was sentenced to 15 years in prison.[292] Unbeknownst to Bazoft and the rest of the world, he was condemned to death. Twenty minutes before his execution on 15 March 1990, Farzad Bazoft received a visitor, British diplomat Robert Keely, in his Abu Gharib prison cell. It was only then that Bazoft learned his fate.

The media storm that followed the execution of Farzad Bazoft had the pronounced effect of dividing world opinion into Moslem and non-Moslem because the Arab states closed ranks around Iraq. Thus, any attack on Saddam Hussein was decried by the Arab press as an attack on Islam. Many analysts believed this to be a clever ploy by the wily, Iraqi dictator to bolster his support among the Arab states for his future invasion of Kuwait.

The anti-Iraqi media view, however, is dependent upon the unproved supposition that Farzad Bazoft was not an Israeli agent *because* journalists do not work for intelligence agencies.

In order to make the Bazoft Affair "walk like a duck," we must point out another incident - the second in the March Massacre - that may cast further illumination on the events.

Seven days after Farzad Bazoft died on an Iraqi gallows, at the end of the traditional period of Jewish mourning, Dr. Gerald Bull, the father of Saddam Hussein's BABYLON gun, died in a hail of gunfire in Belgium. This episode, which has been previously discussed in detail, was, we speculate, a direct result of a biblical reaction on the part of the Israelis. Saddam Hussein publicly mourned the death of his "friend," Jerry Bull, but March was not yet over and neither was the March Massacre.

In the middle of that fateful month, journalist Jonathan Moyle arrived in Santiago, Chile, for the FIDAE (International Air and Space Fair), the annual Chilean military and aerospace exhibition. Moyle was a former RAF helicopter pilot and the editor of *Defense Helicopter World,* a well-respected, British defense publication.

On 31 March 1990, Moyle was found hanging in the closet of his room at the Hotel Carrera in Santiago. The journalist had been brutally interrogated while tied down to his bed and then administered a sedative by injection. His killers wrapped his lower body in a diaper of sorts fashioned from towels and a plastic bag in an apparent attempt to reduce the smell of death, which might have resulted in his premature discovery.

After hanging the unconscious journalist by his neck in the closet, one of his killers called the hotel switchboard and ordered a taxi in Jonathan's name. They then departed with Moyle's briefcase and two of his files. The unconscious journalist slowly strangled to death.

The following morning, the chambermaid noticed blood on the sheets of his bed and found his body in a subsequent search of the room. The reactions of both the Chilean authorities and the British Foreign Office were clumsy and ill-advised.

Initially, the Chilean police declared Moyle's death a suicide and British bureaucrats even hinted darkly about some sort of bizarre sexual practice that had gone horribly wrong. It was an all-too-obvious attempt to smear Moyle's name, but it had the opposite effect. His media colleagues struck back with a vengeance concentrating on Cardoen Industries and the Chilean government in their investigations. When the two key witnesses, the hotel's chambermaid and switchboard operator, disappeared, [293] the journalists went wild.

The findings of a subsequent Coroner's Inquest, combined with the efforts of Moyle's journalist colleagues, destroyed the lies of both the Chilean and British governments. In the media, the blame came to rest on Cardoen operatives, but within *The Trades,* Moyle's murder had all the earmarks of the Iraqi

Mukhabarat, specifically its assassination unit known as "Office 8."

Moyle, as it turned out, was not only covering the FIDAE exhibition for his magazine, but was engaged in an in-depth investigation of Industrias Cardoen. It was an open secret that Carlos Cardoen was involved in an illegal transfer of a number of American-made Bell 206 helicopters to Iraq and Moyle, apparently, was *on the case*. For who Moyle might have been working, other than his magazine, was another question.

Had Moyle published a story on the illegal transfer of American helicopters to Iraq, the Bush Administration might have been forced to take some sort of action. Carlos Cardoen and his client, Iraq, would have suffered as well. In the scheme of things, these three "interested parties" would have gained a great deal by Moyle's untimely death.

British Intelligence stridently disagreed with the pronouncements of their own Foreign Office in the Moyle Affair. To their credit, they provided Moyle's family with enough factual ammunition to force a written, public retraction of the salacious rumor about an unorthodox sexual practice causing his death.

While neither British nor Israeli Intelligence sources would positively confirm that Jonathan Moyle was in their employ, they came close. A British source told us, "One might be surprised at the level of cooperation between 'Six' (MI-6) and Mossad. Certainly Jonathan had friends in both services." Israeli sources spoke of him in sad, reverent terms as if they had lost a close friend.

Two days after Jonathan Moyle was murdered in Santiago, Saddam Hussein gave a speech in which he publicly mourned the death of Dr. Gerald Bull. In the same speech, he threatened to "burn half of Israel with our Al-kimawi al Muzdawaj (binary chemical weapons)."

Farzad Bazoft and Jonathan Moyle

CS 80

SPOOK WAR

CHAPTER 10

VESPERS

"So it is in the Libyan fable that an eagle, pierced by an arrow, gazed at the feathered shaft and said, 'Not by others, but by our own plumage are we smitten.'"

Aeschylus
Fragments

Scud Thursday

"Cry 'Havoc' and let slip the dogs of war."

William Shakespeare
Julius Caesar

In the weeks leading up to the 15 January 1991 UN deadline in the Gulf, the mood was understandably tense throughout the Middle East. The Israelis labored under the idea of having tactically lost the *Spook War* since, as predicted, it had evolved into a shooting war. They resigned themselves to the fact they were now about to suffer the consequences of the secret American buildup of Iraq. Events were completely out of hand and the Jews were determined to retaliate against Iraq if missiles were launched into Israel.

On the American side, the Bush Administration was tap dancing. It faced the likelihood of Israel entering the war, the Coalition falling apart and an American Army being trapped in the middle. The "worst case" scenarios were mind-boggling. The White House did what it could on the political level, assuring the Israelis that American military muscle would eliminate the Iraqi missile threat to the Jewish State.

The American Secretary of Defense, Dick Cheney, had assured his Israeli counterpart, Moshe Arens, that a significant portion of American air assets had been assigned to cover the missile fields in western Iraq around the old British airbases of H-2 and H-3. As matters turned out, Cheney was either badly misinformed or he simply lied. Central Command in Riyadh had assigned no air assets to "Scud hunting" in Iraq's western deserts.

On 15 January 1991, the Jordanian Government announced that Syria had agreed to come to its aid should Israel attack the Heshemite Kingdom and then called up its reserves. (Some Syrian forces were then serving with the Coalition in the Gulf, emphasizing the problem with the potential entry of Israel into the war.) International airlines suspended all flights to Israel and the Israeli Government closed the nation's schools.

At 2:00 AM (Israeli time) the following morning, CNN began carrying the dramatic and sometimes humorous coverage of the air attacks on Baghdad featuring correspondent Bernard Shaw's commentary from under a table in the El Rashid hotel in downtown Baghdad.

The Israeli cabinet met in Tel Aviv at 9:00 PM local time to hear an evaluation by AMAN of the American air attacks. Contrary to what Cheney had told Arens, American aircraft had not attacked the Iraqi Scud sites threatening Israel. Israeli Intelligence believed that Saddam Hussein would make good on his threat to attack the Jewish State.[294]

It was 3:00 AM, local time, on Friday, 18 January 1991, when Major General Giora Rom[295] came on duty at the Kirya, Israel's Pentagon in Tel Aviv. The Air War against Iraq had been proceeding continuously since the previous day. The Israeli Armed Forces were on Alert Gimmel, full war status, and General Rom was pulling a shift as the National Warnings Officer.

It was still Thursday evening in Washington, DC when a satellite warning came into the National Military Command Center. There had been a multiple Scud missile launch from the western deserts of Iraq and they were headed toward Israel. The Americans flashed the warning to Tel Aviv through the HAMMER RICK secure communications line.[296] General Rom did not hesitate to sound the alarm and for the first time in almost twenty years, the air raid sirens began to wail throughout the Jewish State.

The Israeli population put their children into their gas protection equipment and moved into their "sealed rooms."[297] Their national radio station, Kol Israel (The Voice of Israel), delivered terse orders in multiple languages. "The State of Israel is under ballistic missile attack. Go immediately to your sealed rooms. Place your children into their hoods and cocoons and put on your gas masks. Seal your rooms as practiced and await further instructions."

Within four minutes of receiving the American warning, Scuds began falling on Tel Aviv and Haifa. Israel's National Command structure alerted its nuclear forces for a possible counter-launch against Iraq. As Jericho II missiles were erected in their launchers, American KH-11 satellites swept over the Israeli missile fields and picked up the activity.

The Israeli Air Force scrambled under the attack and Jordanian early-warning radar quickly picked up massive formations of aircraft forming up in Israeli air space, apparently for a strike against Iraq. Moments later, the Jordanian radar systems began to malfunction from the effects of Israeli electronic jamming.[298] Matters were running critical and quickly getting out of hand.

In Richard Cheney's Pentagon office, the secure hot line to Israel - HAMMER RICK - began ringing. The Israeli Defense Minister, Moshe Arens, was calling the Secretary of Defense with a personal update. The Israeli spring was coiled and ready to lash out at the Iraqis, but Israel was holding ... for the moment. Arens emphasized that if any of the Scud warheads contained chemical or biological agents, the Coalition's ball game was over.

Cheney knew the Israelis were not bluffing. From the moment the warning came in, American Naval units in the Mediterranean and the Red Sea watched as the Israeli Command and Control communication nets lit up like Christmas trees. He had open lines to his military attachés in the American embassies in Tel Aviv and Amman where pandemonium was reigning as Israeli aircraft were clearly heading across Jordanian airspace toward Iraq. He also had "real time" intelligence feed from the American satellites and knew that Israel's Jericho II missiles were in launch mode. Cheney had a clear read on the probable scenario. He had also heard the resigned inflections in Moshe Arens' voice and knew the world was teetering on the edge of the nuclear abyss. He immediately called the White House.

Vice President Dan Quayle, Larry Eagleburger, Richard Haas and other Bush Administration insiders were huddled in General Brent Scowcroft's White House office when Dick Cheney called. The Defense Secretary briefed them and added his assessment that there was no way to keep Israel out of the war, most especially if the Scuds contained chemical or biological warheads.

Things looked pretty grim. The most dangerous and threatening of scenarios had reared up in the midst of a Middle East war as their Iraqi enemy played the "Israeli card." The "Level Battlefield Doctrine," begun in the Reagan Administration and continued under President Bush, had finally come home to roost.

If matters were not bad enough, their favorite general, "Stormin'" Norman Schwarzkopf, seemed completely oblivious to the implications of the Iraqi Scuds falling on Israel. CENTCOM minimized the Scud strikes to the press and refused to assign more air assets to the "Scud Hunt" in the western deserts of Iraq. (It turned out that no Coalition aircraft were patrolling the western desert on the night of the first attack on

Israel.) Schwarzkopf's behavior over the Scud issue has been likened to the Captain of the Titanic spending his time busily arranging the deck chairs as his ship foundered. Only extreme pressure from Washington caused Schwarzkopf to pay the appropriate attention to the problem.

Just when matters could get no worse, they did. While Cheney was still on the phone to the White House, a preliminary report came in that the Israeli National Police had determined that one of the Scud warheads that landed in Israel contained the deadly nerve agent, Sarin.[299] There was a long silence. There was no way the Israelis could be stopped now.[300]

"What is three feet deep and glows in the dark?" the old saw held. Answer: downtown Baghdad thirty minutes after Iraq hit Israel with a WMD.

"Worst case" scenarios were gamed out. If Israel "lit up" Baghdad with a nuclear strike, how would the Russians react? If the Russians struck Israel, how would the United States react? The Arab reaction to Israel's entry into the war, even short of a nuclear strike, was completely predictable ... Jihad, Holy War against the Jews ... Coalition or no Coalition. Where then would that leave the 700,000 American troops of Central Command?

During those long hours in Washington, it was "heart attack city with a pucker factor edging above the ten mark."[301] At CENTCOM headquarters in Riyadh, General Schwarzkopf fiddled while a few hundred miles away an angry Jewish hand gripped the nuclear trigger, ready to rain all over his parade.

Then, inexplicably, the Israelis backed down. A collective sigh of relief could be felt as the absolute worst night of the Gulf War passed into history. In the years to come, it would be forever remembered by its American participants as "Scud Thursday."

In an American federal prison, far removed from the action, Jonathan Pollard was both excited and satisfied.[302] He was well aware that his information had triggered the change in Israeli civil defense doctrine that not only protected the population, but also gave Israel's political structure a comfort level that allowed them to stay out of the war. Perhaps never before in the history of espionage had a country reaped such a direct benefit from being spied upon as did the United States on "Scud Thursday."

Saddam Hussein, however, had just begun to play the "Israeli Card," and try as they might, the Americans were completely out-maneuvered by the Iraqis in what came to be known as the "Great Scud Hunt." On their side, the Iraqis had a secret weapon that more than offset the tremendous technological advantage the Americans enjoyed during the war. That secret weapon was a spook, whom the Israelis came to call "Herr Mohammed."

ᑢ ᑐ

Herr Mohammed

"Don't rejoice in his defeat, you men, for though the world stood up and stopped the bastard, the bitch that bore him is in heat again."

Bertolt Brecht

Out in their western deserts, near their border with Jordan, the Iraqis had built 28 Scud launch pads around the old British airbases of H-2 and H-3. The construction of these fixed launch pads was part of an elaborate East German ruse to deceive the Israelis and other potential enemies to the west. The deception program included embellished decoys of Scuds on their launch vehicles, which could not be distinguished from the real thing at 50 feet, much less from overhead.

During the Gulf War, the Iraqi Scud crews utilized some 25 mobile launchers, "shooting and scooting," and hiding out while Coalition aircraft bombed the fixed launch positions and the decoys. In this manner, the Iraqis continually bombarded Israel throughout the war. There was, however, more to the Coalition's unqualified failure to find and destroy Iraq's mobile Scuds ... a great deal more.

Jurgen Gietler was a German who had converted to Islam and was a quiet, but ardent supporter of Iraq during the Gulf crisis. Gietler had even taken the name Mohammed when he found his spiritual enlightenment and was considered quite an "odd duck" among his fellow bureaucrats at the German Foreign Ministry in Bonn where he worked as an archivist.

As a member of NATO and supporter of the Coalition against Saddam Hussein, the German government was briefed daily on the tactical intelligence the Allies were developing prior to the Gulf War. Through his job as the archivist, Jurgen Gietler had access to this intelligence data as it flowed into Bonn from the Americans.

After heavy prodding by Washington, as noted previously, CENTCOM spent time and effort trying to destroy Iraq's mobile Scud launchers to keep the Israelis mollified and out of the fight. To this end, the British deployed five Special Air Service teams from their 22nd SAS Regiment into the western deserts of Iraq in January 1991. Operating behind the Iraqi lines for more than six weeks, these elite British commando units were unable to find any of the mobile Scud launchers. The same held true for American Special Forces teams that had also been sent in.

Additionally, theater surveillance assets including JSTARS, AWACS and U-2 aircraft plus KH-11 satellites were employed by the Americans. In spite of all this, the closest they ever came to finding any of the mobile launchers was when American aircraft spotted several Jordanian gasoline tankers, mistook them for Scud launchers and attacked them. General Schwarzkopf showed a video of this attack in his press briefing on 30 January 1991, and declared a victory. The fact that the "mobile Scud launchers" turned out to be gasoline tankers did not dampen CENTCOM's newly found ardor.

There were several other discoveries of the elusive Scuds, which were promptly attacked, but turned out to be some of the East German decoys. The Scuds continued to fall on Israel ... almost 50 throughout the war.

In the end, the survival of Iraq's mobile Scuds was the only tactical victory Saddam Hussein could claim. CENTCOM continued to play down its importance publicly, but the modified Scuds turned out to be Iraq's most potent weapon.

Although Israel never entered the fray, the whole episode did not bode well for the Americans in their lessons learned from the Gulf War. They knew they had been outsmarted, but they did not know how and it bothered them ... a lot.

Shortly before the Gulf War in August 1990, German BfV counterintelligence agents [303] arrested Jurgen Mohammed Gietler and charged him with espionage. In his subsequent trial, Gietler declared himself a "Martyr for Islam" and expressed pride in his work for Iraqi Intelligence. He was found guilty by the court, sentenced to five years in prison, and released in 1994, completely unrepentant for his actions. After his release, Gietler and his Egyptian wife moved to Cairo.

The Germans are tight-lipped about the Gietler Affair, but we have managed to piece together an overall picture that unfortunately still lacks crucial details. Gietler began his career as a spy in 1993 when he converted to Islam. He started out working for Egyptian Intelligence, but he soon felt that somehow they did not appreciate him. In 1990, he by chance met

General Osmat Judi Mohammed and began his six-month career spying for the Iraqi Mukhabarat.

How the strategic and tactical planning, along with the American Order of Battle and German Intelligence reports found their way into the hands of a middle-level bureaucrat in the German Foreign Ministry is easily explained. Gietler was the archivist and he filed the communications coming into the office from the Pentagon. But, instead of filing them in the archives, he filed them in his briefcase, which he delivered daily to his Iraqi handlers.

Gietler met daily with General Mohammed and passed along what amounted to practically "real-time" intelligence to the Iraqis. This treasure told the Iraqis, among other things, exactly what the Coalition knew and did not know about their mobile Scud launchers, and enabled them to stay one step ahead of CENTCOM's efforts to destroy them.

How the Germans discovered Gietler is also clouded with rumors and agendas. One story holds that it was the Israelis who, while watching the Iraqis, "made" Mohammed with the Iraqi Military Attaché. Yet another states that Gietler was picked up on a BfV wiretap of the Iraqi Embassy.

Whatever the truth may be, it is clear that the survival of the mobile Scud launchers allowed Iraq to play their "Israeli card," which constituted the only real threat Saddam Hussein had that might have turned his overwhelming defeat into a victory.

Gietler's espionage amounted to one hell of an intelligence coup.

"Herr Mohammed" gave the Iraqis the "Israeli card," which ironically was defeated, not by CENTCOM, but by the work of Jonathan Pollard.

Cʒ ঔ

EPILOGUE

I believe in la raison d'etat which may outweigh any conventional morality. As one of the longest-standing leaders of Western Intelligence, I have learned that there are two sorts of history. There is the history we see and hear, the official history; and there is the secret history - the things that happen behind the scenes, in the dark, that go bump in the night..."

Count Alexandre de Marenches
Chief, French SDECE

The American-Israeli *Spook War* is like the proverbial elephant in the living room … the spooks know it's there, but no one talks about it publically. It is quite natural for nation-states to have different interests and agendas that often conflict and this is especially true of allied democracies.

The secret arming of Iraq by the Reagan Administration did present a *clear and present danger* to the State of Israel. And, as matters turned out, to Kuwait and Saudi Arabia as well.

In the battles over this secret agenda, the Americans won. Iraq was able to stave off the Shiite Iranians and build and equip its army to the fourth largest in the world. But, it was not a clean and clear victory. In the subsequent Gulf War that inevitably followed, the United States deployed over 700 thousand troops to force their erstwhile ally out of Kuwait. Within nine years of that war, fully one-third of those American soldiers are classified as disabled, to one degree or another, by the Veterans Administration from service-connected injuries. A great number from undiagnosed illnesses loosely classified as the "Gulf War Syndrome." (That is another story.)

In this modern-day David vs. Goliath narrative, the Israelis did inflict very serious damage on the perpetrators of this secret effort to arm the Iraqi dictator. The overt destruction of Iraq's nuclear facilities at Al Tuwaitha in 1981 guaranteed that the American forces of CENTCOM did not have to face that nightmare ten years later. And, for those who would argue that Saddam Hussein would not have used nuclear weapons, even if he had them, one can only point out what he did to the Kuwaiti oil fields. As it was, those American youngsters faced chemical and biological weapons, but the results are still murky and unfocused. It was their own government that not only armed him with CBW, but also financed it.

Try as it might, there is little indication that Israeli Intelligence had any success in closing down Samara and Salman Pak, the Iraqi CBW plants other than exposing them in the media. There is some evidence that they were able to persuade the Carter State Department to stop the designs, blueprints and materials from being exported from the United States in 1978, at least legally. Again, the Germans stepped into the breach and were able to complete both plants. The Jews were, however, seemingly able to neutralize Iraq's best bioweapons scientist, Dr. Abdul Hindawi.

In the matter of Cardoen Industries, the CIA-backed manufacturer in Chile of the "Rockeye" Cluster Bomb Units for Iraq, the explosion of their plant shined an international spotlight on them and International Signal and Control in Pennsylvania. It eventually led to its closure in 1991 and criminal indictments all around in 1993.

The building of the BABYLON Gun, the upgrading of Iraq's Scud C missiles and various other projects came to a screeching halt with the death of Dr. Jerry Bull in 1990. Within a couple of weeks, British Customs was able to wrap up the whole, far-flung venture. Where Customs obtained the detailed information on operations in five different European countries that enabled them to make a clean sweep of matters is still the subject of speculation, but it did close down the British effort to participate in the clandestine arming of Iraq. The subsequent trial of the involved businessmen in 1992 exposed the duplicity of the British Government.

The CONDOR / SAAD 16 missile project would have completely changed the military balance in the Middle East. The technology transfer investigation opened by Jonathan Pollard had to be simply coincidence. But, the convenient "discovery" of information by Swiss Intelligence that Egypt was shipping regulated materials from Baltimore to Cairo led US Customs to an Egyptian spy ring operating in the United States. Not only did American law enforcement publicly expose German firms operating in negation of their own government's policy on non-proliferation, but they also managed to unseat the Egyptian Minister of Defense. Then the total destruction of Iraq's propellant plant at Al Hillah a little over a year later, closed down the project permanently.

Probably the most effective action was that which took down the Banco Nazionale del Lavoro (BNL) in 1989. This completely cut off Saddam Hussein's funding. In the end, the American taxpayer footed the bill for the loan guarantees in the amount of $2.5 billion, but it could have been worse.

The politicians, like George Shultz, who came up with the CCC loan guarantee scheme that eventually cost the United States $2.5 billion, did not suffer for his incompetence. He was too high up on the food chain. So were Caspar Weinberger and even Michael Deaver. Their decisions cost lives, but they went home at night and suffered only their political party's election defeat. The same holds true for Prime Ministers, Cabinet Secretaries, their advisors and the professional bureaucrats who were parties to events.

It was the spooks, the soldiers of this Intelligence War, who paid with incarcerations and sometimes with their lives. Some spent time at the "MCC Hilton" in New York, LA County Central, Abu Ghraib and Her Majesty's Casemates. They were vilified and humiliated and they did not get to go home at night. Most are retired now, dead or simply forgotten with more past than future, and finally at peace with a little time to relax, reflect and perhaps pen a memoir.

BIBLIOGRAPHY

Adams, James, *ENGINES OF WAR*, Atlantic Monthly Press, New York, 1990.

Adams, James Ring, "Iraq's Yellow Rain," The American Spectator, March 1998.

Ammann, Daniel, THE KING OF OIL: THE SECRET LIVES OF MARC RICH, St. Martin's Press, New York, 2009

Arens, Moshe, BROKEN COVENANT: AMERICAN FOREIGN POLICY AND THE CRISIS BETWEEN THE US AND ISRAEL, Simon & Schuster, New York, 1995.

Bani-Sadr, Abol Hassan, LE COMPLOT DES AYATOLLAHS, Editions La Decouverte, Paris 1989.

Bani-Sadr, Abol Hassan, MY TURN TO SPEAK: IRAN, THE REVOLUTION AND SECRET DEALS WITH THE UNITED STATES, Potomac Books, Washington, 1991.

Ben-Manashe, Ari, PROFITS OF WAR, Sheridan Square Press, New York, 1992.

Blitzer, Wolf, TERRITORY OF LIES, Harper and Row, New York, 1989

Brinkley-Rogers, Paul, "People on the run finding themselves at home abroad with Castro," The Miami Herald, 10 March 2001.

Carmel, Chazi, "Expose: The Great CIA Conspiracy against Jonathan Pollard," Ma'ariv, 8 December 2000.
Carter, Jimmy, PALESTINE: PEACE NOT APARTHEID, Simon & Schuster, New York, 2006.

Cherkashin, Victor with Feifer, Gregory, SPY HANDLER: A MEMOIR OF A KGB OFFICER, Basic Books, New York, 2005.

Church, George, "Did Shamir Give Away Secrets?" Time, 28 October 1991.

Claire, Rodger W., RAID ON THE SUN, Broadway Books, New York, 2004.

Cordesman, Anthony H., IRAQ AND THE WAR OF SANCTIONS, Praeger, Westport, 1999.

Crile, George, CHARLIE WILSON'S WAR, Grove Press, New York, 2003.

Darwish, Adel and Alexander, Gregory, UNHOLY BABYLON, St. Martin's Press, New York, 1991.

Deaver, Michael K., with Herskowitz, Mickey, BEHIND THE SCENES, William Morrow, New York, 1987

Dickerson, F. Paul, "Informational Memorandum for Undersecretary Crowder," Department of Agriculture, Washington, 23 February 1990.

Eisenberg, Dennis, Dan, Uri and Landau, Eli, THE MOSSAD, INSIDE STORIES, Paddington Press, London, 1978.

Frantz, Douglas and Waas, Murray, "Bush OK'd Close Ties to Iraq Despite CIA Warnings," Los Angeles Times, 7 August 1992.

Friedman, Alan, SPIDER'S WEB, Bantam Doubleday Dell, New York, 1993.

Goldenberg, Elliot, THE SPY WHO KNEW TOO MUCH, SPI Books, New York, 1993

Goldenberg, Elliot, THE HUNTING HORSE, Prometheus Books, New York, 2000.

Gordon, Michael and Trainor, Bernard, THE GENERALS' WAR, Little, Brown and Company, New York, 1995.

Greenberg, Paul, "Is Jonathan Pollard Next on Clinton's List?" The Arkansas Democrat-Gazette, 7 September 1999.

Haig, Alexander, CAVEAT: REALISM, REAGAN AND FOREIGN POLICY, Macmillan, New York, 1984.

Hafidh, Hassan, "Iraq Says It Produces Vaccine Not Arms at Plant," Reuters, 23 April 1999.

Hamza, Khidhir with Stein, Jeff, SADDAM'S BOMBMAKER, Scribner, New York, 2000.

Hersh, Seymour, "Panama Strongman Said to Trade in Drugs, Arms and Illicit Money," The New York Times, 12 June 1986.

Hersh, Seymour, THE SAMSON OPTION, Random House, New York, 1991.

Herzog, Chaim, THE ARAB-ISRAELI WARS, Random House, New York, 2004

Heyndrickx, Aubin, "Chemical Warfare Injuries," The Lancet, 337, 16 February 1991.

Higgins, Michael R. "Assessment on the Activities of Abdel Kader Helmy, et. al. and the Egyptian/Iraqi Condor Missile Program," Defense Intelligence Agency, Washington, 19 September 1989.

Intelligence and Terrorism Information Center Staff, "Hamas's Military Buildup in the Gaza Strip," The Israel Intelligence Heritage and Commemoration Center, Tel Aviv, 8 April 2007, updated April 2008.

Kadivar, H and Adams, SC, "Treatment of Chemical and Biological Warfare Injuries, Insights Derived From the 1984 Attack on Majnoon Island," Military Medicine, April 1991

Kahan Y, Barak A, Efrat Y, Final Report, The Commission of Inquiry into the Events at the Refugee Camps in Beirut, Tel Aviv, 1983.

Kianifar V, and Balahi M, "Poisoning by Trichothecene Mycotoxin and Analytical Methods for Detection and Determination of T-2 Toxin in Biological Fluids," Poisons Information Center, Iman Reza University, Mashad University of Medical Science, Mashad, Iran, 1990.

Lawrence, T.E., SEVEN PILLARS OF WISDOM, Doubleday, New York, 1935.

Loftus, John, "Will Disclosures Help Unlock Jonathan Pollard's Cell?" The Miami Herald, 23 April 1995.

Maas, Peter, KILLER SPY, Warner Books, New York, 1995

North, Oliver, with Novak, William, UNDER FIRE, Harper Collins, New York, 1991.

Northrop, William, "Just About Everybody vs Jonathan Jay Pollard," New Dimensions, August 1992.

Ostrovsky, Victor and Hoy, Claire, BY WAY OF DECEPTION, St. Martin's Press, New York. 1990

Ostrovsky, Victor, THE OTHER SIDE OF DECEPTION, Harper Collins, New York, 1995.

Parks, Dave, "Accused Weapons Dealer: US Backed Arming Iraq," Birmingham News, May 1993.

Perera, Judith, "Halabja - The Legacy of Chemical Attack," IPS, London, 3 March 1998.

Pizzo, Stephen with Fricker, Mary and Hogan, Kevin, "Shredded Justice," Mother Jones, Jan-Feb 1993.

Rankin, Jennifer, "Marc Rich: Controversial Commodities Trader and Former Fugitive Dies at 78," The Guardian, London, 26 June 2013.

Riegle, Donald W, Jr., Staff Reports 1-3 "Gulf War Syndrome: The Case for Multiple Origin Mixed Chemical/Biotoxin Warfare Related

Disorders," US Senate Banking Committee, GPO, Washington, 1993-1994.

Ritter, Scott, ENDGAME: SOLVING THE IRAQ CRISIS, Simon and Schuster, New York, 1999

Sawchyn, Peter, "Scientist Details Effects of Chemical Attack on Iraqi Kurds," USIS Washington Files, United States Information Service, Washington, 27 April 1998.

Scarborough, Rowan, SABOTAGE: AMERICA'S ENEMIES WITH IN THE CIA, Regency Publishing, Washington, 2007.

Schweid, Barry, "Report Links Russia to Iraq Biological Weapons," Associated Press, 13 February 1998.

Shaw, Mark, MISCARRIAGE OF JUSTICE, Paragon House, St. Paul, 2001.

Thayer, George, THE WAR BUSINESS, Simon and Schuster, New York, 1969.

Thomas, Gordon, GIDEON'S SPIES, St. Martin's Press, New York, 1999.

Timmerman, Kenneth R., THE DEATH LOBBY: HOW THE WEST ARMED IRAQ, Bantam Books, New York, 1992.

Tinnin, David B. with Christensen, Dag, THE HIT TEAM, Dell Publishing, New York, 1977.

Twersky, David, "New Weinberger Bombshell: Judge Asked for Pollard Memo," New Jersey Jewish News, 29 September 1999.

Von Raab, William, "Nothing to Declare: One Nation is More Favored than Others," The American Conservative, July 14, 2003.

Wise, David, NIGHTMOVER, Harper Collins, New York, 1995.

Yergin, Daniel, THE PRIZE, Simon & Schuster, New York, 1991

SPOOK WAR

NOTES AND SOURCES

1Marwan was married to the daughter of the Egyptian President, Gamal Nasser. In May 1973, Marwan warned the Israelis of an imminent attack by Egypt and Syria, the Israelis mobilized (costing millions) but the attack never came.

[2] Controversy surrounds the breaking of PURPLE and the Japanese Naval code, JN-25, by the British cryptanalysts at Bletchley Park. It is said that the Brits knew in advance of the planned Japanese attack on Pearl Harbor, but failed to warn the Americans.

[3] A complete PURPLE machine was never acquired as all were completely destroyed at the close of the war. The only remnants are three parts of one, which were recovered by the Americans from the ruins of the Japanese Embassy in Berlin.

[4] There is particular controversy surrounding JN-25. There is some evidence that this code was broken by HYPO prior to the Pearl Harbor attack. The British also broke JN-25 and on 2 December 1941 intercepted traffic that indicated a Japanese Naval Task Force was enroute to Hawaii and planned to attack on 7 December. These intercepts were passed to London from Bletchley Park, but not onto American Intelligence.

[5] For an excellent biography on Joseph Rochefort, see Carlson, Elliot, *JOE ROCHEFORT'S WAR,* Naval Institute Press, Annapolis, 2011.

[6] The MANHATTAN project was riddled with Soviet spies. Among them was a 19-year-old, Harvard-trained, physics prodigy named Theodore Hall. He passed on the designs of the plutonium "Fat Boy" bomb along with technology for manufacturing plutonium to the Soviets. He was questioned by the FBI, but was not prosecuted because of potential exposure of the American VENONA intercepts. Hall moved to England where he taught biology at Oxford and died there in 1999.

[7] In December 1999, a double informed US Intelligence that China had the designs for our nuclear weapons. This eventually led to the indictment of Wen Ho Lee of the Los Alamos Labs, but the source was determined to be with an American contractor involved in the construction of the weapons. Lee was later cleared and awarded $1.6 million in damages.

[8] The French arrested Sergei Fabiew in 1977 and doubled him in lieu of deportation. He was a KGB Line X (T&S) officer reporting to the Paris Residency.

[9] These four Americans compromised as many as 45 American agents in the Soviet Union and Eastern Bloc and most were executed. Redmond, Paul, Memo from Chief of Counter Intelligence, Soviet Division, CIA, Langley, November 1986.

[10] The Intelligence chief assigned to a Soviet embassy. He runs all sections or lines in the host country.

[11] Cherkashin, Victor with Feifer, Gregory, *SPY HANDLER,* Basic Books, New York, 2005, p. 179.

[12] Prior to the Iraq War of 2003, Britain insisted that the war be tied to the settlement of the Israeli-Palestinian conflict utilizing the so-called "Road Map." Otherwise, Tony Blair could not guarantee British participation because of strong resistance in his Labor party parliamentary faction. Halevy, Efraim, *MAN IN THE SHADOWS,* St. Martin's Press, New York, 2006, p. 244.

[13] In the wake of the Nine-Eleven terrorist attacks, the CIA claimed its' failure was due to lack of funding. In December of 2001, Congress increased its' $30 billion annual budget by 8 percent.

[14] Contemporary historians like to point to the "Team B" controversy as a prime example of the politicizing of the CIA. It happened during the Ford Administration when right-wing politicians criticized the Agency's Estimate of Soviet capabilities, saying it was too low and calling the CIA "a hotbed of Eastern Establishment thinking." President Ford and DCIs William Colby and George Bush agreed to allow the "Team B" estimate, a review process that did nothing but buttress the political standing of well-known conservatives and demoralize CIA analysts. A more current example would be the terrorist attack on the US Consulate in Benghazi, Libya on 11 September 1012 and the subsequent cover up.

[15] "The Director of Central Intelligence shall be responsible for national intelligence ... Such national intelligence should be timely, objective, independent of political considerations." National Security Act of 1947.

[16] AMAN stands for Agaf Ha Modi'in or the IDF Information Branch. (Military Intelligence)

[17] Unit 8200 also handles cyber warfare and is the group that alledgely developed the STUXNET computer virus that crippled the Iranian nuclear program.

[18] Sherut HaBitachon HaKlali or General Security Service.

[19] The Border Police are the muscle of the Israeli National Police and are those "Israeli soldiers" in Green Berets who are usually seen in the news clips in confrontation with the Arabs. Within the Border Police, there is a special anti-terrorist unit called "Ya'amam." (Yehidat Mishtara Meyuhedet) The men of Ya'amam are the veterans who storm the terrorists when the dialogue dries up. Their unofficial motto is "take one prisoner ... so he can tell us all he knows." They have been known to take bullets themselves just to keep one terrorist alive.

[20] Ha Mossad Le Modi'in U'Letafkidim Meyuhadim or The Institute for Information and Special Duties.

[21] The Mossad employs between 1200 and 1700 people worldwide. Of these full-time employees, only 35 to 50 are actual case officers or "Katzas" (Ktzin issuf).

[22] LAKAM stands for Lishka le Kishrei Mada meaning the Scientific Affairs Liaison Bureau.

[23] Staff, "Secret Budget Reveals US Spying On Israel," *The Washington Post,* 29 August 2013.

[24] Ezekiel 44. "The Prince (Messiah) will enter through this gate and will eat bread before the Lord."

[25] Some 11 nations directly supported the Arab forces in the war, including Cuba. Boyne, Walter J., *THE TWO O'CLOCK WAR,* St. Martin's Press, New York, 2002, p.2.

[26] Yitzhak Walker was a German Jew and disciple of Menachem Begin. He fought the British in the Irgun underground, led the Israeli units that took the city of Jaffa during the War of Independence, was Israel's first commander of Paratroops, served as the Israeli Military Attaché to Ethiopia and later was elected the Mayor of the city of Bat-Yam. In his twilight years, he and Yacov Meridor were considered the wise old men of the Likud Party. He died in 1993.

[27] The most recognized "Palestinian," Yasser Arafat, claimed to have been born in Jerusalem. In fact, he was born and raised in Cairo, Egypt.

[28] Like all political movements, Zionism draws its philosophy from a manifesto. The Zionist Manifesto is actually a pamphlet, written by the Austrian journalist, Theodor Herzl, and first published in Vienna on 14 February 1896. Herzl was assigned to cover the trial of Captain Alfred Dreyfus in Paris and was so moved by the rabid anti-Semitism that he wrote his pamphlet espousing a solution to the Jewish question. The name of his work is *DER JUDENSTAAT,* (The Jewish State).

[29] T.E. Lawrence, a British Intelligence officer, advised and led the Bedouin Army of Fisal, during the war. He became the legendary Lawrence of Arabia and wrote about his experiences in a book called THE SEVEN PILLARS OF WISDOM. He was killed in a motorcycle accident a few years after publishing his book and most believe he died of boredom, like the vast majority of adrenaline junkies.

[30] Moshe Dayan, internationally recognized by his black eye patch, actually lost his left eye fighting for the British in the Middle East.

[31] These are the same people who were labeled "Ethnic Albanians" by the politically-correct, American media during the 1999 crisis in Bosnia.

[32] King Feisal of the House of Saud who envisioned the Great Arab Caliphate in the Middle East, always planned to give the Jews their ancient homeland in Israel. In this manner, he expected them to develop culture, industry, and commerce for the Caliphate.

[33] This figure varies from source to source ranging from 62 percent to 90 percent. Since it is doubtful that the truth will ever emerge, we have arbitrarily picked 83 percent, because no one can argue with it. In any case, the vast majority voted for Hamas.

[34] Samantha Power, the Obama Administration's Ambassador to the UN, has advocated an American invasion of Israel to force a peace settlement.

[35] On 11 January 2007, 14 members of the Carter Center Advisory Board resigned in protest over Jimmy Carter's new anti-Israel tome, PALESTINE: PEACE NOT APARTHEID.

[36] Initial intelligence figures listed 230 tanks, 200 APCs, 100 SP guns, 500 towed artillery and 200 aircraft. Herzog, Chaim, THE ARAB-ISRAELI WARS, Random House, New York, 1982, p. 112.

[37] This agent was an Egyptian-born Jew named Eli Cohen, who would go on to greater fame and ultimate tragedy as Israel's greatest spy. He was caught by Syrian counterintelligence in 1965 and executed in a televised event. At the time of his death, Eli Cohen, alias Kamil Amin Taabes, was the number 3 man in the ruling Baath Party of Syria. Even today in Israel, Cohen is remembered as "Our Man in Damascus" and old Mossad operatives like to brag, "He could have been the President of Syria."

[38] In 1967, the Egyptians reneged on their guarantees made in 1957 and closed the Straits of Tiran to all Israeli shipping. They also demanded the UN forces be withdrawn from Sinai, which the UN immediately did and re-occupied the Sinai with a large military force.

This precipitated the third Arab-Israeli conflict, the Six-Day War. All guarantees given to Israel in 1957 by the West flew out the window.

[39] Thayer, George, *THE WAR BUSINESS,* Simon and Schuster, New York, 1969, pp. 287-288.

[40] At the time of his initial employment by the Egyptians, Säenger was the Scientific Director of the Stuttgart Jet Propulsion Study Institute.

[41] These German rocket scientists came to be collectively called Sängerknaben (choirboys), a play on the German word and Säenger's name by the Israelis. Walter Busse was employed in the Helwan Project from 1959-1962 and would later show up in Iraq advising on centrifuge production for their nuclear weapons program. Timmerman, Kenneth R., *THE DEATH LOBBY,* pp. 309-346.

[42] US Department of State, "Military-owned factories profile," *Market Reports,* US Embassy, Cairo, 16 June 1993.

[43] They were the "Al Kahir" (Conqueror), "Al Ared" (Vanguard) and the "Al Zafir," (Victory) three liquid-fuel, surface-to-surface missiles designed and developed at Helwan. Thayer, George, *THE WAR BUSINESS,* p. 288.

[44] There is argument as to whether or not Ben Gurion ordered the operation.

[45] Pilz and the other Germans were not working on a nuclear bomb. They were planning to fire the radioactive material into Israel to induce radiation poisoning, the so-called "Dirty Bomb."

[46] Heberli, Emil (Chief Judge), Sentence, Switzerland vs. Joklik and Ben-Gal, Basle, 13 June 1963.

[47] For an excellent account of the Mossad's efforts regarding the Rockets of Helwan, see Eisenberg, Dennis, Dan, Uri and Landau, Eli, *THE MOSSAD, INSIDE STORIES,* Paddington Press, London, 1978.

[48] Hassib Sabbagh, a Christian Arab, was a large contributor to Jimmy Carter's Presidential Library. Blackburn, Chris, "A Palestinian Enron," *FrontPageMagazine.com,* 6 April 2005.

[49] Timmerman, Kenneth R., *THE DEATH LOBBY,* Bantam, New York, 1992, p. 45.

[50] Arab Projects and Development (APD) closed its operations in 1979 when the fighting in Beirut destroyed their offices. Most of the former APD employees hired on with the Al-Hazen Ibn Al Haitham Institute, a super-secret Iraqi entity engaged in "strategic scientific projects." It eventually metamorphosized into Consolidated Contractors International (CCI) based in Athens, Greece.

[51] Darwish, Adel and Alexander, Gregory, *UNHOLY BABYLON*, St. Martin's Press, New York, 1991. In spite of their heavy anti-Israel – anti-Western bias, Darwish's pseudonymous co-author, and many facts that cannot be checked, it is an interesting and fairly accurate work.

[52] Hamza, Khidhir, with Stein, Jeff, *SADDAM'S BOMBMAKER,* Scribner, New York, 2000, p. 159.

[53] Tamuz is the month of July in Arabic and the 17th the anniversary of the Baath Revolution in Iraq. Also, the Seventeenth of Tamuz (Hebrew: שבעה עשר בתמוז, Shiv'ah Asar b'Tamuz) is a Jewish fast day commemorating the breach of the walls of Jerusalem before the destruction of the Second Temple.

[54] Herzog, Chaim, *THE ARAB-ISRAELI WARS,* Vintage, New York, 1982, p. 339.

[55] Claire, Rodger W., *RAID ON THE SUN,* Broadway Books, New York, 2004, pp. 31-33.

[56] The Osiris was a top-of-the-line, state-of-the-art reactor specifically chosen by the Iraqi nuclear scientists and listed for $150 million. The French sold it to Saddam Hussein for $300 million. Claire, Rodger W., *RAID ON THE SUN,* pp. 39-40; Hamza, Khidhir, *SADDAM'S BOMBMAKER,* p. 83; Herzog, Chaim, *THE ARAB-ISRAELI WARS,* p. 339.

[57] Hamza, Khidhir, *SADDAM'S BOMBMAKER*, p. 133.

[58] Plutonium (Pu239) does not occur naturally in enough quantities to produce nuclear weapons. It has to be manufactured.

[59] Rodger W., *RAID ON THE SUN,* p. 44; Ostrovsky, Victor and Hoy, Claire, *BY WAY OF DECEPTION*, St. Martin's Press, New York. 1990, pp. 1-28.

[60] The warehouse belonged to Constructions Navales et Industrielles de la Mediterranee.

[61] Hamza, Khidhir, *SADDAM'S BOMBMAKER*, p. 133. The French kept Meshad's murder quiet for four days while they convinced the Iraqis that French Intelligence had nothing to do with it.

[62] Hamza, Khidhir, *SADDAM'S BOMBMAKER*, p. 24.

[63] Timmerman, Kenneth R, *THE DEATH LOBBY*, p. 124.

[64] The French technicians were withdrawn from the project when war broke out in September 1980. They returned to Iraq to complete their work in April 1981. Herzog, Chaim, *THE ARAB-ISRAELI WARS,* p. 341.

[65] Colonel Aviem Sella, of whom more later, headed the planning staff for the operation and flew one of the communication relay F-15Bs on the raid – Operation OPERA – on Al Tuwaitha. Twenty-six-year-old Captain Ilan Ramon, one of the F-16 bomber pilots, went on to become Israel's first astronaut and died aboard the Space Shuttle *COLUMBIA* in 2003.

[66] Codevilla, Angelo, Notes, Senior Staff, US Senate Intelligence Committee, June 1981. Of course, Inman was speaking of the Level Battlefield Doctrine.

[67] Jimmy Carter signed legislation in August 1977 that created the Department of Energy.

[68] Yergin, Daniel, *THE PRIZE*, Simon & Schuster, New York, 1991. Democrats usually fund a national, alternative energy program; Republicans generally kill it when they come back into power. This happened with Reagan after Carter and Bush after Clinton.

[69] Bush, George, Memorandum for the Attorney General re: Conflict-of-Interest Wavier, 8 August 1990.

[70] Haig, Alexander, *CAVEAT: REALISM, REAGAN AND FOREIGN POLICY*, Macmillan, New York, 1984.

[71] Arens, Moshe, *BROKEN COVENANT*, Simon & Schuster, New York, 1995, pp. 27-28.

[72] Prince Bandar was initially sent to the United States to head up the Saudi efforts to purchase the AWACS aircraft and air-refueling tankers in 1981. He soon replaced Sheik Faisal Alhegelan as the Saudi Ambassador to the United States.

[73] For an excellent accounts of the entire "Iraqgate" Affair, see Friedman, Alan, *SPIDER'S WEB*, Bantam Doubleday Dell, New York, 1993 and Timmerman, Kenneth R., *THE DEATH LOBBY,* Bantam, New York, 1992.

[74] North, Oliver L., *UNDER FIRE,* p. 184.

[75] The Department of Defense and Department of State control the sale of American military equipment. It is called the FMS program, standing for Foreign Military Sales and is regulated by the US Congress.

[76] AWACS stands for Airborne Warning And Control System. These are the modified Boeing 707 aircraft with the large radar dome on top and are known as "Sentry" planes. It is often described as looking like an airliner being terrorized by a UFO.

[77] James Baker is the Republican's "go to" guy when there is a particular difficulty. He led the legal fight for George W. Bush over the Florida run off in the 2000 election.

[78] One of the caveats was that no F-15s would be based near the Israeli border. The Saudi F-15s were based at Tabouk Air Base near Israel's southern border. Additionally, the Saudis allowed Syrian pilots to fly the F-15s and turned over the aircraft's manuals to them. At the time, Syria was a Soviet client. American Intelligence knew this, but neither Congress nor the Israelis were informed by the administration.

[79] NSC staffer Howard Teicher wrote this NSD. In 1995, Teicher filed an affidavit in Federal Court in Miami on 31 January 1995 exposing the secret political agenda outlined in this National Security Directive. (Teicher, Howard "Declaration," US vs Cardoen, et.al., 93-241-CR-Highsmith, dated 31 January 1995) Teicher is probably best known as the DOD analyst who in 1979 predicted that Iraq would invade Iran and later take over Kuwait. In 1979, his prediction was thought to be too pro-Israel. (Teicher is Jewish.)

[80] Arens, Moshe, *BROKEN COVENANT,* pp. 141-142.

[81] Iraq defaulted on these loans from BNL and the American taxpayer ended up paying $2.5 billion to the Italians because of the CCC loan guarantees.

[82] At that time, Brigadier General Rueven "Rudi" Yerdor commanded Unit 8200.

[83] American intelligence reports from this period and after carried significant information about the trade between the US and Iraq. One report (IIR 22010883.88) specified that American Type Culture Collection of Rockville, Maryland, was shipping pathogens to the Iraqis, who were then using them to manufacture biowarfare agents. Between 1984 and 1990, some of the transactions would become so egregious that even the CIA could not avoid issuing "alert memos" to the US Department of Justice and Law Enforcement agencies.

[84] Walker did provide repair manuals for the machines, which came in handy because the Pueblo crew had managed to damage their encoding machines before they were captured.

[85] The Soviets built six Akula class submarines at Severodvinsk on the White Sea. Each sub carried 20 SSN-20 ICBMs, each with a 10-unit MIRV warhead-payload. The *Akula* became the inspiration for Tom Clancy's 1984 novel, *THE HUNT FOR RED OCTOBER.*

[86] Cherkashin, Victor and Feifer, Gregory, *SPY HANDLER,* Basic Books, New York, 2005, p. 183. PIMENTO was Major Valeri F. Martynov, a

KGB Line X (T&S) officer stationed in the Soviet embassy in Washington. He was fingered by Aldrich Ames (CIA) and Robert Hanssen (FBI) in June 1985, arrested that November, doubled back for a period of time and then executed in May 1987.

[87] Among those murdered in what is now called the "Country Club Massacre" was the celebrated American nature photographer, Gail Rubin, who was taking pictures in a Nature Preserve where the terrorists came ashore.

[88] The first UN intervention was between the Egyptians and the Israelis in 1957. Their departure in 1967 at the demand of Egypt led to the Six-Day War.

[89] Begin, Menachem, Letter to Secretary of State Alexander Haig, 29 May 1982; Haig, Alexander, *CAVEAT*, p. 330.

[90] Ambassador Argov survived. Scotland Yard identified the gunman who was killed at the scene, and three co-conspirators subsequently arrested as being members of Abu Nidal's Black June Organization. Herzog, Chaim, *THE ARAB-ISRAELI WARS,* Random House, New York, 2004, p.351.

[91] SNOWBALL was renamed SHALOM GALIL (Peace for Galilee) for public consumption shortly after the invasion began.

[92] Deaver, Michael K., with Herskowitz, Mickey, *BEHIND THE SCENES,* William Morrow, New York, 1987, p. 165. Deaver resigned his White House post in 1985. In 1986, he was indicted for five counts of perjury, two counts before Congress and three counts before a Federal Grand Jury. He was convicted in 1987. Deaver died in 2007.

[93] Haig, Alexander, *CAVEAT*, p. 334.

[94] In reality, Haig resigned on 25 June 1982, but agreed to stay on until the Senate could confirm George Shultz.

[95] In the first five days of the PLO evacuation, five were killed and over 27 were wounded by stray bullets.

[96] *The Root* was the nickname given to Beirut by the Marine "grunts" who were deployed there. It is reminiscent of *The Nam,* for Vietnam.

[97] Philip Habib actually gave Arafat written assurances that Christian militias would not be allowed into the refugee camps. Carey, T. Elaine, "Destruction At Two Refugee Camps – Witnesses Tell How It Happened," *Christian Science Monitor,* 20 September 1982; Lamb, Franklin, "31 Years After The Massacre At Sabra-Shatila, *Veterans Today,* 20 September 2013.

[98] Elie Hobeika changed sides after the massacres and supported the Syrians. He was killed in January 2002 by a car bomb. Naturally, the Lebanese blamed Israel for his death.

[99] The Soviets were supplying these weapons to Syria and the Syrians were moving them into the Bekaa Valley. American Intelligence was tracking them, but Caspar Weinberger was embargoing the information to the Israelis. One of the American intelligence analysts tracking these weapons deployments at the Navy's Intelligence Support Center in Suitland, Maryland was Jonathan J. Pollard.

[100] This is of course, reminiscent of the French who hate the Americans until the Germans start stirring.

[101] Kahan Y, Barak A, Efrat Y, Final Report, The Commission of Inquiry into the Events at the Refugee Camps in Beirut, Tel Aviv, 1983.

[102] Seventeen members of the "Islamic Jihad" were arrested by the Kuwaiti authorities and incarcerated. Known as the "Dowa 17," the Kuwaitis refused to release them in spite of threats and cajolery by the Arab states. They were freed in August 1990 by the invading Iraqi forces.

[103] As the price of joining the Coalition against Iraq in the First Gulf War, the Bush (41) Administration agreed to give Syria a free hand in Lebanon. For all intents and purposes, Lebanon became a part of Greater Syria, ruled by their Shia surrogate, Hizb Allah. In 2000, the last Israeli soldiers left Lebanon 22 years after they first invaded the country during Operation LITANI.

[104] A great number of these weapons ended up in the hands of the Afghan Mujahedin fighting the Soviets. In fact, Israel became the second largest supplier of weapons for that insurgency that eventually drove the Soviets out of Afghanistan. See Crile, George, *CHARLIE WILSON'S WAR,* Grove Press, New York, 2003.

[105] An embarrassed Cadillac Gage initially claimed that the vehicles had been purchased by the Lebanese Army and subsequently captured by the PLO. There was some truth to that, but among the vehicles captured by the Israelis in 1982 were V-150 armored cars. The Lebanese Army had purchased only the V-100, an earlier version.

[106] Steven Spielberg made his successful movie, "Munich," based on the fictional account of the operation by George Jonas. *VENGEANCE: THE TRUE STORY OF AN ISRAELI COUNTER-TERRORIST TEAM,* Simon & Schuster, New York, 1984.

[107] David's body was picked up by the US Air Force and flown home to Ohio for burial. Today, there is a National Park Service memorial to David Berger and the ten other Israeli victims in Beachwood, Ohio.

[108] Brill, Bruce, "US Failed to Warn Israel in 1973 War," *The Jerusalem Post,* 31 October 1992.

[109] Pollard, Jonathan J., unpublished critique of Wolf Blitzer's book *TERRITORY OF LIES* (Harper and Row, New York, 1989). This 104-page, hand-written document was prepared by Pollard for his attorney, Alan Dershowitz in 1989.

[110] Pollard, Jonathan J., Critique.

[111] Goldenberg, Elliot, *THE SPY WHO KNEW TOO MUCH*, SPI Books, New York, 1993, p. 52; Blitzer, Wolf, *TERRITORY OF LIES*, Harper and Row, New York, 1989, p. 62. Both Goldenberg and Blitzer recount Jay Pollard's participation in the intelligence sharing meetings, but express different views of why information was embargoed by the Americans. Our research indicates that Goldenberg's account is the more accurate.

[112] After receiving a compendium of American intelligence documents classified at the "Secret" level, the Israelis were shocked to see that the Pentagon had denied the very existence of 75 percent of the documents which should have been made available to them under the sharing agreement.

[113] Technology transfer is a growth industry. Stealing technology that has been developed at the cost of millions of dollars by American industries is far cheaper than paying to develop it yourself. Most technology transfers are illegal, whether by espionage, industrial espionage, or simple smuggling.

[114] Kadivar, H and Adams, SC, "Treatment of Chemical and Biological Warfare Injuries, Insights Derived From the 1984 Attack on Majnoon Island," *Military Medicine,* April 1991; Heyndrickx, Aubin, "Chemical Warfare Injuries," *The Lancet,* 337, 16 February 1991.

[115] This information was confirmed to us by sources at Eglin Air Force Base, Florida, in 1995. Our sources were primary, part of a team of advisors from the DOD's Intelligence Support Activity.

[116] Kianifar V, and Balahi M, "Poisoning by Trichothecene Mycotoxin and Analytical Methods for Detection and Determination of T-2 Toxin in Biological Fluids," Poisons Information Center, Iman Reza University, Mashad University of Medical Science, Mashad, Iran, 1990.

[117] The UN reacted in outrage. A later investigation on the Majnoon battlefield by UN inspectors identified residue of the biological toxin T-2, a component of the infamous "Yellow Rain." The Israelis later

discovered that a German company, Josef Khum GmbH, had shipped the T-2, along with its weaker cousin, TH-2, to the Iraqis.

[118] Kadivar, H and Adams, SC, "Treatment of Chemical and Biological Warfare Injuries, Insights Derived From the 1984 Attack on Majnoon Island,"

[119] As an interesting aside, some scientists believe that the Mycotoxin, Stachybotrys Atra, caused God's Tenth Plague, which killed the first born of Egypt just prior to the Israelite Exodus.

[120] While there has been a great deal of talk about Aflatoxin, this family of agents barely meets the needed Military Specification (MilSpec) for a bioagent, unless you are trying to ruin someone's peanut crop. That being said, there are some indications that the Iraqis employed an altered Aflatoxin in their attack on the Kurdish village of Halabja in 1988. For an interesting account of "Yellow Rain" see Adams, James Ring, "Iraq's Yellow Rain," *The American Spectator,* March 1998.

[121] This information was passed from Achmed Tashkandi, a Saudi diplomat, to Jonathan Pollard in 1985.

[122] President Jimmy Carter secretly assured the Iranians that the Americans would not allow Iraq to defeat Iran. See Bani-Sadr, Abol Hassan, *LE COMPLOT DES AYATOLLAHS*, Editions La Decouverte, Paris 1989. Some historians and participants have linked the Reagan Administration's approval of these early Israeli arms shipments to the "October Surprise." While this cannot be ruled out, Israel was never a real "fence-sitter" in the Iran-Iraq War and supported Iran in spite of the anti-Israel rhetoric emanating from the Islamic Republic.

[123] Nothing of this sort could possibly happen in Israel without the full knowledge and cooperation of the government. "Civilians" are always used to provide the state with plausible deniability.

[124] This clandestine air link between Israel and Iran would come to be called, "The White Pipeline" or in some versions, "Channel One."

[125] Wines, Michael and McManus, Doyle (Staff), "US Sent Iran Arms for Hostage Releases," *The Los Angeles Times,* 6 November 1986.

[126] North, Oliver L., *UNDER FIRE*, HarperCollins and Zondervan, New York, 1991.

[127] A good account of this incident can be found in Perry, Mark, *ECLIPSE,* William Morrow & Company, New York, 1992. The incident resurfaced in William Webster's confirmation hearings as the DCI-Designate in April 1987. The story remains tantalizing because the

reported date of the sighting was August, not September and the CIA has continued to deny any knowledge of the shipment. That it was an unmarked American-made plane was never in doubt. We have concluded that it was the early September shipment since there is no real evidence to the contrary. Of course, it could have been an Israeli CHANNEL ONE shipment.

[128] The Lockheed Key Hole 11 is a 27,600-pound, imaging (photo reconnaissance) satellite that orbits the earth at a mean altitude of 115 miles. The entire system was compromised in 1978 when William T. Kampiles, a CIA employee, sold the system's technical manuals to the Soviets. In spite of this and the turning over to the Iraqis of KH-11 "overhead" during the Iran-Iraq War (1980-1988), the American Intelligence Community insists that Jonathan Pollard compromised the system when he turned over satellite pictures to the Israelis. Out of necessity, Israel began launching its own satellites, the "Ofek" (Horizon) series, in the early 1990s.

[129] After the American invasion of Iraq in 2003, the Kurdish north of the country has been the only area free of insurgent violence.

[130] Azad, "The Incident at Halabja," Lulea Technical University of Sweden, 3 May 1996. This benign attitude toward the Halabja attack is also noted in Darwish, Abdel, and Alexander, Gregory, UNHOLY BABYLON.

[131] Azad, "The Incident at Halabja."

[132] Professor Christine Gosden is an expert in Fetal Medicine and Oncology who has conducted numerous international studies for the Medical Research Council, the British equivalent of the American National Institutes of Health.

[133] Gwynne Roberts' documentary is called "Saddam's Secret Time Bomb."

[134] The Gulf War Syndrome.

[135] Perera, Judith, "Halabja - The Legacy Of Chemical Attack," IPS, London, 3 March 1998.

[136] Perera, Judith, "Halabja - The Legacy Of Chemical Attack."

[137] Perera, Judith, "Halabja - The Legacy Of Chemical Attack."

[138] Sawchyn, Peter, "Scientist Details Effects of Chemical Attack on Iraqi Kurds," USIS Washington Files, United States Information Service, Washington, 27 April 1998.

[139] An excellent account of the Samarra Project can be found in Timmerman, Kenneth R., THE DEATH LOBBY, Houghton Mifflin, New

York, 1991, pp. 151-157. The good doctor Al Ani showed up in April of 1999 as the "factory boss" of the French-built, "vaccine factory" in the Baghdad suburb of Daura. He denied to the press that the factory could be used to produce biological weapons as UNSCOM insisted. Hafidh, Hassan, "Iraq Says It Produces Vaccine Not Arms at Plant," *Reuters,* 23 April 1999.

[140] Timmerman, Kenneth, *THE DEATH LOBBY*, pp. 154-155.

[141] This is the conclusion drawn by UNSCOM inspection teams after the Gulf War. At Salman Pak, they discovered large inhalation chambers that could easily accommodate a human being. The "test subjects" were thought to have been Kurdish prisoners, many of whom have simply disappeared.

[142] Ritter, Scott, *ENDGAME: SOLVING THE IRAQ CRISIS,* Simon and Schuster, New York, 1999, p. 86; Cordesman, Anthony H., *IRAQ AND THE WAR OF SANCTIONS,* Praeger, Westport, 1999, pp. 574-575.

[143] Our information is that Israel is the only country to have a copy of this document and they have not shared it with their American counterparts. They have however, informed the Americans and the UN Inspections teams. As of late 1997, Iraq continued in its refusal to make a copy available to the UN. It is presumed to have fallen into the hands of American experts in 2003.

[144] Like government entities involved in the Iran-Contra scandal, records from the CDC and ATCC were only available back to 1985.

[145] Staff, US Senate Committee on Banking, Housing and Urban Development, Don Riegle, Chairman, Reports of September 1993, May 1994 and October 1994, *"Gulf War Syndrome: The Case for Multiple Origin Mixed Chemical/Biotoxin Warfare Related Disorders,"* Government Printing Office, Washington, 1993-1994.

[146] Staff, US Senate Committee on Banking, Housing and Urban Development, Don Riegle, Chairman, Reports of September 1993, May 1994 and October 1994, Government Printing Office, Washington, 1994. These 1985 shipments of West Nile Fever virus raised suspicions in 1987 with an outbreak in the Golan Heights in Israel and once again in 1999 when the disease magically appeared in New York.

[147] According to Iraqi declarations made to UNSCOM inspectors, 1900 liters of weaponized Botulinum toxin was produced, a portion of which was mated to delivery vectors.

[148] The politically connected Rihab Taha - she is married to Iraq's oil minister, General Amir Rashid Ubaydi - is often characterized as the

leading official in charge of Iraq's bioweapons program. We would point out that she is an acolyte, a protégé of Dr. Hindawi.

[149] Schweid, Barry, "Report Links Russia to Iraq Biological Weapons," Associated Press, 13 February 1988.

[150] The Iraqis confirmed these tests to UN weapons inspectors in 1995. See UNSCOM Report S/1995/864, dated 11 October 1995. The seed cultures for these agents were purchased from ATCC on 2 May 1986.

[151] Pulmonary Anthrax was called in the media "inhalation" Anthrax in wake of the post Nine-Eleven bioweapon attacks in the United States.

[152] The strain was identified at the US Department of Agriculture lab in Ames, Iowa in 1932 … hence the Ames strain.

[153] Messerschmitt-Boelkow-Blohm (MBB) is an old established German airframer. During World War II, it designed and produced the famous ME-109 fighter and the first operational jet fighter, the ME-262. After the war, during the 1950s and 1960s, it was active in the secret Helwan Project in Egypt. They are now an industrial giant in Germany.

[154] The Cosen Group was well-known to Israeli Intelligence. On 27 May 1988, an automobile belonging to Ekkehard Schrotz, head of Cosen, was blown up with a car bomb. Schrotz was not in the car at the time, but disappeared some time later. Timmerman, Kenneth R., *THE DEATH LOBBY,* pp. 379-380.

[155] Dickerson, F. Paul, "Informational Memorandum for Undersecretary Crowder," Department of Agriculture, 23 February 1990.

[156] This agreement was formally called the Missile Technology Control Regime (MTCR) and under it the CONDOR was classified as a Category 1 Missile System. There were 7 member nations: USA, Germany, France, Canada, Great Britain, Italy and Japan.

[157] Dickerson, F. Paul, Memorandum. Dickerson wrote in his now-famous memo that "there would be considerable adverse Congressional reaction and press coverage" if BNL investigators found the "direct link to financing Iraqi military expenditures, particularly the Condor Missile."

[158] Surprisingly, the Israelis have an excellent working relationship with British Intelligence, which evidently informed them about the CONDOR project. The British kept a watchful eye on Argentina and the Israelis, who supplied clothing and other non-lethal material to the Argentine military, kept the British informed.

[159] As an intelligence officer tasked with tracking technologies, Pollard was authorized to open counter-intelligence investigations.

[160] Interestingly, Aerojet-General was a major contractor in the area of biological warfare. For Fiscal Year 1969, it was the 5th largest recipient of appropriations for the Army's biological weapons research. Transcript of Hearings, House Subcommittee of the Committee on Appropriations, 91st Congress, First Session, Washington, Part 5, 1969.

[161] Higgins, Michael R. "Assessment on the Activities of Abdel Kader Helmy, et. al. and the Egyptian/Iraqi Condor Missile Program," Defense Intelligence Agency, Washington, 19 September 1989.

[162] Higgins, Michael R., Assessment.

[163] This was first brought out by Adel Darwish and Gregory Alexander in their book, *UNHOLY BABYLON*. American and Israeli Intelligence sources confirmed this shipment of the CONDOR missiles from Egypt to Iraq.

[164] The Iraqis confirmed these tests to UN weapons inspectors in 1995. UNSCOM Report S/1995/864, dated 11 October 1995.

[165] These bioagents were sold to Iraq by American Type Culture Collection of Rockville, MD. They were shipped on 2 May 1986 with the approval of the US Department of Commerce.

[166] Frantz, Douglas and Waas, Murray, "Bush OK'd Close Ties to Iraq Despite CIA Warnings," *Los Angeles Times,* 7 August 1992. The quote is from George Bush.

[167] Historically, the Israelis have often done this. David Ben-Gurion supported the British in the fight against Nazi Germany, but opposed them when it came to the restrictions on Jewish immigration to Palestine.

[168] Slang for killing.

[169] Fully one third of the 700,000 American servicemen and women are officially disabled, to one degree or another, from service-connected injuries received during the 1991 Gulf War. US Department of Veterans Affairs, Washington, 2000. Many of the disabilities have been classified as "undiagnosed illness," read: Gulf War Syndrome.

[170] Many believe it is in the Arabs' culture to blame others for their own mistakes.

[171] Timmerman, Kenneth R., *THE DEATH LOBBY,* p. 185.

[172] Morris Weinberg, Jr., the Assistant US Attorney assigned to prosecute Marc Rich claims that he was first tipped off about Rich by two convicts in Texas before Rudy Giuliani arrived in New York. Weinberg proffers that Washington in general and Giuliani in particular had no prior knowledge of the prosecution before the latter's arrival in the Southern District of New York in 1983.

[173] Rich and his wife were also heavy contributors and politically active in the Democratic Party.

[174] Writing in March 2003, after the Supreme Court had reviewed the RICO statues and greatly narrowed their application. John Leo of *U.S. News & World Report* observed: "Congress passed the loosely worded and maddeningly vague Racketeer Influenced and Corrupt Organizations Act in 1970 to make conspiracy indictments of mobsters easier. From Day 1, it was obvious that someone would use the law to hammer political opponents."

[175] The three Israelis were Zakaria, Baumel, and Katz. Interestingly, Baumel was a dual national, who was born and raised in New York. The matter of these prisoners was first raised in the publicity surrounding Rich's indictment.

[176] Safir, Howard, Former US Marshal in charge of the Marc Rich case, interviewed on "Larry King Live," *CNN*, 8 February 2001. Howard Safir is best known for orchestrating the seizure of the international drug trafficker Juan Ramon Matta Ballesteros in Tegucigalpa, Honduras on 5 April 1988.

[177] Lewis, Samuel W., American Ambassador to Israel (1978-1985), deposition in Howard and Tucker Vs. US, US Court of Claims, Washington, 1987.

[178] Ammann, Daniel, *THE KING OF OIL: THE SECRET LIVES OF MARC RICH,* St. Martin's Press, New York, 2009, pp.; Rankin, Jennifer, "Marc Rich: Controversial Commodities Trader and Former Fugitive Dies at 78," *The Guardian,* London, 26 June 2013.

[179] Eric Holder shepherded the Rich pardon through President Bill Clinton's office. He was appointed Attorney General under President Barack Obama.

[180] Giuliani, Rudolph W., Testimony before the House Committee on Government Affairs, Washington, 8 January 2001.

[181] Cardoen received his PhD in Metallurgical Engineering from the University of Utah in 1969. He was also a former pilot in the Chilean Air Force.

[182] Ben-Manashe, Ari, *PROFITS OF WAR,* Sheridan Square Press, New York, 1992.

[183] ISC was an American defense contractor partially owned by foreigners and under DOD regulations, a proxy Board of Directors made up of Americans suitable to the Pentagon, had to be appointed. Former Deputy Director of the CIA, Bobby Ray Inman, former General John Guthrie and former Assistant Secretary of Defense Barry Shillito, were appointed and approved.

[184] Inman, Bobby R., letter to Judge Louis Bechtle on behalf of James Guerin, dated 27 April 1992. Guerin was convicted of fraud and illegal technology transfers to South Africa and Iraq in 1992. Inman's letter was an effort to have Guerin's sentence reduced.

[185] The Israeli CBUs employed in Lebanon were not, as portrayed in press accounts, American-made. The Israelis manufacture their own CBUs designed for their own tactical needs at Israel Military Industries (IMI). Chief among the "Israel bashers" within the Reagan Administration was Michael Deaver of the White House "troika." Deaver was an intimate of Nancy Reagan, which accounted for his position within the White House. After resigning from the White House, Deaver was tried and convicted of Perjury in 1987. Deaver died in 2007.

[186] Friedman, Alan, *SPIDER'S WEB*, Bantam Doubleday, New York, 1993.

[187] Parks, Dave, "Accused Weapons Dealer: US Backed Arming Iraq," *Birmingham News,* May 1993.

[188] US vs Cardoen, et. al., 93-241-CR-Highsmith, Southern District of Florida.

[189] There is some speculation that Dr. Cardoen currently resides in Cuba along with 76 other federal fugitives. Brinkley-Rogers, Paul, "People On The Run Finding Themselves At Home Abroad With Castro," *The Miami Herald,* 10 March 2001.

[190] As it turned out, Iraq was directing Abu Nidal and his Black June Organization, which was responsible for the London attack on Sholomo Argov that triggered Israel's invasion of Lebanon and the Paris attack on Joe Goldenberg's restaurant which left six innocents dead.

[191] This was a $2.65 billion contract to provide Iraq with four Lupo-class frigates, six Assad-class corvettes, a floating dock, munitions and support craft.

[192] Valsella was half-owned by Fiat. The Italian land mine deal became a *cause celeb* after the Gulf War. Thousands of them were found by

the 37th Engineers, 82nd Airborne Division at Kamasiyah. Because they were air dispersible, they remain a hazard to this day.

[193] Chris Drogoul died in 1999.

[194] US vs. Christopher Drogoul, 1:CR-91-078-MHS, US District Court, Northern District of Georgia, Atlanta, Court Order issued 5 October 1992.

[195] William Hinshaw retired from the FBI in April 1992 and became the Inspector General of the Tennessee Valley Authority.

[196] This matter does not seem so far-fetched when one notes that Israel maintains a large consulate in Atlanta.

[197] Friedman, Alan, *SPIDER'S WEB*, Unless otherwise noted, most of this information is found in Friedman's definitive work on the BNL scandal.

[198] Pizzo, Stephen with Fricker, Mary and Hogan, Kevin, "Shredded Justice," *Mother Jones,* Jan-Feb 1993.

[199] Quoted in Friedman, *SPIDER'S WEB*, p. 283.

[200] Goldenberg, Elliot, *THE SPY WHO KNEW TOO MUCH*, p. 55.

[201] Katza is short for the Hebrew words Ktzin Issuf meaning "harvester" and is used to designate an intelligence officer, a trained operative who recruits and runs spies. The American Intelligence counterpart is called a "case officer."

[202] In 1985, Pollard passed information on the Iraqi threat to Saudi Intelligence through his agent in the Saudi Arabian embassy in Washington. He correctly deduced that Iraq would target Saudi Arabia after the Iran-Iraq War ended.

[203] The Intelligence Business, "The Trades."

[204] Prior to the Arab surprise attack on Israel in October 1973, American Intelligence assured the Israelis that there was no cause for alarm. The Egyptian and Syrian military build-up on their borders was assessed by the Americans as only "exercises," not a prelude to war. This is part of the reason Israel was strategically surprised.

[205] All intelligence services have a "No Foreign Dissemination" classification. Israel uses JUMBO, the US uses NOFORN and the Brits use GUARD.

[206] Pollard's official codename was DANIEL COHEN, but this was only known to a handful of senior Israeli officials. His nickname, "Hunting Horse" was given to him by AMAN officers in 1984. It is a transliteration from the Hebrew, which loosely meant that he would

"hunt" up information on request and he was a "horse" for his handlers. "Horse" (Sus in Hebrew) means an exceptional agent on whose back his handler rides up the promotion ladder. The term is also applied to a superior who favors a particular Katza and sees to his advancement. In American Intelligence slang, such a superior is ironically called a "Rabbi."

[207] Timmerman, Kenneth R., THE DEATH LOBBY, p. 436.

[208] Washington-based Saudi diplomat, Ahmed Tashkandi, provided Jonathan Pollard with notes on these meetings, which were used as "talking points" in subsequent meetings between the Saudis and the Iraqis. Pollard passed this information onto Israeli Intelligence.

[209] Timmerman, Kenneth, THE DEATH LOBBY, p. 390. General Al Saadi was in charge of building the Samarra chemical complex which began in 1981.

[210] It should be noted that a vast majority of the American citizens kidnapped in Lebanon came from the expatriate (ex-pat) community, had Arab wives and had lived there for many years. The Reverend Benjamin Weir had lived in Lebanon for 31 years and when the Israelis won his release, he turned on both the Americans and the Israelis. NSC staffers Ollie North and Mike Ledeen took to calling him "The Reverend Weird" and even suggested that they trade Weir back to the Arabs for another hostage. With the exception of CIA Chief of Station, Bill Buckley, and US Marine Intelligence Officer, William Higgins, one also has to factor in the old admixture of money for ransom, an Arab tradition going back centuries. In 1986, the Libyans had to "purchase" Peter Kilburn from his Arab kidnappers in Beirut. He was then killed in retaliation for the American raid on Libya.

[211] Osama bin Laden became the most wanted terrorist in the world in the late 1990s as a result of his attacks against the United States. He was held responsible for the simultaneous destruction of the American embassies in Kenya and Tanzania, has been linked to the attack on the USS Cole and, some even say, to the bombing of the Murrah Building in Oklahoma City prior to Nine-Eleven. On 2 May 2011, US Navy SEALs killed him in Pakistan.

[212] Gulbuddin Hekmatyar was the largest recipient of CIA weapons during the war. Crile, George, CHARLIE WILSON'S WAR, Grove Press, New York, 2003, pp. 212-213.

[213] The Egyptian officer, who provided the critical information to Israel and through Israel to Washington, was discovered by Egyptian counterintelligence because of a Newsweek article detailing the interception and diversion of the EgyptAir 737 carrying the Achille Lauro hijackers to Tunis. The officer was executed and because of the

subsequent controversy, *Newsweek* was forced to name the source of their article: LTC Oliver North, under orders. Within days of their agent's execution, the Israelis smuggled the officer's family out of Egypt and resettled them in Israel.

[214] This air raid was in response to a terrorist attack in Larnaca, Cyprus on 25 September 1985 in which three Israelis were killed. The attack on the Israeli yacht "First" was an operation carried out by the PLO's "Force 17." The Israeli attack on Hammam Lif killed 61 PLO terrorists, including Mohammed Natour, the commander of "Force 17." Subsequently, "Force 17" became Yasser Arafat's personal bodyguard and part of the security apparatus for the Palestinian Authority.

[215] One of those tactical planners was Israeli Air Force Colonel Aviem Sella.

[216] This changed somewhat when the PLO relocated its headquarters from Beirut to Tunis in 1982 after being driven out of Lebanon by Israeli forces.

[217] The First Law of Analysis holds that "If it walks like a duck, looks like a duck, swims like a duck, then it probably is a duck." Read: Common Sense Prevails.

[218] Pollard, Jonathan J., (Critique).

[219] Pollard, Jonathan J., undated letter to Rabbi Morris Werb. (Circa 1989)

[220] Goldenberg, Elliot, *THE SPY WHO KNEW TOO MUCH*, p. 111.

[221] Goldenberg, Elliot, *THE HUNTING HORSE*, Prometheus Books, New York, 2000, p. 25.

[222] The Shin Bet is the Israeli equivalent of the American FBI. It is tasked with security at Israeli diplomatic mission abroad. It is also known as Shabok or the General Security Service (GSS).

[223] Eddy Rubinstein was later promoted to Cabinet Secretary, then to Attorney General and at this writing, is a Justice of the Supreme Court of Israel. Many blame him for the Pollards' arrest and the subsequent scandal. Whatever the case, he has been a prime mover in the Israeli Government seeking Pollard's release.

[224] Northrop, William, "Just About Everybody Vs Jonathan Jay Pollard," *New Dimensions,* August 1992. It should be pointed out that the clash between diplomats and spooks working out of the same embassy is not unheard of in *The Trades.* In the summer of 1963 a man begged an American couple in Moscow to pass a package of papers to the American embassy, which they did. Diplomats thinking it was some sort of provocation, over the protests of the CIA Chief of Station,

SPOOK WAR

turned over the material to the Soviet Government. The material was classified documents from the KGB's Second Chief Directorate and the provider, who was trying to make contact with the CIA, was discovered and executed. His name was Aleksandr Nikolaevich Cherepanov.

[225] Several interviews with Dr. Morris Pollard from 1996 to 2001; Shaw, Mark, *MISCARRIAGE OF JUSTICE,* Paragon House, St. Paul, 2001, pp. 89-90.

[226] Leeper, Charles and Geneson, David, "Victim Impact Statement," US Vs Pollard, CR 86-207 AER, US District Court, District of Columbia, Washington, DC, 3 March 1987.

[227] Leeper, Charles and Geneson, David, "Victim Impact Statement." We are reminded that the Intelligence Sharing Agreement was a Congressional fiat and arguably not subject to interpretation by bureaucrats.

[228] Weinberger, Caspar, "Supplemental Declaration of the Secretary of Defense," in US Vs Pollard, CR 86-207 AER, US District Court, District of Columbia, Washington, DC, 3 March 1987.

[229] US Vs Pollard, CR 86-207 AER, US District Court, District of Columbia, Washington, DC. Declaration of Jonathan Jay Pollard in Support of 2255 Motion for Re-sentencing, 28 August 2000; Shaw, Mark, *MISCARRIAGE OF JUSTICE*, pp. 207-214.

[230] Robinson was appointed to the Federal Bench by Lyndon Johnson in 1966. In his judicial career 85 of his 300 decisions were reversed on appeal. He died in March 2000 at age 77.

[231] Transcript of Proceedings, US Vs Pollard, 90-3276, US Court of Appeals, District of Columbia Circuit, 10 September 1991.

[232] US Vs Evans, et.al., CR 86-384 LBS, US District Court, Southern District of New York. The name "Brokers of Death" was bestowed upon the defendants by William Von Raab, then Commissioner of US Customs.

[233] One of those arrested in New York on 22 April 1986 was Manucher Ghorbanifar, but his incarceration was short lived. Giuliani released him that night after a call from Oliver North. Report of the President's Special Review Board (Tower Commission), Appendix B, "Iran/Contra Affair: A Narrative," Note 64, Washington, February 1987.

[234] Transcript of bail hearings, US Vs Evans, et.al., CR-86-384-LBS, US District Court, Southern District of New York, June 1986.

[235] Sporn, Michael, Motion to Produce all CIA records, In re: VE/GOLF, KK/SASHA, Transcript of hearings on Defense Discovery Motions, US

Vs Evans, et.al. CR-86-384-LBS, US District Court, Southern District of New York, August 04, 1988; Lubasch, Arnold H., "Defendant In Arms Case Says Casey Backed Him," *The New York Times,* August 05, 1988; Honegger, Barbara, *OCTOBER SURPRISE,* Tudor, New York, 1989, p. 68, 207; Jones, Stephen and Israel, Peter, *OTHERS UNKNOWN,* Public Affairs, New York, 1998, p 156.

[236] CBS News, Transcript, "The Arms Game," *60 Minutes,* 30 November 1986. Maxwell Rabb was a New York lawyer who had been appointed to various positions by five (5) US Presidents. He was also a member, along with Bill Casey, of the Knights of Malta. He died in 2002.

[237] Wines, Michael and McManus, Doyle (Staff), "US Sent Iran Arms for Hostage Releases," *The Los Angeles Times,* 6 November 1986. While the four Israelis were incarcerated in Bermuda, over fifty Bermudan nationals were arrested in Israel as "illegal immigrants."

[238] Staff, *The Observer,* London, 30 August 1986; Adams, James, *ENGINES OF WAR*, Atlantic Monthly Press, New York, 1990, p. 145; Staff, "1986 Death of Iranian Informant in Arms Plot Prosecution Studied," *The Los Angeles Times,* 7 March 1987.

[239] The government dropped all charges against the defendants in the "Brokers of Death" case in January of 1989, almost 3 years after indicting them, citing the untimely death of their chief witness, Cyrus Hashemi. In his book, *THE OTHER SIDE OF DECEPTION*, Victor Ostrovsky blames the Mossad for Hashemi's death. Most observers agree, but Ostrovsky's account of the "Brokers of Death" case, into which he injects himself, is a complete fabrication. Ari Ben Menashe in his book, *PROFITS OF WAR,* opined that Hashemi was killed by the US Customs Service.

[240] Adams, James, *ENGINES OF WAR,* Atlantic Monthly Press, New York, 1990, p. 144.

[241] Samghabadi, Raji, Transcript of Testimony, US Vs Ben-Menashe, et. al., CR 90-010 LLS, Southern District of New York, November 1990.

[242] *Al Shiraa,* 3 November 1986. Ben-Menashe was arrested on 3 November 1989 in Los Angeles on trumped up charges, was moved to New York and spent 11 months in jail before being acquitted by a jury on 28 November 1990. He became disenchanted with Israel, moved to Australia, wrote a book, and became one of the Jewish State's harshest critics, revealing some of its secret operations to the media. He later moved to Montreal, Canada and on 2 December 2012, his home there was firebombed. The resulting fire destroyed most of his documents and computer records.

[243] In the month following the November 1986 disclosures about Iran-Contra, President Reagan's job performance approval with the American people fell from 67 to 46 percent, the steepest decline ever recorded for an American President. Further, 48 percent of the American public thought he should resign.

[244] Operation STAUNCH was a Customs Service program, which targeted individuals doing business with Iran. After the Iran-Contra scandal broke Operation STAUNCH disappeared.

[245] US Vs Caspar W. Weinberger, CR 92-235. Indictment by Grand Jury 91-1, dated 16 June 1992. Weinberger was indicted for Obstruction of Congress, False Statements and Perjury. He was indicted for an additional charge of False Statements in CR 92-0416 on 30 October 1992.

[246] Staff, "Report on Reagan role in Iran-Contra Released," The Nation section, *News and Record,* 26 November 2011, Washington.

[247] Combined Chiefs of Staff, "Yalta Conference Agreement – US, UK, USSR," Re: Handling of Liberated PoWs, 1945, pp. 175-180, 242-243, Dwight D. Eisenhower Presidential Library, Abilene, Kansas.

[248] Clark, Mark W. Text, Speech of May 1954, Mark Clark Papers, The Citadel, Charleston.

[249] Rita Van Wees identified her son, Ronald "Dutch" Van Wees, in a published picture of American PoWs. In 1957, she received a report from an eye witness who saw her son in a Soviet labor camp. She became a founding member of National Alliance of Families.

[250] Shalit was held incommunicado for five (5) years in spite of the efforts of the Red Cross, the United States, the European Union, etc. Three (3) letters and a DVD were passed to the Israelis in exchange for the release of twenty (20) terrorists during his long incarceration. Israeli sources estimate that the 1027 ransomed terrorists were responsible for the deaths of over 550 Israelis.

[251] Glavnoye Razvedyvatelnoye Upravlente (GRU).

[252] Tatro, Nicolas, "Syrians Parade Israeli Tank Through Damascus," Associated Press, Damascus, 11 June 1982; Staff, "Israeli Prisoners in Damascus," *La Stampa* (Italy), Damascus, 12 June 1982; Magnuson, Ed, "Israel Strikes at PLO, But the Attack May Make Peace More Remote," *Time* (US Edition), 21 June 1982.

[253] The victim's room was locked and chained from the inside and the findings of the post-mortem examination were changed ten (10) days after the original conclusion of natural causes.

[254] US Customs Service "Chronology of Association: Bickel, Robert F. Sr., Op Code YOUNGBLOOD," 13 November 1990.

[255] US Bankruptcy Court, Records in re: Commercial Helicopter, Inc., Baton Rouge, LA, 1986.

[256] The Boland Amendment is actually Section 8050 of Public Law 99-190, which forbade all entities of the American Government from using taxpayer funds to provide assistance of any type to the Nicaraguan democratic resistance (Contras).

[257] In January 1986, President Reagan signed Executive Orders 12543 and 12544 forbidding all commercial intercourse with Libya by American citizens and firms.

[258] Dr. Khidir Hamza, one of Iraq's key nuclear physicists, defected to the West in 1994. In a speech on nuclear proliferation given to the Carnegie Endowment for International Peace in November 2000, Hamza confirmed Bickel's suspicions that Iraqi students were used to gather technical information on nuclear weapons in the United States prior to the Gulf War. See also Hamza, Khidir, *SADDAM'S BOMBMAKER*, Scribner, New York, 2000.

[259] US Vs Brenneke went to trial in Federal Court in Portland, Oregon in May of 1990. In a landmark case, the jury had to decide who to believe ... Dick Brenneke or George Bush. They acquitted Brenneke of all charges.

[260] The essence of the scandal was that the Reagan campaign made a deal with the Iranians to hold their American hostages until after the election, damaging Jimmy Carter's reelection campaign. Nothing actionable came out of the scandal. There was a precedent in the efforts of the Nixon campaign against Johnson when they contacted the South Vietnamese and convinced them to hold out for a better deal to end the Vietnam war.

[261] The two lawyers who defended Dick Brenneke were Mike Scott of Denver, the brother of Congresswoman Patricia Schroeder, and Richard Mueller of Portland, a Lieutenant Colonel of Intelligence in the Marine Corps Reserves.

[262] When President George Bush lost the 1992 election, then Secretary of Defense, Dick Chaney, became the CEO of the Halliburton Corporation. He retired from Halliburton to run as George W. Bush's Vice Presidential candidate in 2000.

[263] Report of Investigation, US Customs Service, Case HOD3RROHOD14, dated 8 May 1990.

[264] US Customs Memorandum dated 21 June 1990, requesting consolidation of two strategic cases, AUO3SF8AU003 and AUO3SF0AU002, the investigations of KEM & Associates and CHAUDCHEM for the illegal transfer of carbon-carbon technology for the Condor missile project. It should be noted that this memo was written only days before Houston's whole technology transfer effort was closed down.

[265] A complete set of the "Bickel Papers" is archived at the Texas Woman's University in Denton.

[266] Generally, Customs lore holds that when the service wants to get rid of an agent, he is indicted for perjury usually concerning imported parrots. Brumfield was indeed indicted for this exact thing.

[267] State of Texas vs. Robert F. Bickel, Sr., Harris County, Houston, Texas.

[268] The Brown Helmet Society formed during the Iran-Contra Affair when the Reagan Administration began cutting its losses by jailing and generally discrediting their clandestine operatives. Many were jailed during this period on various trumped-up, federal charges with an average sentence of 54 years. When the Spooks began fighting back, the conviction rate dropped drastically. Among the members-in-good-standing were such Spook notables as Robert Sensi, Ari Ben-Menashe, Robert Bickel, Harry Rupp, David McMichaels, Richard Brenneke, Gary Howard and Ron Tucker.

[269] Gejdenson, Sam, Chairman of the Subcommittee on International Economic Policy and Trade, House Foreign Affairs Committee, personal letter to Attorney Ronald Tonkin re: "Your client, Robert F. Bickel, Sr.," dated 20 November 1991.

[270] We have taken license in reconstructing what happened based on the belief that the Israelis hit Jerry Bull. (Victor Ostrovsky, the ex-Mossad agent who turned against his former employer, also believes that the Israelis were responsible, as does Ari Ben-Menashe.) If that was indeed the case, the "Kidon" (bayonet) unit came into Belgium specifically for this mission. Unlike gangsters or movie spies, the Israelis carefully plan and kill with precision, utilizing a "hit team" of at least 15 people.

[271] Frickey, Curt, 20/20, ABC News, 23 November 1997. In his interview with 20/20, Frickey told of Bull's access to the supercomputers at the facility where he ran the calculations to "increase range and stability of liquid filled payloads" (cocktails).

272 US Select Senate Committee to Study Governmental Operations with Respect to Intelligence Activities, 94th Congress, 1976.

273 The interviews took place on 20 November 1986 and 29 January 1987 at the Federal Correctional Institute in Petersburg, Virginia. In both instances, Blitzer had US government permission. Later, the government claimed in court that Blitzer did not have permission, although one is hard pressed to understand how a reporter gained admission to a federal prison without permission.

274 US Vs Pollard, CR-86-207-AER, US District Court for the District of Columbia, Declaration of Jonathan Jay Pollard in support of Motion For Re-sentencing, 28 August 2000.

275 The 46-page, ex-parte memo haunted Caspar Weinberger until his death in 2006. In an interview in the September 1999 issue of *Middle East Quarterly*, he stated that Judge Aubrey Robinson "made a formal, official request" for the memo. If true, which many doubt, it is completely improper for a federal judge to secretly solicit information about a case. Robinson put it in the court record that the Weinberger Memo was introduced by the US Attorney, which if Weinberger's 1999 statement is true, is a lie. The US Attorney agreed with the judge, making Weinberger's statement a lie. Twersky, David, "New Weinberger Bombshell: Judge Asked for Pollard Memo," *New Jersey Jewish News,* 29 September 1999.

276 Hersh, Seymour, "Panama Strongman Said to Trade in Drugs, Arms and Illicit Money," *The New York Times,* 12 June 1986.

277 Hersh, Seymour, THE SAMSON OPTION, Random House, New York, 1991.

278 Hersh, Seymour, THE SAMSON OPTION, p. 285. Interestingly, this entire statement is false. As near as we can determine, Pollard worked for Israel not because of loyalty, misguided or otherwise, but for solid moral reasons. The money statement is also completely false. Pollard's expenses in his work for Israel left him with a shortfall of over $5000. Hersh's entire statement is nonsense.

279 Church, George, "Did Shamir Give Away Secrets?" *Time,* 28 October 1991.

280 Carmel, Chazi, "Expose: The Great CIA Conspiracy Against Jonathan Pollard," *Ma'ariv,* 8 December 2000; Cherkashin, Victor and Feifer, Gregory, *SPY HANDLER,* Basic Books, New York, 2005, pp. 224-225. Cherkashin, the KGB case officer who handled Aldrich Ames and Robert Hanssen, also denied that Pollard supplied any material to the KGB, directly or indirectly.

[281] Hersh, Seymour, THE SAMSON OPTION, p. 300.

[282] As fate would have it, Aldrich Ames was the CIA officer who did the damage assessment for the Intelligence Community in the Pollard case.

[283] Hersh was sued for libel in Great Britain over allegations made in his book, which had nothing to do with Pollard.

[284] Church, George, "Did Shamir Give Away Secrets?" Time, 28 October 1991.

[285] Loftus, John, "Will Disclosures Help Unlock Jonathan Pollard's Cell?" The Miami Herald, 23 April 1995.

[286] Editorial Staff, "Self-hating Jews," The Jerusalem Post, 6 March 1992.

[287] For excellent accounts of the Aldrich Ames case, see Maas, Peter, KILLER SPY, Warner Books, New York, 1995 and Wise, David, NIGHTMOVER, Harper Collins, New York, 1995.

[288] Upton, Fred, Congress of the United States, House of Representatives, "Dear Friend" Letter, 5 March 1999.

[289] Greenberg, Paul, "Is Jonathan Pollard Next on Clinton's List?" The Arkansas Democrat-Gazette, 7 September 1999.

[290] Kurtz, Howard, "Drug Czar Up in Arms Over Gulf War Inquiry," The Washington Post, 18 April 2000. The quotes are from letters sent to Hersh's editor at The New Yorker, by the angry interviewees.

[291] Kurtz, Howard, "Drug Czar Up in Arms Over Gulf War Inquiry."

[292] Daphne Parish was released on 16 July 1990. She subsequently wrote a book with Pat Lancaster, PRISONER IN BAGHDAD, Chapman, London, 1992.

[293] It should be remembered that "disappearing" was a way of life in Chile. Thousands of innocent people "disappeared" while Chile was ruled by Pinochet.

[294] Arens, Moshe, BROKEN COVENANT, pp. 175-176.

[295] Giora Rom was an Air Force fighter pilot, a former POW and Israel's first jet ace.

[296] HAMMER RICK was a single, secure telephone line from the Kirya in Tel Aviv to the Pentagon in Washington (Virginia). It became operational on 4 January 1991 and was officially inaugurated on 7 January 1991. On the Israeli side, it was located in a small hut within

the Ministry of Defense compound and manned by a small team of American technicians and Israeli Air Force officers.

[297] In 1985, HAGA, the arm of the Israeli Army in charge of civil defense, changed its doctrine from bomb shelters to sealed rooms. This doctrine change came about because of intelligence provided by the HUNTING HORSE (Jonathan Pollard) and was implemented so quietly that the world did not realize it until the international media covered the Gulf War in Israel.

[298] Israel's ability to jam up Jordan's air defenses came as a total surprise to the Americans and the Arab countries. The effects of this electronic jamming were felt as far away as Iraq where Coalition AWACS suffered from it while conducting the air campaign in the early hours of 18 January 1991 (local time). As a general rule, Middle East countries prepare for air strike packages made up of a maximum of 40 aircraft. It was determined post-war that Israel launched three times this number of airplanes in its strike package headed for Iraq on 18 January 1991 and again on 20 January 1991. In both instances, the Israelis recalled their planes before they penetrated Iraqi airspace, while they were still over Jordan.

[299] Israeli experts rechecked the initial field findings and determined that the warhead did not contain Sarin, only high explosives that failed to detonate. They issued a correction to the Americans the following afternoon. Still, the initial report continues to surface to this day in some sectors of the Gulf War veterans' community, while the correction seems lost to everyone.

[300] One of the best accounts from the American side of "Scud Thursday" and "The Great Scud Hunt" that followed can be found in Gordon, Michael and Trainor, Bernard, *THE GENERALS' WAR*, Little, Brown and Company, New York, 1995.

[301] This quote is from an American military source who was present in the American Embassy in Tel Aviv during the first Scud attack on Israel.

[302] Many discussions with Amnon Dror, the Special Assistant to the Prime Minister for the Pollard Matter. Pollard would often call Dror (collect) during the Gulf War.

[303] Bundesamt fur Verfassungsschutz (BfV) literally "The Federal Office for the Protection of the Constitution," German Counterintelligence.